Hatteras Keepers
Oral and Family Histories

Edited by Cheryl Shelton-Roberts

Family History Research by Sandra MacLean Clunies

Outer Banks Lighthouse Society

Family members must have viewed the lighthouse many times from the beach and watched as fathers and husbands lighted the kerosene IOV (incandescent oil vapor) lamp at dusk.

ADVOCATES FOR NORTH CAROLINA LIGHTHOUSES

To our readers: This book is a "work in progress." We have been pleased with the amount of information gathered to date. A great deal has been discovered about many of the Cape Hatteras keepers; however, there are others who remain a mystery. Our deadline for submissions to this first edition was 31 January 2001, and any information gathered after that date will appear in another edition. Material presented in this publication has been extensively researched and comes from various sources including interviews with keepers' descendants, family histories as submitted by family members, family Bibles, census reports, pension records, war draft cards, Record Group 26 at the National Archives in Washington, D.C., Internet genealogy sites, the Outer Banks History Center, and other libraries credited in specific chapters. Corrections and additions are welcomed by writing the Outer Banks Lighthouse Society at P.O. Box 1005 Morehead City, N.C. 28557.

Copyright 2001 by the Outer Banks Lighthouse Society

All rights reserved. No part of this book may be reproduced or transmitted in any form by any means, electrical or mechanical including photocopying and recording or by any information storage and retrieval system, except as may be expressly permitted by the 1976 copyright act or by the Outer Banks Lighthouse Society. Requests for permission should be made in writing to the Outer Banks Lighthouse Society P.O. Box 1005 Morehead City, N.C. 28557.

Book design by Bruce Roberts. Printed in USA by Letton Gooch Printers, Inc., Norfolk, Virginia.

First edition/first printing

Acknowledgements

*Thank you to the many people who helped to make this publication a reality.
All of you know who you are and in listing names,
there is always the risk of missing someone deserving of recognition.*

First, acknowledgement goes to the Outer Banks Lighthouse Society's board of directors who approved the undertaking of the Hatteras Keepers Descendants Homecoming by the lighthouse society: President John McPherson, Betty Parrish, Bill Parrish, Dr. Mabry O'Donnell, Dr. Jim O'Donnell, Lloyd Childers, Charlene Wiles-Perry, Ralph Burroughs, Bett Padgett, Bruce and Cheryl Roberts.

Sandra MacLean Clunies, Board-certified genealogist, put into action her tremendous research skills and produced volumes of information on keepers' ancestors and descendants. Sandy, like others in this volunteer effort to produce this first edition, gave freely of personal time, even vacations, to work on this project. Contributors to the genealogical research include Rhetta Williams Quidley, Almarie (Midgett) Brothers, Gregory Williams, Jo Ellen (Jennette) Luscombe, Annie Miller (Parker) Hodges, Ormond Fuller, Ellen Fulcher Cloud, Coley Jordan, Ann Marie Ladue, Susan Rollinson, Richard P. Farrow, Angel (Billhimer) Roller, and many others who sent photocopies from unknown sources. Each registrant offered information on their forms, which gave us further leads, and well, you get the idea. Beatrice "Beatie" (Barnette) McAruthur and Earl O'Neal of the Hatteras Island Genealogical and Historical Society (HIGHS) have worked closely together to help locate descendants and record accumulated material from the search for keepers' descendants. The HIGHS goal is "To determine the history of this Island and the surrounding areas and its people; to protect, preserve, and promote our history. History is People."

Lynn Jennette worked tirelessly to amass the descendant's registration forms, copy pertinent information, and forward it to Sandy Clunies and the editor. She sought out sources for photographs and kept the database for the descendant's replying to the committee's contacts. She also chaired planning committee meetings and juggled the many details that made the homecoming event possible and this publication a success.

Bruce Roberts worked with me every day for months to plan and design this book. His vision worked creative wonders while he, too, juggled details that ranged from copying photography and fundraising to every detail involved with self-publishing a book.

Bob Woody, Chris Eckard, Patty Lockamy, and the rest of the National Park Service administrators and staff along with Judy Basnett and Rulaine Keggeris of Eastern National, who saw our vision and arranged for seed money to begin the planning, all deserve special recognition. Charlie Votaw and Shirley Votaw worked side by side with us on the planning committee, helped with the fact gathering, and gave financial backing for the printing of this book. Charlene Wiles-Perry, Allen Perry, and John Howard helped with any computer-related issues. Lynne Jacques was the planning committee's secretary, Judy Basnett served as treasurer, Rick Polad and Norma McKittrick assisted with copy proofing, and Dr. Margaret Harker conducted intense research for medical information relative to Hatteras Island of the 1800s through 1940s.

Keepers' family members who gave special help with the research, writing, and sharing of photographs from family albums and collections made over several decades and are owed recognition include: Annie (Fulcher) Pellegrini, Bobby Pellegrini, Sabra (Gray) Jennette, Jackie Jennette, Lynn Jennette, Annie Miller (Parker) Hodges, Paul Sharp, Jr., Jo Ellen (Jennette) Luscombe, Sybil (Austin) Skakle, Renae Brabham, Allene (Quidley) Gaskins, Ruth (Fulcher) Rickert, Marie E. Riddick, Norma (Gray) Rhoden, Connie (Rhoden) Manley, Marilyn (Austin) Meads, Verna (Austin) Wall, Agnes (Wallace) Haddaway, Marie (Wallace) Mulvaney, Sybil (Gray) McDaniel, Edna (Casey) Gray, Donna Schlag, Jean Lewis, Sally Davis, Reese Folb, Dallas Quidley, Rhetta Quidley, Hilda (Austin) Williams, Norma Deane Skinner, Melita (Midgette) Harris, Rebecca (Midgette) Mastros, Walter Garrish, Dr. J. Charles Jennette, Ben Price, Mike Shepherd, Winnie (Austin) Minson, Faye (Baum) White, Ophelia (Baum) Smith, Ruth Ann Geer-Lloyd, William L. Quidley, Jim Lewis, Ronnie Quidley, and Brian Edwards and Sarah Downing of the Outer Banks History Center.

Ms. Lloyd Childers offered valuable information about the homecoming held at the Currituck Beach Light Station of which she is Executive Director for the Outer Banks Conservationists, Inc.

Letton Gooch Printers, especially Jean Burke and David Muscarella, did an excellent job in the professional layout and printing of this book. Their patience and caring attitude during each step of the publishing process is greatly appreciated.

To all the volunteers who worked on this project, you are the best. And finally, one more attempt to say it with all the meaning it's intended to carry: to all of you who helped with any part of this project, thank you.

Cheryl Shelton-Roberts
Cofounder Outer Banks Lighthouse Society
Cochairman Hatteras Keepers Descendants Homecoming
Editor *Hatteras Keepers Oral and Family Histories*

One of the greatest improvements to the Cape Hatteras Lighthouse occurred in 1913 when this huge incandescent oil vapor lamp (I.O.V.) was installed. It vaporized the kerosene before it burned, similar to a Coleman lantern, providing a light of 80,000 candlepower, much brighter than the old kerosene wick lamp. Lighting the I.O.V. lamp took great skill on the part of the keepers who were specially trained to handle this task. Photo courtesy National Park Service

Hatteras Keepers
Oral and Family Histories

This book is dedicated to all Cape Hatteras Lighthouse keepers and their families. We are all keepers of the light, for all of us who learn to appreciate the history of a lighthouse, we become part of its heritage. *Hatteras Keepers Oral and Family Histories* has been published in recognition of those who served in the U.S. Lighthouse Service to guard the beacons of the lighthouses, lightships, and the river and sound lights and who served aboard the lighthouse tenders.

The purpose of the Outer Banks Lighthouse Society is to preserve the lighthouses and history of the old U.S. Lighthouse Service and honor the men and women who kept the lights burning.

For their financial support for the research for this book, the Outer Banks Lighthouse Society thanks Eastern National, serving America's National Parks.

Keepers and wives posed in the yard of the principal keepers house when this 1893 photograph was taken by U.S. Lighthouse Service photographer Henry Bamber.

*This magnificent first-order Fresnel lens now resides in the Pigeon Point Lighthouse in Petaluma, California. It is the same lens that was removed from the original Cape Hatteras Lighthouse prior to its destruction when the second lighthouse was activated in 1870. This particular lens was a replacement for the first-order lens that had been stolen by Confederates in 1862 when Rebel and Union forces struggled to gain control of Hatteras Island and the coastal and sound lighthouses. The linen curtains in the photo are kept closed during the day to protect the prisms of the lens from intense sunlight. When keepers manned lighthouses, drawing the curtains during the day also provided a cooler environment in which to work.
Photo courtesy Nancy A. Pizzo*

Table of Contents

Acknowledgements iv
Introduction xii
What's in a Name *by Sandra MacLean Clunies* xvi
Foreword *by Sybil Austin Skakle* xviii
Cape Hatteras Lighthouse Keepers List xx
Keepers Describe Their Duties xxii
Lighthouse Keeper, *Poem by Renae Brabham* xxiii
Homer Treadwell Austin
  with *Maretta (Austin) Derrickson and Hilda (Austin) Williams* 2
M. Wesley Austin *by Walter P. Garrish* 4
Julian Haywood Austin *by Cheryl Shelton-Roberts* 8
Thomas Hardy Baum *by Cheryl Shelton-Roberts* 20
James Oliver Casey *by Cheryl Shelton-Roberts* 24
Amasa G. Fulcher *by Fannie Pearl Fulcher* 34
Benjamin T. Fulcher *by Ruth Fulcher Rickert* 36
Charles Haywood Fulcher *by Cheryl Shelton-Roberts* 38
James Wilson Gillikin *by Sandra MacLean Clunies* 48
The Jennett(e) Family Group *by Sandra MacLean Clunies* 52
John Benjamin Jennette with *Christopher Roy Jennette* 54
Unaka Benjamin Jennette *by Lynn Jennette with Rany Jennette and family* 57
Ephraim Meekins *by Brian Edwards* 66
John Evans Midgette *by Norma Deane Skinner* 70
Christopher Columbus Miller *by Sandra MacLean Clunies* 76
Amasa Jones Quidley *by Cheryl Shelton-Roberts* 80
John Bunion Quidley *by William L. Quidley* 82
William Edward Quidley *by Cheryl Shelton-Roberts* 84
Simpson Family of Keepers *by Sandra MacLean Clunies* 92
Tilman F. Smith and the Cape Hatteras Beacon 96
Thomas Levi Wallace
  by Agnes (Wallace) Huddaway and Marie (Wallace) Mulvaney 98
Alpheus B. Willis *by Cheryl Shelton-Roberts* 104
Quiet Voices *by Sandra MacLean Clunies* 106
My Keeper Heritage with *Beatrice (Barnette) McArthur* 112
Lightships of Diamond Shoals *by Charles and Shirley Votaw* 116
Medical Resources on Hatteras Island of the 1800s through early 1900s 122-131
  M.B. Folb, *A Navy Pharmacist Mate* 122
  Rovena Rollinson Quidley, *Midwife,* and her son, T.D. Quidley 123
  Dr. Joshua Judson Davis, *Dr. Josh* 124
Life and Living 1830-1930 *by Margaret Harker, M.D.* 126
Keepers of the Light, *Lyrics by Bett Padgett* 131
Index 132

This book is dedicated to the

Cape Hatteras Lighthouse Keepers *and their*

Wives

Children

Grandchildren

Introduction

*Happiness at the Cape Hatteras Lighthouse was
a beacon working well and the laughter of children.
Neighbor helping neighbor was a way of life on Hatteras Island.*

Thomas Jefferson appointed the first keeper for Cape Hatteras in 1802, the year before the original Cape Hatteras sandstone tower was completed. One-hundred and thirty-four years later, the last keeper left the second and present striped tower after it was darkened and an automated light was put atop a steel skeleton tower in Buxton Woods on May 13, 1936. Three years earlier, keepers' families had been ordered to leave the light station after back-to-back storms caused extreme island overwash and put the keepers' quarters too close for comfort to Atlantic breakers. The families never returned.

In an attempt to preserve memories of life at this light station, an extensive search for surviving descendants, many born in the keepers quarters, and for their family photographs, was launched in April 2000. Keepers' children and grandchildren have been recorded for the oral histories during personal interviews. The family histories, based on genealogical research, add depth to our knowledge of the various men who once served at Cape Hatteras.

According to Board-certified genealogist Sandra MacLean Clunies, during the more than one dozen decades when the Cape Hatteras Light Station was manned, there were basically eight families under whose stewardship this important aid to navigation was entrusted. Their surnames are Austin, Farrow, Fulcher, Jennett(e), O'Neal, Quidley, Simpson, and Williams, pioneer Outer Banks family groups which had first settled there in the late 1700s. It was also common for sons, brothers, sons-in-law, and nephews to become assistants to the primary keeper, although many may have had a different surname. Each appointment carried a federal salary, however modest, and this provided much economic stability for many Outer Banks extended families. Most of those appointed to the federal position of keeper were experienced mariners who were born and raised on the Outer Banks.

Information on one of the keepers illustrates the many interesting discoveries made while working on this project. Family histories researcher Clunies summarized the lineage started by Benjamin T. Fulcher. "Benjamin T. Fulcher (1810-1867), keeper in 1860, had one grandson, Randolph Fulcher, and one great-grandson, Unaka Jennette, who became keepers. It was his female descendants who married many keepers: daughter Sabrah married William B. Jennett, while daughter Emma married Christopher Columbus Miller. Four granddaughters, one great-granddaughter, and one great-great-granddaughter married keepers, many of whom themselves were from multiple keeper families."

There were several duty stations that included the word "Hatteras" listed in official records of the U.S. Lighthouse Service. One crew staffed the Cape Hatteras Lighthouse together with the Beacon Light at Cape Point. A separate and distinct team staffed the Hatteras Inlet screwpile light in Pamlico Sound. A keeper did not move from Cape Hatteras to Hatteras Inlet without a separate federal appointment

This is an aerial view taken during late 1930s. It shows the "highway" running between the lighthouse and the keepers quarters south to the CCC camp. Prior to the dune system built by the CCC and groins put in place in the 1960s, the beach ran straight as an arrow by the light station. This would become the scene of a constant battle with nature to retain the wide beach. This picture became a popular postcard upon which Sudie Jennette wrote to her son Rany while he was in service. After the families left the light station in 1936, Sudie always longed to return to Cape Hatteras and have all the family together. The families never lived there again. Photo courtesy Annie Miller (Parker) Hodges

Ships that washed ashore after big storms were no stranger to Outer Bankers like this one beached near Rodanthe. If lucky, a ship could be put afloat again and taken to port, usually Norfolk, and sent on its way again. These vessels often traveled twelve and more miles from their encounter with rough weather off Diamond Shoals, and if fortunate to make the unplanned journey without extreme damage, a ship was restored. If not so lucky, it was sold at auction right where it landed and salvaged for parts. Circa 1920s
Photo courtesy Annie Miller (Parker) Hodges

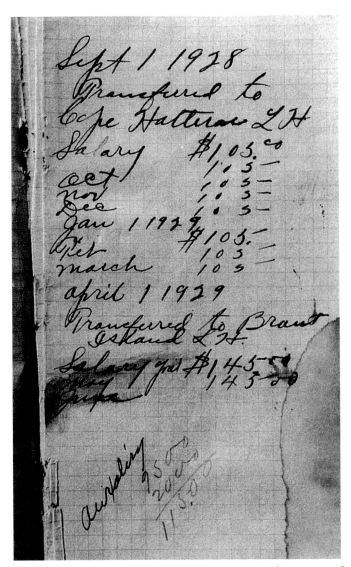

Keeper Julian Austin kept meticulous records, many of which his children preserve. In this note he was keeping track of his salaries after transferring to the Cape Hatteras Lighthouse and later to Brant Island. 1928
Photo courtesy Marilyn (Austin) Meads

"Stuck again," Marilyn (Austin) Meads commented while looking at this picture of their family car. Brave islanders took the "beach road," literally two ruts along the beach at low tide, but often did a lot more pushing and shoving than riding. But the thrill of the ride was worth it.
Photo courtesy Marilyn (Austin) Meads

Prior to a bridge spanning the gap between Hatteras Island and Bodie Island, a car and passenger ferry did the job. The Herbert Bonner Bridge was the final link to unite Hatteras Island to the mainland. Upon its completion in 1963, cars full of visiting family members and tourists poured forth onto Hatteras Island. Circa late 1930s.
Photo courtesy Annie Miller (Parker) Hodges

Before the advent of the motorized boat and the automobile, islanders traveled three ways: on foot, by sail, or in a horse-pulled cart. Even the luxury of owning a horse and cart required maintenance of the cart and the feeding and housing of the animal. But one has to admit- what a relaxing way to go along the beautiful beaches of the Outer Banks.
Photo courtesy Annie Miller (Parker) Hodges

transferring the duty station. Although several men served at different periods at both the Cape Hatteras Light Station and the Inlet Light, including other screwpile lights of North Carolina, this publication focuses on the keepers and their oral and family histories of the primary Cape Hatteras Light Station in Buxton. Keepers of sound and river lights, as well as lighthouse tender and lightship crews, deserve due recognition for their dedicated service to mariners and they will be covered in a future publication.

Lighthouse keepers worked for the U.S. Lighthouse Service, which was considered the best aids to navigation system in the world for the first half of the twentieth century. It was hailed as one of the most efficient government agencies, consistently developing state-of-the-art technology including the advent of radio navigation, which enabled the automation of lighthouses to begin in the late 1920s.

Underlying a passel of children's laughter, braying of wandering, free-range animals, the rush of fresh winds, and the peaceful lull of the waxing and waning tides, there was an ever-present tension that the district superintendent's report could put a keeper's job on the line. Families knew well that they were living in housing provided by the government for the keeper, who tended the tower, that held the light, that guided the mariner, who was the backbone to the lucrative shipping business of the nation. Keepers worked long, tedious hours to fulfill their duties. Happiness at a light station was a beacon working well.

Sons and nephews worked alongside their fathers and uncles. They were multiskilled with equal talents in fishing, raising a productive garden, refurbishing a house after a flood, keeping a light station in top condition, and maneuvering a boat in roguish waves. It was only natural for many to follow in the footsteps of their role models and also become keepers. In several families, a keeper's daughter had become accustomed to the duties carried out by her mother; therefore, it was only natural for her to marry a keeper's son who grew up next door at the light station, thus perpetuating the heritage of this profession.

Moreover, Outer Bankers of the era upon which this book focuses, lived by the unwritten rule that in order to survive, neighbor helped neighbor. They took care of one another. A friend in need was a friend in deed. With natural disasters always at their doorstep, scant medical resources, few secure jobs upon which to depend, and large families for whom to provide, island families were a tightly knit community in and of themselves, and a neighbor was the same as family.

Keepers expected children to do their chores, obey strict rules of the light station, and yet, to be children. These are the young ones who watched storms not as a feared enemy, but as a welcomed treasure-producing machine. As soon as allowed, children and adults took to the beaches to see what the waves had brought to them from far away. Gifts in the form of beach lumber are still part of many Hatteras Island homes; they still cherish seashells kept from decades ago, buttons, coins, and whittled wood from mariners passing the time while risking the Graveyard of the Atlantic on their way to port.

The people in these stories are those who witnessed the ravages of tuberculosis, diphtheria, and hurricanes. They saw the ghost ship *Carol A. Deering*; they lived during the sinking of the Diamond Shoals Lightship by a WW I German submarine; a war later, they thrilled at the words, "Sighted sub, sank same." These are the same children who roller skated on the sidewalks that connected the keepers' houses, mimicked the terns, skirted the incoming waves, played in the shallow pools left by receding tides, and flew over the incoming waves while seized with laughter. Every surviving keeper's child speaks of Cape Hatteras as heaven on earth for a youngster. "It was the best place for a child to grow up," Keeper William E. Quidley's granddaughter, Norma (Gray) Rhoden said.

Rany Jennette, son of the last Cape Hatteras keeper agreed. "Growing up at the lighthouse was like a fairy tale. I remember the beacon seemed to throw off a constant series of flashes, creating a glow that filled my bedroom and lulled me to sleep at night. I spent the first thirteen years of my life here. I can't think of a better place for a boy to grow up."

Annie (Fulcher) Pellegrini commented, "I was born in the keepers double quarters and have always been bonded to it and the lighthouse." Her father, Charles Fulcher, was an assistant keeper for fourteen years, 1906-1920.

Cora Edna (Casey) Gray, Keeper James O. Casey's daughter, spent eight years at the lighthouse from 1920-28. At ninety-three years of age, she has extended this invitation, "I want you to come to my island home near the lighthouse and do some serious porch sitting with me while we talk. In case Daddy needs me to help him light the lamp, I'll get my lantern ready."

Rany Jennette added, "Many times I climbed the lighthouse with my father and helped with the routine maintenance, I shined lots of brass. My fondest memory at the top of the lighthouse was going out on deck, looking through the huge (spy glasses) or binoculars and observing ships passing - so close you could see crew members on the ships."

Their love for lighthouses and pride in the keeper's title carried by their fathers and grandfathers are bridges to childhood memories. Through interviews completed between 1995 and 2001, amazingly, we can still look into the eyes of these people who called Cape Hatteras "home." And to them, it is still home.

Cheryl Shelton-Roberts
Cheryl Shelton-Roberts

This is a rare photograph of the two keepers quarters. At right is the principal keeper's house and at left is the double assistant keepers house. The picture was taken during a time when the light station was run as a visitors lodge by private individuals after the lighthouse was darkened in 1936 due to the threat of erosion. Both houses have been restored and were moved to the new location in 1999. Circa late 1930s
Photo courtesy Annie Miller (Parker) Hodges

Terms Used for United States Lighthouse Service (USLHS):
There were three distinct periods of organization in the history of the "Lighthouse Service."
    1789-1852 U.S. Lighthouse Establishment (USLHE)
    1852-1910 Light-House Board
    1910-1939 Bureau of Lighthouses; in 1939 it was merged into the U.S. Coast Guard
An overall term used in referencing the civilian-staffed government agency that took care of aids to navigation from 1789-1939 is "U.S. Lighthouse Service," or simply the "Lighthouse Service."

What's in a name?

There are many family surnames in the Outer Banks, which have been present there since the 1700s. Census enumerators and citizens alike paid little attention to spelling in prior centuries, and names were often written as they sounded to the person writing them down. The following surnames of later Cape Hatteras keepers appear in 18th century and deed records, often with many spelling variations:

Austin	Miller
Baum	O'Neal, O'neal, Neal, Neale
Burris, Burrus, Burrows, Burroughs	Quigley, Quidley
Bunnett, Barnett	Rollison, Rolison, Robinson
Farrow	Rue, Rew
Gray	Scarboro, Scarborough, Scarbro
Jinnett, Jennett	Smith
Midgett, Migyett, Midyett	Thomson, Thompson

Some later branches of three families in particular have modified the spellings of these surnames:

Barnett and Barnette   Jennett and Jennette   Midgett and Midgette

First offspring were named (and still are), often following a tradition of honoring the names of parents and grandparents. Many babies were named to recognize another relative, friend, historical figure, national political leader, favorite biblical figures - even the family doctor!

There are some wonderful-sounding names in the old records of Cape Hatteras Lighthouse keepers' families.

Pharoah Farrow (leading to an unproven fable that he was a shipwrecked Arab)
Barzilla Brittannia Midgett (mother of keeper Randolph Fulcher)
Christopher Columbus Miller
Martin Luther Fulcher
Malachi Daniel Swain
George Washington Farrow (father-in-law of John E. Midgette).

By Sandra MacLean Clunies,
Board-certified genealogist

Sandra MacLean Clunies

Adam Gaskins

Adam was the first. And he is a good example of how this publication is a work in progress.
We continue to look for earlier records on this man and his descendants.
It's like fitting pieces of a puzzle together in order to see the picture of a man named
Adam Gaskins, the first keeper at the 1803 Cape Hatteras Lighthouse.

Who was Adam Gaskins? Research into his life and family has been challenging. We do not have a precise birth or death date. The surname is sometimes written as "Gaskill", or "Gaskell" even though there is a separate family group of that name. Adam was listed in the 1790 census of Carteret County. There were two men of the name in the 1800 census, one in Craven County, and one in Hyde County.

The two Adam Gaskins listings clearly reveal two separate and distinct families. The Craven County man was much younger, married in 1798, with no children listed in 1800, and with no documented military or mariner experience, and is thus unlikely to be the man later appointed lighthouse keeper. The new Federal government preferred to reward military veterans, and those with proven understanding of the seafaring life.

Other researchers have added information, especially R.S. Spencer of the Hyde County Genealogical Society and Kay Lynn Midgette Sheppard, a frequent contributor of Outer Banks records transcriptions to the North Carolina resources on the Internet. Data from all sources on this Adam Gaskins of Carteret and Hyde Counties strongly suggest that he was the first lighthouse keeper at Cape Hatteras.

Adam was born before 1755, possibly as early as 1748, and he gave his age as "over 45" in 1800. He signed a petition in 1773 with other "legal pilots of Oacock Bar" [Ocracoke], revealing his mariner experience. He was a veteran of the American Revolution, appointed a Second Lieutenant in 1776, and served as a Captain in 1779 in the Carteret County Regiment of Militia.

In 1789, he was among those appointed commissioners to erect a lighthouse at "Ocacock Island". This collection of records, which includes many other documents, clearly points to this man as the one qualified to assume the position of lighthouse keeper in 1803.

He married Sarah "Sally" Gibbs, the widow of Cason Jones, with whom she had one son. She was the daughter of another Revolutionary veteran, Cason Gibbs, who may have sired twenty-one children in three marriages. Besides a daughter Polly and son Caswell, named in the estate papers, Adam and Sally are reported to have had: daughter Esther "Hetty" who married Joseph Tunnell, daughter Dianna who married Hardy Swindell, and son Samuel Treadwell who married Matilda Swindell. Note the last son was named Samuel Treadwell Gaskins, perhaps in honor of the local Collector of Customs who had recommended Adam for the position as keeper.

Of his duties at the Cape Hatteras Lighthouse during its first years of operation, we have no lighthouse journals or reports. But from the fragments of records which survive, it appears that a very mature man of the sea, and man of the military, had all the necessary skills and experience to handle the job.

The research on Adam Gaskins emphasizes the fact that when researching a particular man and finding his descendants, we must keep in mind that more than one man may have gone by the same name. In this case, all sources including family, local, county, and state records must be studied. Separating two men with the same name and then deciding which man is the one we are looking for is frequently a continuing process. Thanks to increased interest in family history, we are finding more information on Cape Hatteras keepers and their descendants while we also learn about their remarkable families.

The appointment letter remains, sent from Commissioner of Revenue William Miller, Jr. at the Treasury Department to Samuel Treadwell, Esq. in North Carolina, who was Collector of Customs and locally responsible for the new lighthouse. Gaskins' service would begin when the light was completed, at an annual salary of $333.33.

Foreword

We Are All Keepers of the Light

By Sybil Austin Skakle

When I was a little girl at Hatteras I remember my parents taking us up to Buxton to visit Mr. Unaka Jeanette and his family in their quarters near the Cape Hatteras Lighthouse. We climbed all those steps and Mr. Unaka explained to us about the light. From the vantage of that tower the keepers' house and everything on the ground looked very small. That was a marvelous discovery to the little girl I then was.

Cape Hatteras Light has been part of my life forever. As a teenager, visiting a girl friend in Buxton, we went out to the Cape Hatteras Lighthouse to take pictures and see the boys. When we were older we had a picnic and a swimming party at its foot. Or we climbed to the top with our favorite fellow and got kissed.

Summer of 1946

World War II over
boys were home again and
after sophomore year at Carolina
so was I
We climbed Cape Hatteras Lighthouse
to the black metal balcony
atop the spiraled black and white tower
Sea gulls flew below us.
White clouds soared above us
Brisk breezes tousled his brown hair
and tangled mine
Our clothing clung to young hungry bodies
as we stood surrounded by
Sea and shore, birds and breeze,
God and Spirit
between earth and heaven
Cape Hatteras Light stands, threatened
by ocean currents
He has been gone a long while
I recall that moment - the breadth of a kiss-
in space
and our summer passion

One night in the hospital pharmacy in Durham, North Carolina where I worked the work was caught up and it was a bit dull. I began to think of the Cape Hatteras Lighthouse standing on the shore of the Atlantic Ocean at Buxton. Words began to form in my mind and I wrote a poem I named "Giant." It was published, one of my first, in 1990 *Anthology of Southern Poetry*.

Giant

Cape Hatteras Light stands vigil
Protecting shore, identifying position
Warning ships of dangerous shoals
Black and white spiraled body-
Sand-blasted, salt-crusted, sun-baked -
Threatened by Atlantic currents.
Around its maroon, kilt-like skirt
The sands advance, retreat-
Propelled by tides and wind.
Summer breeze, northeaster, hurricane, rain
Buffet and batter
Caress or abuse the ancient lamp
Pluck the metal parapet railings
Reverberate tympanic balcony
Disperse into the ether-
Transcending emotion and time-
Cacophony and cadence blend
For Giant's symphony

    I remember how we watched for the first sweep of the light's beam as we drove down the beach from other parts of the state or Virginia. Walking on the beach at night we saw it, clearly or hazily, depending on the weather.

    Cape Hatteras Lighthouse has been a part of my life always. When talks of moving it began, I opposed. I believed it would tumble into the ocean when they tried to uproot that tall structure. How glad I am that I was mistaken. How grateful I am for the modern technology and feats of engineering that made it possible for men to accomplish the feat and make our light safe.

    Lighthouse keepers do not have to take care of the modern light in the tower as they once did, climbing all those steps as often as needed to keep the light burning. The light is now powered by electricity and controlled from the ground. We are indebted to Lighthouse Keepers for their faithful vigilance in all kinds of weather to keep the light burning bright for the sailors on the sea and for those who depended on its constancy on the shore. Are we not all keepers of the light? Keep your memories bright in your hearts.

Signed, Sybil Austin Skakle

Sybil Austin Skakle

Cape Hatteras Lighthouse Keepers List

	Primary Keeper	Assistant Keeper
Angell, Nelson P. (c. 1831-1887)		1871-1873
Austin, Homer T. (1881-1949)		1912-1913
Austin, Julian H. (1898-1970)		1928-1929
Austin, M. Wesley (1864-1941)		1885-1893
Barnett, Hezekiah	1849	
Barnett, James J. (1844-1937)		Mar-July 1907
Barnett, Oliver N. (1829-1892)		1873-c.1875
Baum, Thomas H. (1877-1938)		Apr - Dec 1905
Bliven, George A. (1859-1920)	1880	
Brady, John D.		1917
Burfoot, Jabez W. (c. 1878-1969)		May - Oct 1907
Burrus, Ethelburt D. (1856-1936)		1876-1878
Casey, James O. (1873-1937)		1920-1928
Daniels, Joseph B.		1892-1893
Daniels, Louis G.		1888-1889
Farrow, Abraham C. (1824-c.1883)	1862	
Farrow, C.P. (c. 1824-?)		1869-1871
Farrow, Harvey L.		1873-1875
Farrow, Isaac (c.1785-c.1842)	1830-1842	
Farrow, Joseph (c.1760-1822)	1809	
Farrow, L.B. (1811-1869)		1864-1867
Farrow, Pharoah (c.1775-1847)	1821-1831	
Fulcher, Amasa G. (1876-1946)		1903-1904
Fulcher, Benjamin T. (1810-1867)	1860-1861	1845-1860
Fulcher, C.		1858
Fulcher, Charles H. (1878-1942)		1906-1920
Fulcher, Christopher		1865-1869
Fulcher, Martin L. (1875-1927)		1900-1905
Fulcher, Randolph P. (1872-1946)		Apr - Aug 1928
Gaskins, Adam (c.1750-1819)	1803	
Gillikin, James W. (1857-1925)	1897-1900	
Gray, Abner H. (c. 1835- ?)		1865
Hause, Selwyn		1878
Jennett, Benjamin C. (1846-1874)	1868-1871	
Jennette, John B. (1871-1951)		1889-1903
Jennett, Joseph C. (1805-1866)	1843, 1849	
Jennett, Joseph E. (c. 1842-1881)		1869
Jennett, Wallace R. (1829-1908)	1873-1878	1863-1865, 1867
Jennett, William (1820-1862)		1860
Jennett, Zion B. (1814-1888)		1870
Jennette, Unaka B. (1882-1965)	1919-1939	
Meekins, Ephraim (1861-1940)	1900-1906	
Meekins, Isaac C. (1868-1948)		1905-1906
Midgett, John E. (1895-1982)		1929-1930
Miller, Christopher C. (1844-1927)		1887-1892

	Primary Keeper	Assistant Keeper
O'Neal, E.D. (c.1837-?)		1856-1860
O'Neal, E.F.	1860	
O'Neal, W.B.		1854
O'Neal, William (c.1811-?)	1853-1860	
O'Neal, William B. (c.1833-?)		1867
Quidley, Amasa J. (1877-1962)		1917-1923
Quidley, John B. (1877-1936)		1904-1905, 1909-1911
Quidley, William E. (1874-1961)		1928-1934
Riggs, Ephraim H. (1853-?)		1889-1892
Roach, Louis C.		1871
Rodgers, George W.	1864-1866	
Rollinson, Sylvester (1822-1893)		1864
Rollinson, William G. (1873-1959)		1905-1906
Rue, Oscar (1827-1880)	1878-1880	
Salter, Albert G.B. (1852-?)		1888
Scarborough, Henderson (c.1826-1881)		1872-1873
Scarborough, R.		1855
Shepperd, John S.	1871-1872	
Simpson, Alpheus W. (1844-1905)	1866-1868	1869, 1876, 1894
Simpson, Amasa J. (1856-1919)		1883
Simpson, Fabius E. (1858-?)	1907-1919	1884-1885, 1893-1899
Smith, Sanders B. (1867-1929)		1892-1899
Smith, Tilman F. (1852-?)	1887-1897	1878-1887
Stowe, John M.		1930-1931
Swain, Malachi D. (1868-1927)		1913-1917
Thompson, Augustus C.	1881-1887	
Tolson, William G. (c.1871-?)		1905
Twiford, John T.		1907
Wallace, Thomas L. (1900-1987)		1931-1933
Watson, Victor L. (1874-1925)		1907-1909
Whedbee, Miles F. (1852-?)		Oct 3-10 1909
Whitehurst, John E. (c.1856-?)		1879-1880
Whitehurst, Joseph B.		1878
Williams, Andrew (c.1810-?)		1860
Williams, Bateman A. (c.1822-1866)		1860-1865
Williams, Nasa S. (c.1818-?)		1864-1871
Willis, Alpheus B. (1868-1924)		1905-1907, 1911-1912
Willis, David		1885-1887

List entries are based on extensive research of official United States Lighthouse Service Records. Corrections will be an ongoing process based on future research. Anyone having documentation which differs with information provided herein is encouraged to write us at OBLHS, P.O. Box 1005, Morehead City, NC 28557

Keepers Describe Their Duties

Periodically, keepers were asked to fill out "Personnel Classification Board Form No. 14- Field Questionnaire. In it, keepers were asked to fill in their name, field station, number of hours worked per week during the summer and winter, a description of their training/experience/education, and a description in detail of the work the keeper did. We can get a glimpse at what our Cape Hatteras Keepers were doing in 1928.

Unaka B. Jennette wrote part of the report in his own hand and part of it was typed. He was serving at Cape Hatteras Light Station, having first been assigned March 16, 1919. After a seventh grade education, he had trained as a "Seaway Quartermaster, Mate and Master on U.S. Light Vessels for the 15 years prior to entry upon present position." The keeper indicated his gross rate of pay was $1740 and that he had to furnish the house provided for him and his family. $240 was deducted from his gross pay each year for the following allowances: an unfurnished house, light, and fuel. He also had to pay for a replacement uniform, $15 per annum.

Keeper Jennette described his duties thus: "This station comprises a 200 ft. masonry tower (the tallest lighthouse tower in the U.S.) surmounted by glazed lantern, in which is mounted 1st order Fresnel lens, revolved on ball bearing chariot by weight driven clock-work. The illuminant is incandescent oil vapor. There are extensive grounds, quarters and outbuildings to be kept in order including painting and minor repairs.

"The principal keeper is in responsible charge of station to see that lens and lantern are kept properly clean and polished and clock work clean and running on time, and that buildings and grounds are kept clean and orderly, well painted and in repair within capacity of keepers. He is also responsible for keeping of station records and for all property and supplies. His time is estimated to be divided as ..." and the description ends there. Obviously Keeper Jennette had more to say but his attached sheet has been misplaced.

He detailed his duties. "I have two assistants whose duties are standing their watches which takes one third of their time. Their other regular duties are the keeping up of their dwellings and grounds, the work consisting of cleaning, scrubbing, painting and other work necessary [to] keep station premises in good condition. Each man being held responsible for his watch.

"20%: My individual work consists of my regular watch in the tower beginning one hour before sunset and running continuously until one hour after sunrise making about 14 hours in 72 when all men are present at the station. 14 in 48 with one man on leave.

20%: Remainder of each day in three is spent on day watch.

In 1933, Unaka B. Jennette posed for National Geographic photographer, Clifton Adams. The magnificent first-order Fresnel lens was comprised of eighteen panels of crown-glass prisms, specially designed, manufactured, and polished in Paris, France in 1870. The lens was cleaned with jewelers' rouge and soft, lint free cloth such as chamois to prevent scratching. A keeper took great care with the glass prisms, never allowing direct contact of skin and glass as oil could dull the prism's surface, lessening the light's intensity. The great care taken in a keeper's duties kept the lighthouse in top running order.
Photo courtesy National Park Service

40%: My other duties consist of from 4 to 8 hours each day in scrubbing, cleaning & painting dwelling and grounds, painting cleaning, & chipping tower inside and out, whitewashing and cementing fences, and other duties necessary to the upkeep of the reservation.

"20%: I personally attend to all reports and correspondence, which consist of Official reports and correspondence and the writing of the daily log.

"In my opinion, I judge that a fair estimate of the daily time devoted to official duties, would be about 10 hours per day.

Signed,

The meticulous upkeep of a lighthouse under the care of such an able man as Jennette is precisely why lighthouses were kept in consistently good condition. The presence of a human hand and a few tools, constantly wielded as both restorative and preventative maintenance, kept the light station in top working condition.

To do this tremendous job, both physically and mentally challenging, Keeper Jennette estimated it took him an average 70 hours per week during the summer and winter.

No, there was no overtime pay, just a keeper who took pride in doing a good job, no matter the number of hours required.

Assistant Julian H. Austin

In 1928, Julian Haywood arrived at Cape Hatteras as an assistant keeper along with his wife, Katherine, and two-year-old Julian Jr. Keeper Austin stated he had an eighth grade education and "...five years of experience at sea. Three of which were served as machinist on steam ships." As assistant keeper, Austin made $1,500 gross pay with $240 deduction, yielding $1,260 net pay. The range of pay at Cape Hatteras made it possible for an assistant, depending on his years of experience and rating by the principal keeper as an employee in good standing, to make as much pay as his superior.

Second assistant keeper Austin wrote that he had watch duty every third night,

"beginning one hour before sunset, and lasting continuously until one or one and one half after sunrise. Work in the tower consisting of carrying up oil for lamp, dusting off lens, lighting up lamp and adjusting same in afternoon. In morning, after extinguishing light, I get up the curtains and cover the lens, fill reservoir with oil, wind up lens machinery, and wipe up watch tower. The watch averaging fourteen hours."

Austin further detailed his required duties as

"painting and scrubbing tower and dwellings inside and out, handling supplies such as oil, coal...[intelligble]...whitewashing fences, mowing lawn, and general work suggested by the keeper in charge. Averaging about six hours a day."

Signed,

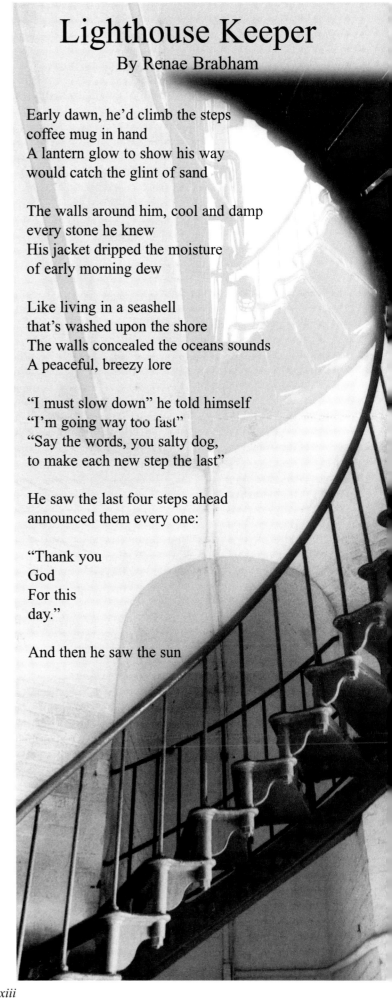

Lighthouse Keeper
By Renae Brabham

Early dawn, he'd climb the steps
coffee mug in hand
A lantern glow to show his way
would catch the glint of sand

The walls around him, cool and damp
every stone he knew
His jacket dripped the moisture
of early morning dew

Like living in a seashell
that's washed upon the shore
The walls concealed the oceans sounds
A peaceful, breezy lore

"I must slow down" he told himself
"I'm going way too fast"
"Say the words, you salty dog,
to make each new step the last"

He saw the last four steps ahead
announced them every one:

"Thank you
God
For this
day."

And then he saw the sun

*Two Different Austin Families
Served First at Cape Hatteras and Later at
Currituck Beach Light Station*

Homer Treadwell Austin

With Maretta (Austin) Derrickson and
Hilda (Austin) Williams

Homer Treadwell Austin served for two years as assistant keeper at Cape Hatteras 1912-1913. He was born the son of Henry Bunyon Austin and Patsy (Willis) Austin. He married his pretty Orphia (Midgett) in June 1907. Homer and Orphia had a large family including Willie Alford (1907-1990), Elice (1908-1908), Sibyl Gates (1911-1990), Sidney (1914-1934), Maretta (1916-1999), Mildred (1918), Homer T. Jr. (1925-1998), Hilda (1927), Lovie (1930-1930).

Maretta "Ret" and Mildred "Mill" were not only sisters, but fast buddies while growing up, according to Ret. She told a story about staying at a sparkplug lighthouse in the Chesapeake Bay. These lighthouses were named for their sparkplug shape and they were located in the bay, totally surrounded by water, often a mile or several miles from land. In other words, it wasn't exactly a place to take your dog for a walk...or to host two young girls. But Ret said they loved to accompany her dad wherever he was stationed, so they spent two weeks on one particular trip to the light that Ret remembered as Middle Ground .

"We fished, played cards, anything we could think of," Ret recalled. And often we got bored, so we made up lots of games. Once we sneaked my father's hammer out on the deck. We found some slate and broke it up into little pieces so we could play 'tiddly winks.' Oh, no! Daddy was not happy! But he was such an understanding parent and he didn't punish us."

Another daughter, Hilda, wrote of her family and growing up on Roanoke Island. Hilda gives us a good idea of this family's priorities and how the nurturing of two caring parents carried on with the Austin children. "My father was a lighthouse keeper and my mother was a homemaker. I didn't realize it at the time, but I was not only blessed with having such good parents but also older brothers and sisters."

"My brother, Willie, was the first member of this union. 'Buddy,' as he was so affectionately known to everyone in the Austin family, was born in 1907...so you can see there was a 'little' bit of difference in our ages. My mother and father adopted [him] when he was about seventeen months old and could not have loved him anymore had he been their biological son... "

"...At the time I was born he [Keeper Homer Austin] was the keeper at Currituck Lighthouse in Corolla, North Carolina. Daddy was stationed there for a number of years and all of my brothers and sisters remember when the family lived there. I have some memories of it when Estelle [Estelle Jones, Hilda's sister's child who was the same age and they grew up like twins] and I played around the lighthouse as well as the old Knight estate [hunt club] which remains close by. The keepers house at Corolla is on the National Historic Register. The principal person in securing this in its abandoned and vandalized state is John F. Wilson, IV, great-grandson of Orphia and Homer Austin. Much work has been done to preserve the house, which is so beautiful... A large portrait of Orphia and Homer Austin hangs inside this house. My older siblings remember going to school in the little one-room schoolhouse located nearby the lighthouse. They have many memories of living there and I've enjoyed listening to Ret and Mill reminisce about those days. Mill says 'they were some of the happiest days of my life.' Mill talks about driving our mother to Virginia Beach to grocery shop. She was probably too young to be at the wheel of an automobile, but with no police patrol and riding the 'wash,' one did not have to be concerned with speeding or getting a 'ticket.'"

Mill is the sister that Ret called the "bold one. "She'd do anything!" Ret laughed. "We had such great areas to explore on our own. Daddy took care of the lighthouse and Mama took care of everything else."

Hilda added, "Growing up in Manteo was an 'easy' life. There was always so much love. I always think of wanting to stay up and listen to Mama and Daddy and relatives and friends tell stories of 'olden' times. We always had a 'daybed' in the 'sitting room' where I would fall fast asleep listening to the tales."

> *"My father was a lighthouse keeper and my mother was a homemaker. I didn't realize it at the time, but I was not only blessed with having such good parents but also older brothers and sisters."*

Timeline

Homer Treadwell Austin (1881-1949)
Assistant Keeper 1912-1913

Orphia and Homer T. Austin probably never realized how many people would admire their picture decades into the future. A large portrait of this image hangs in the keepers quarters at the Currituck Beach Light Station. "Mother was a homemaker and gardening was her number one hobby and one could easily tell by taking a look at our yard," daughter Hilda stated. The Austin family endured separation at times due to their father's remote lighthouse service duty, but maintained their home in Manteo, even rebuilding it after a tragic fire. Photo courtesy Hilda (Austin) Williams

Contributing information on Homer T. Austin were Willie Austin, Jr., Gregory W. Williams, Hilda (Austin)Williams. Quotes also were taken from Maretta "Ret" (Austin) Derrickson during an interview November 1997 at her home in Florida. For more on this family, see Currituck Beach Lighthouse Oral Histories *To Illuminate a Dark Space* by Jenny Edwards for the Outer Banks Conservationists 2000.

He Saved a Lighthouse During a Dedicated Career
M. Wesley Austin

Born in 1864, Wesley Austin spent his formative years aboard windjammers traveling the East Coast. Austin's career spanned over four decades as keeper at Cape Hatteras, Currituck Beach, and Ocracoke Light Stations from 1885-1929.

By Walter P. Garrish

M. Wesley Austin, my grandfather and whom I called "Papa Austin," was born on Hatteras Island in 1864 to his parents Isaac Farrow Austin, Sr. and Sarah Ann Midgett. Not much is known of his early years of growing up on Hatteras. His formal education was from the school he attended on the island. His first appearance on the U.S. Census reports was in the year 1870. At this time, Wesley was age seven and at home with his parents and his brothers, William, Isaac, and Robert, and his sister Charlotte. An older sister Charlotte had died prior to 1870 and a subsequent sister became her namesake. His father, Isaac, was listed on the census as a carpenter.

Wesley next appears on the 1880 census at age sixteen. He was living at home as were his brothers William, Isaac, Robert, and John, and sister, Charlotte. A younger sister Rebecca and a younger brother Edward both had died in 1878. It was not too long afterwards that Wesley would leave home for a new life that would forever tie him to the sea.

Papa spent his late boyhood and early manhood aboard windjammers, plying the coastal waters between ports of the eastern seaboard. He endured the hardships which mariners had to accept as the norm back in those days of sail- standing watches on bitter cold nights aboard vessels that were often blown off course during gales and living aboard craft that were often water-logged and in danger of sinking.

In the year 1885, at age of twenty-one, Wesley decided it was time to give up the life at sea and try something that would keep him closer to home. His life was now becoming more closely tied to his future wife, Isabelle Frances Barnett, and this, no doubt, had some influence on Wesley's decision. Isabelle was a local girl, the daughter of James J. Barnett, (Cape Hatteras assistant keeper in 1907) and Salome Dailey.

On July 6, 1885, Wesley joined the U.S. Lighthouse Service. He served part of his freshman year aboard the tenders that transported supplies to the various lighthouses along the coast. On September 26 of the same year, Wesley received his permanent appointment at the Cape Hatteras Lighthouse as third assistant, (keeper of the Hatteras Beacon at Cape Point). His salary was $400 a year.

On January 12, 1886, Wesley and Belle Barnett, "Mama Austin" as all her grandchildren called her, were married. On July 19, 1887, their first daughter, Iola was born. Three years later, on January 12, 1889, Wesley received a promotion to second assistant keeper with a salary increase of fifty dollars. These promotions were important because every dollar was needed for his growing family. On September 27, 1890, their second child, another daughter, Sarah Salome, was born. In April of 1892, Wesley received his promotion to first assistant keeper, and on July 12, their third daughter, Maude Hunter, was born.

At Cape Hatteras, one of Papa Austin's main assignments early in his service was to keep the old Hatteras Beacon Light burning. This was located about a mile southwest of the big striped tower. Often during his later years, he told of the night during a hurricane that he fought the force of the breakers to apply a flame to the old wick so that mariners might be warned of the dangerous sandbars nearby. It was during this attempt to keep the light burning that the old beacon gave a lurch and was toppled to a 45-degree angle from the force of the sea.

> *"Papa spent his late boyhood and early manhood aboard windjammers, plying the coastal waters between ports of the eastern seaboard. He endured the hardships which mariners had to accept as the norm back in those days of sail..."*

In Papa's obituary, written by my father, James D. Garrish, July 13, 1941, the story is told. The account reads, "...Often during his [Austin's] later years he tells about 'the night that he fought a hurricane and sweeping breakers to gain a foothold on this old beacon - how, while applying a flame to the oil wick, the old beacon soon to be abandoned, gave a lurch and toppled over to a 45 degree angle.' With a prayer on his lips, this man of great faith, clung to the leaning structure, lighted and adjusted the lamp so that its beam of light might warn mariners of the dangerous sand bar nearby. An unselfish prayer was his." His exemplary conduct distinguished Austin as a dedicated keeper early in his career.

My grandfather remained at the Cape Hatteras Light until November 15, 1893, when at the age of twenty-nine, he transferred to the Currituck Beach Lighthouse at Corolla, as first assistant keeper. There, Papa shared the double keepers quarters with his brother William Riley Austin, who had entered the service on January 16, 1888, and had been transferred from the Hatteras Inlet Lighthouse (screwpile) on June

TIMELINE

M. WESLEY AUSTIN (1864-1941)

ASSISTANT KEEPER AT CAPE HATTERAS 1885-1893:

Wesley Austin joined the U.S. Lighthouse Service during the heyday of American lighthouses. After reorganization of the old U.S. Lighthouse Establishment into the Light-House Board in 1852, the majority of lighthouses were rebuilt and new ones replaced old light vessels. The boom lasted until the Civil War. After the war, rebuilding began again with a frenzy in order to light the seaways for increasing maritime trade. By 1885, when Wesley began his Lighthouse Service career, the tall lights of North Carolina and the dozens of sound and river lights lit the waters like diamonds in the night.

2, 1891. It was at Corolla that five more children were born: Walter, Leon, Monford, Ruby, and Wilma. He was now receiving $500 per year.

At Currituck Beach Light Station, the keeper and his family were assigned one half of the quarters and Papa and his brother, William Riley, had the other half. They now had fifteen children between them and one can only imagine the crowded quarters! The primary keeper had an only child and it was through this only child, Nellie Swain, that some insight on the individuals and family life of the keeper and his two assistants has been gained. Before she passed away, her daughter made a voice tape of Nellie relating her memories of her childhood at the Currituck Beach Light. Her memories of Wesley were a reflection of how he lived his whole life. "He was a very religious and good man." There was no minister at the small Methodist Church at Corolla, so Wesley held services every Sunday morning and Sunday School for the kids.

In 1912, Papa Austin transferred to the Ocracoke Island Light Station at Ocracoke as primary keeper. He and Mama Austin took five of their eight children from the Currituck Beach Light Station to the Ocracoke Light Station (the three older girls had married and stayed in Corolla). Here he gave seventeen more years to the Lighthouse Service. This is where he retired in 1929 at the age of sixty-five after forty-four years of faithful and unblemished service. He said, "Yes, I'm getting too old and shaky to serve my country as a Light Keeper, but I will continue to serve my God. I will never be too old to serve Him and by serving God, I serve my country best. God and my country will be first with me until the end."

He died after a long career in the U.S. Lighthouse Service on July 13, 1941, on Ocracoke Island.

Wesley Austin and his lifelong friend and mate, Belle (Barnett) Austin, remain side by side in a composite picture. Both Wesley and Belle had many family members who were outstanding servicemen of the U.S. Coast Guard, U.S. Lifesaving and Lighthouse Services.
Photo courtesy Walter P. Garrish

Source: Register of Lighthouse Keepers 1845-1912, NC-TX, 5th District. Microfilm at Nat'l Archives, M1373.

Ending quote is from an article entitled "Greater Faith Had No Man," written by his son-in-law James D. Garrish, Sr. and published in the *Beacon* in 1941.

M. Wesley Austin's grandson, Walter "Potter" Garrish has researched his family's genealogy and gathered documents from the National Archives in Washington, D.C. on his grandfather's U.S. Lighthouse Service career.

For information on Nellie Swain and family life at the Currituck Beach Light Station, see *To Illuminate a Dark Space* by Jenny Edwards published for the Outer Banks Conservationists, Inc. 1999.

Papa Austin

With Keeper Wesley Austin's Daughter, "Miss Ruby" (1906-1997)

"Miss Ruby," as the islanders on Ocracoke knew her, was born January 27, 1906, in the double keeper's house at the Currituck Beach Lighthouse in the village of Corolla, North Carolina. She was the second youngest daughter of Keeper Wesley Austin's eight children. Her "Papa" had transferred from the Cape Hatteras Light Station, where he had served for eight years. At Cape Hatteras, his career progressed as he worked his way up the roster from third to first assistant.

In an interview at Miss Ruby's home in 1997 on Ocracoke Island, she described one of her strongest memories, the storm of 1913. "The waves were terrible. The boats washed up on the island and over the fences around the lighthouse."

Principal Keeper Wesley Austin stood in the yard of the Ocracoke Lighthouse in his U.S. Lighthouse Service uniform. After taking care of the Hatteras Beacon Light and serving at the Currituck Beach Lighthouse, Austin became the primary keeper at Ocracoke for seventeen years from 1912 until 1929. Wesley Austin is remembered by family members as a deeply religious man, a devoted husband and father, and a dedicated lighthouse keeper. Photo courtesy Walter Garrish

One of the reasons she admired her father was shared. "Papa shook with a kind of palsy just like this," and she demonstrated by moving her hand side to side. "Papa drank 'postum,' you know what 'postum' is? It's coffee. And he never lost a drop."

Austin had learned to compensate for the unsteadiness of his hands and never skipped a beat on the job. At Ocracoke as the primary keeper, he had the tedious job of lighting the fourth order Fresnel lens on time and the same cleaning and maintenance duty expected of any keeper.

Miss Ruby's uncle was Captain Benjamin Baxter Dailey, brother to her mother, Salome. Dailey was winner of the congressional gold medal for lifesaving in 1884 for leading the rescue of the *Ephraim Williams*. "We called him 'the Hero' in the family," she proudly recounted.

Her entire family made a life from the sea. With Coast guardmen, Lighthouse Service keepers, Lifesaving Service surfmen, and fishermen on all sides reaching back as far as genealogy will allow, her relatives are deeply rooted in the civilization of the Outer Banks of North Carolina.

Miss Ruby speaks of "Uncle Walter." Her grandfather was James L. Barnett, Jr. whose brother was the celebrated Captain Walter Barnett. Barnett was in charge of the Diamond Shoals Lightship when it was approached and sunk by a German submarine in 1918 during World War I.

Staying close to the sea and her home on Ocracoke came naturally for Miss Ruby. She enjoyed the island lifestyle and became one of the most respected women there. She played piano and organ for her church for over forty years for worship services, weddings, and funerals. She made "old-fashioned frame quilts for all my children through grandchildren."

"I remember we played tag in the lighthouse yard, and marbles. There were children who lived all around the lighthouse [Ocracoke] and I had friends to play with even though we were on an island."

Miss Ruby also remembered the visits of the U.S. Lighthouse Service tender *Holly* and the coal, oil, and wood brought once a year. The inspector often came on this trip and gave Captain Austin the top score for a keeper's job well done. She recalled that her father had to keep close records, even for the lamp oil used for lights in the keeper's home. She commented, "That tender had a dog on it. The biggest blonde lab I've ever seen. That dog would jump up on me and it felt like he put his arms around me. I had never been so frightened! Papa raised his own beautiful vegetable garden, and we had chickens. Making only $450 a year, how did he live and send me to school and raise eight children? He had to pay my high school tuition," she stated incredulously.

"We didn't have a Christmas tree at Christmas but we hung our stockings at the mantel." Christmas for Wesley Austin and his family was celebrated for its traditionally religious meaning.

A big loss to the Garrish, Austin, and Barnett families happened in 1917. Ruby's brother, Monford Lambert Austin, joined the Revenue Cutter Service in February, following in the footsteps of his heritage at the age of seventeen. Only two weeks passed before Monford was called to duty to rescue victims from the steamer *Louisiana* near Ocean City, Maryland. The young Monford, along with a friend from Ocracoke who had joined the service with him, drowned in this valiant rescue attempt.

Resuming talk about her parents, Miss Ruby said that her mother, Belle, "... didn't help in the lighthouse, but she helped in other ways. She took care of all us kids and she was a great seamstress. She made clothes for us and for others. There were no clothes stores on the island and everyone would bring their dresses to Belle to be made for them. Of course, other things that we needed we ordered from Sears way back."

"Papa?" Ruby summed up about her father. "I was very proud of my daddy. He was a good father. I loved him. As a lighthouse keeper he got a lot of respect. He gave me good training. He always went to church and he took us with him. It was an inspiration to me to love the church and love people. You get to know others and have good friends. Sometimes we need each other."

Keeper Austin strictly recorded each time he left the light station. In the logbook from the Ocracoke Light Station there are dozens of entries that read, "Went to church." Rarely are there other notations of going anywhere else. His dedication kept him close to his family and his lighthouse.

Walter Riley Austin, son of Wesley Austin and Nell Swain, lounge upon what appears to be the tramway at the Currituck Beach Light Station. The lighthouse is in the background. Nell is the daughter of another Currituck Beach Lighthouse keeper, Nathan Swain.
Photo courtesy Walter Garrish

Keeper Wesley Austin's grandson, Walter "Potter" Garrish offered this recently discovered photograph. "It appears the family is at the keepers quarters at the Currituck Beach Light. Left to right in back: Leon, Wilma, and Walter; in front are Monford and Ruby.
Photo courtesy Walter Garrish

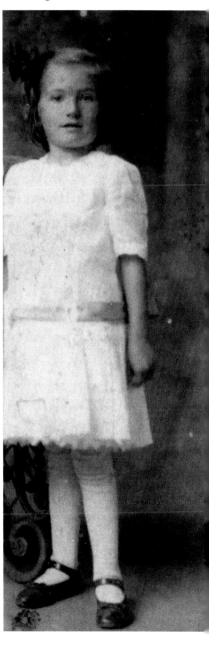

As a young girl, Ruby loved to dress up. Originally her sister, Wilma, appeared in this picture with her, but many years ago when copies of photographs were difficult to obtain, especially on Ocracoke Island where they lived, Wilma simply cut off her part of the picture and took it with her. Circa 1912
Photo courtesy Walter Garrish

Source: Personal interview with Miss Ruby on Ocracoke, 1997 and The LIGHTHOUSE NEWS Vol. III No. 1 by Cheryl Shelton-Roberts 1997.

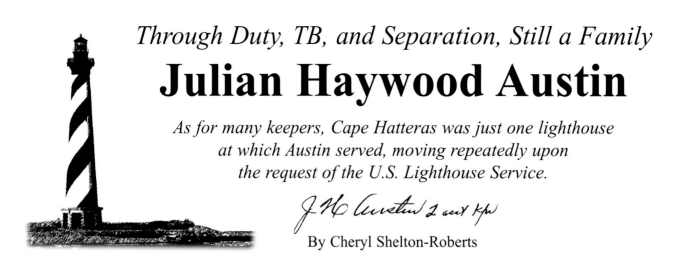

Through Duty, TB, and Separation, Still a Family

Julian Haywood Austin

As for many keepers, Cape Hatteras was just one lighthouse at which Austin served, moving repeatedly upon the request of the U.S. Lighthouse Service.

By Cheryl Shelton-Roberts

In the living room of the Cape Hatteras double keepers' quarters in 1928, Katherine Dobson Austin placed a mirror on cotton batting under the Christmas tree that her husband, Julian, had cut for her in nearby Buxton Woods. Upon it she rested various animals and fish, creating a Christmas scene for her family. It was her favorite time of year! She hung angel-faced ornaments and old Kriss Kringle paper ornaments while arranging and rearranging a string of glass beads on her Hatteras Christmas tree. She took great care with these ornaments that she had carefully packed and brought with her from her Maryland family home. As she looked out the window, she saw her young husband stride across the wide light station grounds, carrying the responsibility of a respected Cape Hatteras keeper.

Assistant Keeper Julian Haywood Austin, son of John Lotson Austin and Arkey "Empie" (Poyner) Austin, had been born February 20, 1898, at their family home in Trent, now known as Frisco, North Carolina. From mid-1916 until Christmas Day 1917, Julian served on three lightships, including #71 stationed on Diamond Shoals off Cape Hatteras. He hopped jobs from one "oiler" to another and returned to the United States Lighthouse Service (U.S.L.H.S.) June 27, 1921. Julian began work on LV #49, which would begin an uninterrupted career. After he transferred to Choptank River Light, Maryland, Julian began courting a lovely young lady, who would soon become his lifetime partner.

Katherine married Julian on September 27, 1923, and they spent a month-long honeymoon at the Choptank River Light, enjoying every moment as a new bride on the old Chesapeake Bay Light. After Julian transferred to the Cape Charles Light Station on Smith Island, Virginia, in 1925, Katherine bore Julian a fine son, his namesake on May 18, 1926.

Julian Jr. took to lighthouses right away; in fact, when only eighteen months old, he climbed his first lighthouse to the very top- on his own. Katherine had left her young son on the grass near the Cape Charles tower while she quickly went inside to check something cooking on the stove. Julian made a fast escape, entered the tower, and started to explore. Appearing from around the corner of the house where he had been painting, Keeper Austin found a frantic Katherine trying to locate their vanished toddler.

All they heard was "Clunk... clunk... clunk."

Keeper Julian Sr. ran into the lighthouse and looked up the winding steps. Above him was the speedy crawler, Julian Jr., taking each step deliberately, holding a big shell in one hand. Every other iron step echoed the "clunk...clunk...clunk" of the shell that the baby held determinedly. How he didn't fall through the wide gaps between each steep step is a miracle.

> *"For this young family, it would perhaps be the most carefree time they would ever have together...And Julian Jr.'s strongest memory at Hatteras as a wee lad is how he loved to swing on the porch at the double keepers quarters at Hatteras."*

For this young family, it would perhaps be the most carefree time they would ever have together. In 1928, with hope and the energy of youth, the family had moved with Keeper Austin to the Cape Hatteras Light Station, near Julian's family home in Frisco.

Christmastime at Hatteras was a festive one for Katherine. Away from her family for the first time, she felt comfortable amongst the network of friends and Julian's family, learning to bake Miss Sudie Jennette's famous biscuits while shaping their half of the double keepers quarters into a welcoming home for her, Julian Sr., and their son. Keeper Jennette's son, Rany, often told Katherine that her Christmas tree was the prettiest he'd ever seen. The colorful, hand-blown glass ornaments depicting a pipe with Santa's head at the end of the stem, and the festive round ornaments became a lifelong memory for this young boy. And Julian Jr.'s strongest memory at Hatteras as a wee lad is how he loved to swing on the porch at the double keepers quarters at Hatteras. Contented days continued as Katherine was expecting her second child.

Marilyn Ione Austin was born in the family home in Frisco, the next village south of the Cape Hatteras Light Station, on April 14, 1929. Just days before her birth, Julian

Timeline

Julian Haywood Austin (1898-1970)
Assistant Keeper 1928-1929:

While Keeper Austin served at Cape Hatteras,
America went from boom to bust on Wall Street.
At the lighthouse, little changed. Kerosene lamps glowed in the keeper's homes and an incandescent oil vapor lamp was lit in the tower each evening.

Sr. transferred from Cape Hatteras to Brant Island Lighthouse in the southerly part of the Pamlico Sound, and later to the Roanoke River Lighthouse at the mouth of the Roanoke River, North Carolina. One of the "water lights," this rectangular wood-trimmed house built on pilings offshore, the lighthouse was accessible only by boat.

Though Julian was often absent from his young and growing family, Katherine was safely in the charge of Julian's widowed mother. Empie had returned many years earlier to live with her father, William Poyner, in the home he had built in Frisco. Just across the road, Julian Sr. had built a home for him and Katherine the year they married.

Katherine was a venturesome young woman who took her two little ones with her to visit Julian at the Roanoke River Light and lived at the river light for several months over a period of time. When going to the mainland, the family would go by boat. Once on the mainland, they walked to Mr. Askew's farm near Mary Hill where Keeper Austin parked his car in a barn. After visiting Julian Jr.'s favorite spot- the natural spring where the farm family kept their cold milk- they would take the car into town to buy supplies and catch up on family news and world events. If Keeper Austin were alone on these trips, he would occasionally drop in and visit the Askews for a little friendly conversation and share news. One of the tenant farmer's children had measles, and shared them generously with Keeper Austin.

During an interview, daughter Marilyn recalled that the family was not supposed to be at the river light; indeed, she recalled Julian, Jr. and her mother hiding under the steps with her when the U.S. Lighthouse Inspector came- forever amazed that they all remained quiet. It was good fortune that they went against this rule, for it saved the keeper's life.

Katherine asked her husband if he'd had the measles. "No," was the dreaded answer, and in a short time Keeper Austin became gravely ill and eventually went unconscious. "Daddy would have died if Mama hadn't been there to help him," Marilyn explained. Katherine, who had trained as a nurse, took care of Keeper Austin, tended to two young ones, kept the light going, and sounded the foghorn for the duration of her husband's illness. Her strength would be fleeting, however.

Julian Haywood Austin, Sr. stood for a studio picture at age seventeen. His expression foretells a serious career man. 1915
Photo courtesy Marilyn (Austin) Meads

(Below) Christmastime was always very important to Keeper Julian H. Austin's wife, Katherine (Dobson) Austin. Verna wrote, "These handblown delicate Christmas ornaments, the lovely paper angel and Kris Kringle, the celluloid lion... were only a few of the lovely things that Mother used to decorate the fresh tree at Christmas, the same way her mother decorated her tree. Mother's love of Christmas trees was passed down to me and I'm usually the last one to take down my tree." The ornaments are snug in a longleaf pine basket woven by Katherine during her years in a sanatorium away from her family. "Some had dainty pinwheel designs in them made out of raffia," Verna added.
From the private collection of
Verna (Austin) Wall

(Above left) Katherine (Dobson) Austin smiles in spite of the long separation from her young family during her recuperation at a sanatorium. She was a resident of the McCain Sanatorium near Pinehurst, N.C. "Pine ozone" from trees along sandy paths in what was a drier climate in the 1930s was thought the best treatment- antibiotics had yet to be created. Claiming old and young alike, TB affected an estimated 45% of the South through the 1950s (source: Tufts Archives, Pinehurst, NC). The spread of TB has always been unpredictable since it can lie dormant in a healthy person. Circa 1937
(Above right) Arkey "Empie" (Poyner) Austin, Keeper Julian H. Austin's mother. She helped with Julian's two young children after he left Cape Hatteras. Upon her death in 1935 from TB, while her own daughter was away at a sanatorium, Julian took his family of three, including nine-month-old Verna, to Katherine's mother in Maryland. Circa 1930
Photos courtesy Marilyn (Austin) Meads

This was the home of William A. Poyner and his wife, Margaret B. (Rollinson) Poyner in Frisco. Julian's father, John Lotson Austin, married their daughter, Arkey "Empie" in 1897 and there were two children born in Hatteras: Julian in 1898 and Myrtle after 1900. In the 1910 census, Empie was listed as a widow and had returned with her two young children to live with her parents in Trent (now Frisco). She apparently never remarried. Julian spent his youth in the home of his grandparents. He returned in 1928 to build a home of his own across the road from his grandparents for his growing family in Frisco. Circa 1928
Photo courtesy Marilyn (Austin) Meads

A letter from the Lighthouse Service dated May 2, 1933, told Austin that, due to the economy, the Roanoke River Light was being discontinued and he was to report to Bodie Island Light Station and Keeper Vernon Gaskill, Sr. on June 2, 1933. Austin reported alone because he sent Marilyn and Julian Jr. back to the family home in Frisco with Katherine. Julian, Jr. attended the two-room schoolhouse there in the second grade.

During the early 1900s, residents accepted violent storms as a natural part of island life, nature's housecleaning, so to speak. They occurred without forewarning, leaving residents little or no time to prepare. Two such storms, today called "hurricanes," struck the Outer Banks in 1933. The keepers' families never returned to the Cape Hatteras Lighthouse due to the extreme flooding from the wallops of these back-to-back blows.

The first tempest struck early September 15 while Katherine's parents were visiting her in Frisco. Marilyn looked back. "A bad storm blew all the water out of the sound. Granddad and Grandmom were down there picking up oysters and fish and he looked- and a wall of water was rushing back across the sound! He ran up to the house and told Mama to get everything up off the yard. Mama went across the road to Grandmom Austin's to help her get her chickens and ducks up to the top part of the barn, and when Mama got back to our house, the tide was up to her neck."

Marilyn continued to describe this destructive storm. "It cut New Inlet between Frisco and Hatteras and Little Inlet above Rodanthe. The houses were fenced to keep out cattle, sheep, and pigs...any kind of livestock. People knew which animals belonged to whom by the notches in the ears. But Mama made an exception when a young calf floated by in the storm's flood. She got the calf and brought it into the fenced area and onto the porch that had a foot of water on it.

"All kinds of things were going by, including snakes and rabbits. Mama and Granddad tried to put the furniture up before it got wet. Mrs. Rosa Fulcher and her children Graham, Maxine, and Florine came over and stayed with us until the tide went down. This hurricane destroyed the Methodist Church and a store that was on the sound. We went to church in the schoolhouse until they built the Little Grove Methodist Church."

The second leviathan storm struck in the fall of 1933, quite an introduction for Julian and Marilyn who were visiting their keeper father at Bodie Island at his new duty station. The light station at Bodie Island, set back farther from the ocean, fared better than the Hatteras Light Station, and would continue to be manned for another seven years by Keepers Gaskill and Austin until after the merger of the Lighthouse Service and the U.S. Coast Guard.

Continuing her family's story, Marilyn chronicled, "We were at Grandmom Austin's in Frisco and at Bodie Island in 1934 when Mama was expecting Verna. The doctor told her if she had another baby that it would probably break down her health. So we went up to Maryland to stay on a farm with her cousin Elsie Stevens and her husband Elmer. Mama stayed in bed and I would help carry her food up to her and help take care of her when I was only five years old.

"Verna was born in the Easton Memorial Hospital in Maryland on October 29, 1934. We went back to Frisco shortly after that."

Grandmother Austin, to whom Katherine had been close during her time in Frisco, died of tuberculosis at Christmas, 1935, approximately nine months after Verna was born. And then, disaster struck again; it was an event that would separate the family for years.

Marilyn stated, "When Verna was nine months old, Mama contracted tuberculosis. She got real sick and she went to the McCain Sanatorium in Pinehurst [also known as the Sanatorium for the Treatment of Turberculosis of Hoke County], North Carolina, where she stayed for two and one-half years."

Marilyn recalled the trip when her dad was taking Julian nine, Marilyn six, and Verna barely one-year old away from Frisco and their mother to stay with Grandmother Dobson in Maryland. "We took the Little Creek Ferry and Mama said, 'Now, don't cry-big girls don't cry.' Mama was down there on the dock waving and waving-I chewed my lip to pieces trying not to cry. And while we were on the way to Grandma's, Verna needed her milk. Granddad went into a farmhouse and explained to the family there that he needed to warm the bottle up. And they let him and after that they became friends."

When the family arrived in Oxford, Katherine's mother, suffering from scarlet fever, greeted them. Grandmother Dobson struggled to care for her three grandchildren.

History was repeating itself: Empie had returned home after her husband, John, died, making her parents key figures during Julian's and his sister Myrtle's childhood. In turn, Julian had returned to the same home, making Empie a key figure in her grandchildren's lives. After her death in 1935, Katherine's mother became the caretaker while she convalesced in a sanatorium.

In keeping with the professional that he was, Julian Sr. returned to Bodie Island alone to handle his keeper's duties, in spite of his great concern for his wife and three children.

Those many hours standing solitary vigil at the Bodie Island Lighthouse, one of the most remote light stations in the 1930s, were filled with the solace of reading.

All three Austin children have agreed that their father loved history. "He had his own fine collection of books; he could have taught history, he knew so much," an admiring Verna remembered.

Only a few months after he had left the three children in the charge of ailing Grandmother Dobson, Keeper Austin decided that she couldn't handle the enormous task. He announced that Marilyn and Julian Jr. would have to transfer to Bodie Island with him, leaving only Verna in Maryland.

Son Julian's first memories at Bodie Island in 1934 are of the ...."MOSQUITOES!" he said with emphasis. His two sisters nodded in complete agreement.

At nine years of age, Julian was accustomed to adult

responsibilities; in fact, he had often taken care of baby Verna in Maryland, and had always treated both girls like his own children. At Bodie Island, Julian did what he could to help Keeper Austin while Marilyn washed dishes, cleaned for the family, and learned to cook from the time she could reach the wood stove.

"Daddy was a good cook," Marilyn said. "Everybody pulled together."

"If he didn't burn it up!" Verna laughed. "He learned to read directions."

"HOTBLAST IT! I done burnt it up!" Julian Jr. imitated his father. The keepers' kids laughed together at the good memories.

"I did a little of everything for Daddy to help out at Bodie Island, " Julian Jr. recounted. And it was black out there on the island- no lights, no nothing. Once in a while headlights would pass on the way to the hunt club or Oregon Inlet."

"Julian slept in the bathroom," Verna began with a big smile towards her brother. "There was a bathroom on both sides of the double keepers' house, but we didn't' use it as a bathroom."

The bathroom, which had been officially assigned bedroom duty by night, was a playroom for the girls by day. Keeper Vernon Gaskill had requested a bathtub repeatedly from the Lighthouse Service. When it was finally installed, he pumped water from the cistern up one flight to the bathroom and prepared for the finest bath of his life. Just after Gaskill came rocketing out of the icy bath water, it was officially designated a bedroom/playroom. Keeper Gaskill's daughter, Erline, played with them during the 1930s.

Sometimes both Keeper Gaskill and Austin and their families were at the light station together, but more often than not, only one keeper and his family were present due to two technological advances. A "call bell" was installed over the flame during the late 1920s, alerting the keeper on duty that something wrong was afoot with the lamp; a sensor positioned over the flame sent out an alarm along a wire that connected in the keeper's bedroom. Then, around 1933, the light was electrified, and since no foghorn was installed at Bodie Island, often one keeper was capable of running the light station. While one family was off the island, the other made use of the entire house. John Gaskill, son of Primary Keeper Vernon Gaskill, says, "We were one big family."

"Bodie Island is home to us," said Julian, Jr., and his sisters nodded readily in agreement. "It's the one that comes to mind when you say 'home.'"

Visually remembering their home at Bodie Island, Verna continued, "The outdoor toilets were really fixed up snazzy. It was a wood house with a foundation."

Julian added, "It had a vent pipe and we kept a screen across the windows."

"There were two small windows," Verna joined in, "with a two-seater and the two small windows were at the back."

With a hearty laugh, Julian pitched in, "If you didn't keep screens across the windows, the mosquitoes would've eaten you up!"

Julian recalled the toilet was furthest out from the house. "There was also a shed for a workshop where paints, and a push mower, work supplies and cleaning materials for the Coleman lanterns we used to light in the house. Three was a garage about fifty feet from the house."

Marilyn and Julian clearly described the generators. There were two Westinghouse generators in the south workroom in the entrance building (once used to store oil) of the Bodie Island Lighthouse. They would be run about eight hours, twice a week, and used gas that ran like a car engine with approximately 250 (two banks) batteries on each side on shelves.

There was a bulb indicator on one battery of each bank. When charged by generator, the bulb indicator would be at the top; when the indicator was almost at the bottom, the generators were run to charge them.

These batteries supplied the electricity after the Bodie Island Light was automated, switched from the incandescent oil vapor (IOV) kerosene lamp to a 1,000-watt bulb. The light then (circa 1933) was changed from fixed to flashing and only one keeper had to stay at the light station.

Electricity was also supplied to a flash controller to change the beacon's steady white beam to its present flash characteristic: 2 1/2 seconds on, 2 1/2 seconds off, 2 1/2 seconds on and a 22 1/2 second eclipse, in 2 cycles-per-minute.

There was no fluid stored in the lighthouse. All gasoline and kerosene were housed in a cement oil storage building just southwest of the lighthouse. A small cement walkway remains as reminder of the building's location where the oil was stored separately to protect against fire in the lighthouse. Since Bodie Island was notorious for its dramatic lightning storms, fire was an imminent possibility.

Marilyn vividly remembered the heart-stopping bolt of lightning that hit one of the generators in the tower, jumped to the phone wire, and thus entered the keeper's house. She can still see and hear the glass shattering all around her and the telephone exploding off the wall at the bottom of the stairway. This was an emergency device that kept the surfmen (coast guard) in touch with the lighthouses as keepers of the lifesaving stations and lighthouses watched sea and horizon together.

The generators created direct current. When the light went out it was usually because the generator had broken a belt and the flash controller was knocked out.

"One time," Julian cited, "Daddy and Keeper Gaskill were down at the hunt club. We walked outside and looked up and the light was not on!"

Marilyn and Julian lit out for the hunt club to save the day because momentary darkness of the light meant sure disaster for passing ships. Southbound ships hugging the coast to ride the swift, southerly flowing cold current needed the light of Bodie Island to know when to head southeast to get out and around Cape Hatteras and its infamous Diamond Shoals. The shoals reach out fourteen and more miles off the Hatteras headland and have witnessed the demise of hundreds of ships that ran afoul of them.

In 1943, Keeper Austin transferred to the Wade's Point screwpile lighthouse near Elizabeth City. Austin is with one of his assistants. "Daddy looks like he was in his socks!" daughter Marilyn chuckled.
Photo courtesy Marilyn (Austin) Meads

Wade's Point Lighthouse was located at the mouth of the Pasquotank River to guide seafarers from the north side of the Albemarle Sound into the Pasquotank River and the bustling port at Elizabeth City. Like many of the river and sound lights, it was badly damaged by fire during the Civil War, rebuilt in 1899. Known as a "screwpile" lighthouse, it had large metal screw caps on the end of each piling to help grab the soft, muddy bottom of the sound. Wind and ice were capable of causing great damage to these lights. Old sailors tell of the comfort they received from the sound and river lights along the North Carolina coast. In the pitch black of night with no other landmarks to follow, these lights were the guides for many passing boats and ferries.
Photo courtesy Marilyn (Austin) Meads

The fearless crusaders ran through one-half mile of marshland, teeming with snakes and other nocturnal critters. When they got to the hunt club, they breathlessly delivered the news. "The light is out!"

Daddy said his favorite line, "HOT BLAST IT!" Julian added.

In utter panic, Keeper Gaskill jumped in the car and took off, leaving the Austins standing there is disbelief.

"And it was Daddy's car that he took off in!" Verna chuckled.

Julian commented, "They both knew their jobs were on the line if that light didn't flash."

The keepers regularly cleaned the big Fresnel lens at least twice weekly. Soft, lintless chamois cloth was reserved for this special job. Also, the keeper used large bags of "waste cotton string" for cleaning up in the entrance building to the lighthouse. "I cleaned the lens," Marilyn smiled, "as far up as I could reach." The six-by-eleven-foot, nearly 1,000-prismed giant beehive of glass towered above little Marilyn.

All the Austin children remembered the fenced-in "back" area of the house. The double keepers quarters had been designed so that the "front" of the house faced the light tower. Should he not be at the top of the lighthouse, a keeper could look out his bedroom window and watch the light.

Julian Jr. helped keep the big area of grass cut with a twenty-two inch push mower. "That was a lot of grass, wasn't it Julian?" Verna asked.

"That was a lot of grass," Julian repeated while nodding affirmatively. "Or at least it looked like it to me!"

The children reminisced about the fence. "Wasn't that fence wire below and boards above the top?" Verna questioned.

"Cement posts and wire," Julian answered his younger sister.

Some of Julian's chores included bringing in coal for the living room stove during the wintertime. He also had to keep the wood box by the cook stove in the kitchen filled while sister Marilyn chopped wood. In the absence of their ailing mother, the kids took care of everything possible when their father was on watch at the lighthouse.

Two hundred miles inland at the sanatorium, Katherine kept her own watch from her hospital room, eagerly awaiting a visit from her children. With great anticipation, she thought she recognized some of the people approaching the hospital. Excitedly, she went into the hall by her room and listened to echoes of her children's footsteps that reached her long before sight confirmed their presence. Katherine waited.

"I was trembling as I walked down the long hall," Marilyn shared in her soft voice.

Katherine was a thin woman with long hair wound into a circle at the back of her neck. She stood in the hall with pleading, smiling eyes. She did not speak, so Marilyn walked on.

Then the woman called to her, "Marilyn!"

Marilyn spun about and saw the open arms of her mother. She ran to her and her mother's embrace held all the warmth that had filled her dreams for nearly two years.

Katherine cried while she cradled her daughter. The regrets and time spent waiting for the moment dissipated. A mother comforted her young child, hoping that body language would ease the pain of having to grow up too quickly. But things were as they were. Only time and healing would help bridge the distance between them.

Separation was required for tuberculosis patients prior to the advent of antibiotics. Katherine spent many hours weaving beautiful long-leaf pine baskets. "But she didn't have any strength," Verna added.

Verna remembered her visit to her "Mother Katherine" when she was allowed to briefly see her. "When I was three years old, Grandmother Dobson took me to the sanatorium. Mother saw me and sat down in the middle of the hospital corridor and held her arms out like this," Verna told while dramatically demonstrating outstretched and eager arms. "And I went to her and she was just BAWLING. And she says 'Do you know who I am?' and I said 'You're my mother Katherine' and she bawled once more. And that's really the first time I saw her to know her in person because I was nine months old when she left. I was blessed to have Mother Dobson because she was my earth mother and taught me to love my Mother Katherine by showing me pictures and telling me stories. Mother Katherine was a warm and loving mother...overprotective, but very careful to kiss on the cheek. She didn't want to risk our health...even a remote possibility...until they were absolutely sure she had healed."

The family was together. "Things were as good as they were going to get," Julian whispered. Then he abruptly changed the subject, "The buoy tender dropped off coal, wood, paint and other work supplies, but no food. We had to supply our food ourselves. And the government charged us twenty dollars a month for rent."

For several years Keeper Austin had faced the possibility his ailing wife would leave them a bachelor family. To ease the expense of food and ensure the availability of vegetables on the island, Keeper Austin had labored to raise a garden. Judging by the tentative hold that any life has on the windblown island, it is hard to imagine anyone could coax a garden to yield fresh produce. Marilyn remembered the magic Julian Sr. had worked with his garden. "It looked big to us kids, and he grew all sorts of vegetables."

For other supplies, Keeper Austin would make a trip across the sound to L.D. Tarkington's store in Manteo. "It was in front of the court house but disappeared when Manteo burned," Julian Sr. recollected solemnly.

Julian continued, "If we went to the store, most of the time on Saturday, we'd buy some ice and bring it back. Daddy built two boxes together...one box built on another

These two lighthouse children are Julian Haywood Austin, Jr. and his sister, Marilyn Ione, about five and two years old, respectively. Another sister, Verna, was born in 1934. Circa 1931
Photo courtesy Marilyn (Austin) Meads

Left to right are Keeper Austin's three children, Marilyn, Julian Jr., and Verna, at the wedding of Julian Austin III in 1986. Verna arranged for David Evans of O'Neal's Studio to take the picture at the special occasion.
Photo courtesy Marilyn (Austin) Meads

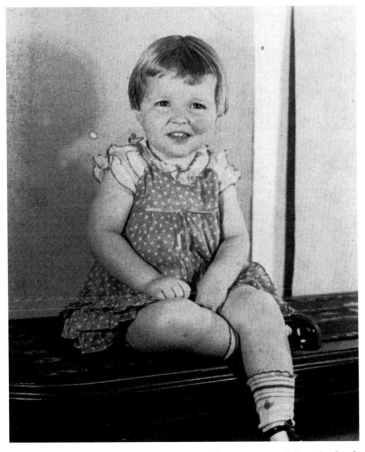
In this image, Verna Lee Austin is three years old in Oxford, Maryland, while she stayed with her Grandmother Dobson and her mother, Katherine, was in a TB sanatorium. 1937
Photo courtesy Verna (Austin) Wall

with sawdust all around it. He'd put ice in another box, set it inside and it'd keep ice for two or three days." And on top of having to get our own food, we were charged $20 a month for rent at the lighthouse and there was no food allowance! We had a kerosene refrigerator, but didn't get it until we'd been there for four years, around 1937."

The children were often alone with their father on Bodie Island. One of their playmates came from the hunt club "next door." George Mann and Julian loved to find mischief between chores.

One day, George, Julian, Marilyn, and Verna were on the brick walkway between the keepers' quarters and the lighthouse, admiring George's new bicycle. "There was a good six-inch drop off the brick walk then," Marilyn remembered.

Verna told the story, "George Mann, the son of the manager of the Bodie Island Hunt Club was over at the lighthouse with his bike and we were playing. George put me on the back 'carrier seat' of the bike to ride behind him along the walk. Some of the other kids must have come up and George was straddling his bike and talking and forgot I was sitting on the back, I was just little. He must have decided to do something else, swung his leg over the bike to get off and knocked me off! It broke my arm in two places! And I remember the ride all the way to the doctor in Manteo because my arm jiggled all the way! I remember he strapped it to my body and all I could do was wiggle my little finger. It was terrible. This was around 1938-39. I remember Dr. Johnson on the corner in Manteo."

Sixty years later, her big brother, Julian, still shakes his head in sympathy. George Mann never forgot either, and he apologized to Verna every time he would see her.

Though they were largely on their own, the children enjoyed island life. Julian said of this time, "Mr. Linquist owned the Bodie Island Club and he'd bring me something for Christmas. He was president of the Otis Elevator Company. He had a room in the clubhouse as big as this living room and had every kind of gun you wanted. We used to sneak them out and shoot them once in a while."

"He was so kind," Verna said with a faraway look. "He brought me a little blue glass tea set one time. I still have one of the cups."

"We left Bodie Island Lighthouse in June of 1940," Marilyn stated, "and after taking our furniture to Frisco to our family home, we moved to Tilghmans Island because Dad had been transferred to the Sharp's Island Lighthouse.

"In 1940, Verna started to school and I was in the sixth grade and Julian in the seventh. The doctor that Mama had seen in Norfolk had told her to never stop taking the artificial air they put through her ribs with a long needle. He said the lung wall would get like leather and she wouldn't be able to collapse the lung to help it heal. Her doctor in Salisbury at the sanatorium stopped the treatment. When she mailed her sputum to be checked, as she regularly did, she tested positive for TB again and had to submit to a physical on Christmas Eve.

"Meantime, Dad had received word he had been transferred to Holland Island Bar Lighthouse out of Chrisfield, Maryland. We moved back to Oxford, and in April, Mama returned to the sanatorium in Salisbury, Maryland. That was another very sad day for me. I went to school and laid my head on my desk until Ms. Ella Haddaway (she had been my mother's teacher also) sent me to the bathroom with my best friend, Iris Retallack, to see if she could find out what was wrong. This was when we had to go back and stay with Grandma Dobson. Mom was away again for another year and a half.

"While she was in the sanatorium, she was sent to John Hopkins Hospital to have seven complete ribs on her right side removed, from breast bone to spine.

"In May of 1942, she came home again until school was out and then we moved to Crisfield, Maryland, Julian, Verna, and me.

"Mom had to stay in bed most all the time. At this time, Verna was in the second grade, and I was in the eighth, and Julian was in the ninth grade.

"Then again, Dad received a transfer to Wade's Point Lighthouse, near Elizabeth City, NC in 1943. So we were again on the move as soon as school was out.

"Verna stayed with Grandma Dobson until 1945 since Mom was still very sick. It was difficult for Verna to leave the only mother she had really known, her beloved Grandmother Dobson. Julian and I started school in Elizabeth City. The war was going on and Julian quit to go into the Merchant Marines. He traveled all over the Atlantic and Pacific, carrying supplies to the troops and of course, this was very hard on Mom and Dad.

"Since everything was rationed during the war, it was difficult to have good food often. But when Julian came to visit, we would have his favorite food. I would go to Mr. Onley's Store on Road Street and get two live chickens (that was the only way you could buy them in those days) and take them home and chop their heads off and clean them," Marilyn ended.

Verna shared her memories of when she left her Grandmother Dobson and moved in with her parents. "Mama would come in late at night to check on me," Verna admitted, "and I would cry softly into my pillow. I didn't want to hurt her! Grandma Dobson had always showed me pictures of her and told me how to run to her and hug her, to never want to ever hurt her."

There had been enough disappointment and hurt, and this was a time for healing, laughter, and the future at last.

Marilyn commented, "In 1946 a new doctor came to town and some new drugs were available for tuberculosis, including Streptomycin. After being treated with the antibiotic, she was cured.

"Julian was drafted into the Army after the war although he had a certificate from President Truman stating he had fulfilled his service. His only choice was to join the Army Reserve and be left with a commitment of one more year's duty.

"1950 was the year my dad retired from the U.S.

Standing almost eleven feet tall, the 1872 Fresnel lens at Bodie Island is one of the few first-order lenses in North America still working today as an active aid to navigation. The center of the versatile lens, first used in America in 1841, could accommodate any source of light. As a child, Marilyn was dwarfed by its immense size and marveled at the hundreds of rainbows that the precision-machined prisms cast all around the lantern room. This 1872 cathedral style lens is made of special crown-glass prisms, designed by Augustin Fresnel in Paris. The most recent valuation of a first order lens was in 1900 at $6,500, but today they are irreplaceable. 1994
Photo courtesy Bruce Roberts

Verna Lee Austin hugged her puppy, Rex. She had returned to stay with her Grandmother Dobson so she could attend the second grade at Oxford, Maryland, when her mother returned to the sanatorium for further treatment. 1942
Photo courtesy Verna (Austin) Wall

"Uncle John" (white shirt) and a friend visited Julian Jr. and Marilyn at Bodie Island. Getting to the island from the north involved using the main road to Whalebone Junction (now Hwy 158) and then following ruts in the sand along the shoreline at low tide. Circa 1934
Photo courtesy Marilyn (Austin) Meads

Lighthouse Service with 32 years of faithful service and should have been a happy time, but Mom began worrying again," Marilyn continued her memoirs. "The Korean War had broken out and Julian Jr. was sent there right away. He was captured in February of 1951 and became a prisoner of war for two and one-half years."

Marilyn said matter-of-factly, "Mama received some letters from Korea verifying that her son was deceased, but she would not give up hope. She never believed he was dead. Something kept her going. And he came back from Korea, but he was legally blind and 100% disabled."

"Mom and Dad retired at the family home in Frisco where she was able to love and keep her grandchildren as much as we'd let her," Verna said with a smile.

Katherine became the third grandmother in this family to serve as a significant influence in her grandchildren's lives. The young mother had been denied closeness to her children due to her contagious illness.

The Austin children cherish memories of their family. Marilyn released her tight grip on two small pieces of paper from sixty years ago that she had been holding for hours and waiting to share. She took them from an autograph book Katherine had given her when they were preparing to move from Bodie Island. Realizing the difficulties in leaving her friends again, Marilyn's mother wanted her to be able to take her friends' autographs with her. Katherine and Julian, Sr. also signed the book on Marilyn's eleventh birthday. Julian's beautiful handwriting was read aloud by Verna:

"May 11, 1940
Dear Daughter,
I think your freckles are cute although I tease you a lot about them. My time here at our Bodie Island Lighthouse Station is short, our happy days here past. I couldn't picture what the future will be. But let us hope we will be located at some station together. I will never forget our Bodie Island.
Love,
Dad"

The second note reads,

"Darling, Marilyn, this is April 14, 1940. Sometime when you're grown and look over this little book you'll remember the night I wrote this. Bodie Island has been taken over by the Coast Guard and we're soon to leave here. It's farewell to this lighthouse and it makes us all sad. I love my little freckled-face girls so much and I hope you'll have a long, happy life. Give to the world the best that you have and the best will come back to you. Your ever-loving mother. Happy Birthday, sweetheart. Katherine Austin."

Indeed, these are "keepers."

Verna wrote of two of her most cherished toys from her childhood. "Teddy and Miss Rachel sit in Keeper Austin's highchair. The Teddy Bear was given to me when I lived in Chrisfield, MD, by Mr. Owl [Verna was living with her Grandmother Dobson while her mother was recovering in a sanatorium and brother Julian Jr. and sister Marilyn were with Keeper Austin at Bodie Island]...when I was in the third grade. Rachel was named after Mrs. Rachel, a friend of Mother's, who came to Manteo on the Adam's Floating Theater. The winning token was in my box of taffy and Mrs. Rachel let me choose my gift from the ones on the shelves on stage. Mother gave me Daddy's highchair to use for my last baby, Rachel Dobson Wall. All of them are very dear to me and will be passed down through my children who appreciate their history."
Teddy, Miss Rachel, and Keeper Austin's highchair private collection Verna (Austin) Wall
Photo courtesy Bruce Roberts

(Left) Marilyn (front) became quite the young entrepreneur while living with her brother and keeper father at Bodie Island. When visitors came to the island, keepers were expected to oblige with a light station tour. Marilyn does the honors this time and received $.50 for her efforts. "That was a lot of money in those days!" she said of this picture. Circa 1938
Photo courtesy Marilyn (Austin) Meads

(Right) Left to right, Ann Austin, Katherine Austin holding Brenda Austin, and Julian Austin, Sr. Julian Austin Jr. did not see his daughter, Brenda, until she was nearly three years old because he was a Korean prisoner of war. Keeper Austin had recently retired and had been awarded the coveted Gallatin Award for his outstanding U.S. Lighthouse Service career. Circa 1951
Photos courtesy Marilyn (Austin) Meads

Quotes and stories are taken from extensive interviews with Marilyn Austin Meads, Verna Austin Wall, and Julian Haywood Austin, Jr. for over three years, 1997-2001. Thanks to Marilyn and Verna for sharing of family pictures and artifacts and helping to edit their story.

Keeper of Sound Lights
Thomas Hardy Baum

Keeper Baum earned a prized appointment to Cape Hatteras and after a brief stay, he transferred to the sound lights of the inner waterways to make a Lighthouse Service career. He married a keeper's daughter and his son worked for the U.S. Lighthouse Service.

By Cheryl Shelton-Roberts

Thomas Hardy Baum was born the son of Somers Baum and Mary Anne (Wright). As a waterman, he developed strong hands, excellent tools for use as a first assistant keeper at Cape Hatteras Light Station in 1905. During his lifelong career with the U.S. Lighthouse Service, Thomas served at several of the lighthouses that had been built on inland waters of the Pamlico, Croatan, and Albemarle Sounds during the years just following the Civil War including Long Shoal, Tangier Island, and the Croatan Light from which he retired. His son, Wayland, born in 1904, spent much of his childhood growing up at a river light. He initially worked for the Lighthouse Service on the sidepaddle steamer tender *Holly* and later as substitute lighthouse keeper for several years.

By 1891, about two dozen river and sound lights provided more reliable navigational aid than their predecessors, lightships, which were prone to break from their moorings and confuse mariners.

In Personnel Classification board Form No 14- Field Questionnaire in 1928, Thomas Hardy Baum was keeper at the Croatan Light Station. He described his experience and training. "Two and one-half years in Life Saving Service, a General experience in Boating, in Small Boats for about 10 Years, Painting and Mechanical work for about 5 years." He checked his education as the equivalence to fourth year, high school. He wrote a great deal about the reason for stating this. "In answering questions 21 and 22 I have given the grade of school that I believe would about correspond to the school I attended while I was a boy, as we had no such schools at that time as we have now, hence this is the best way I know to answer this question."

A clue as to why he felt he had received the best education came in his description of his duties as keeper of a river light. "A Light Keepers duties are very exacting and require that a man know something about most every kind of ordinary work, from the tidying up of a house to the rough work of scraping and painting and handling of boats in all kinds of weather, then we are required to keep books and answer all letters, (which is at times very difficult for us) but we always do the best we can in everything. I should say that our work requires us to be busy when on duty for as much as 15-16 hours every day at some kind of work, this does not always mean that it is hard work, but it is work that requires our time..."

Baum went on to describe that he had to take rough trips at all times of the night in order to keep the small lanterns burning in the sound for "a distance of 8 or 10 miles and it takes about 3 hours to make the round trip." And if the weather were icy, sometimes the keepers had to stay up for three and four days to make sure ice was kept off the lantern room glass because icy windows obscured the light for passing vessels. He also described his constant worry about leaks that developed in the lantern room of the Croatan Light Station and his responsibility to protect the lamp.

"Life at a sound light was quite different than being at Cape Hatteras. Often only one keeper was on duty and had no one to rely on for help. The mainland was accessible by boat only, and family stayed in a home in a nearby town, visiting occasionally."

Life at a sound light was quite different than being at Cape Hatteras. Often only one keeper was on duty and had no one to rely on for help. The mainland was accessible by boat only, and family stayed in a home in a nearby town, visiting occasionally. During the summer months while children were out of school, the families were able to spend more time together.

Ophelia, Thomas and Lillie Baum's daughter, shared recollections of her father's concern for the isolation of his duty stations. His wife, Lillie, was an epileptic. "Mama was never really well. She had seizures come on her often, and she didn't know when it was going to happen. Papa tried to always be around for her. When I wasn't in school Mama and I would go out with Papa to stay for a week. The men on duty would then go home. I remember two of the men, a Mr. Twiford and a Mr. Tolson were with Papa. Before we went out to the Croatan Lighthouse, that was a water light you know, we would go to the store and buy bags of apples, oranges, candy, and such. We took books. I loved to read like Papa did, so we took reading for the entire week, and coloring books, and playthings. So it was a good time, too.

"Friends ask me if I felt lonesome out there," Ophelia

TIMELINE
THOMAS HARDY BAUM (1877-1938)
ASSISTANT KEEPER 1905:

Keeper Baum liked serving at the sound lights of North Carolina. He lived and served when travel was by sail and steam power. The inland water route from the Albemarle Sound through the Croatan Sound to the Pamilico Sound to the south was a busy liquid highway and would remain so until the advent of the automobile two decades later. Supplies and news traveled quickly and efficiently to all parts of the coasts to and from larger ports. In the world news, Robert Koch won the Nobel Peace Prize for his research on tuberculosis and the development of the science of bacteriology.

Keeper Thomas Hardy Baum and his son Wayland sat for a photograph taken in a Norfolk, Virginia, studio. Wayland grew up working with his father as a keeper and a fisherman. He and his sister, Ophelia, are rare witnesses to everyday life at a sound light. Following in his father's footsteps, Wayland began his work for the U.S. Lighthouse Service on the side-paddle steamer tender Holly. *Today, at ninety-seven-years-young, Wayland is the oldest living Cape Hatteras keeper's descendant.*
Photograph courtesy of Willie Hearne Mann

spoke easily of this time during the 1920s. "I tell them, 'No, I never got lonesome. When it was time to go home, I was ready, but I never was so unhappy that I refused to go back.'"

"There was a place under the lighthouse where I could fish. I wasn't too crazy about fishing, but my mother- she could fish all day! She used to catch the biggest croakers you ever did see. She could clean and cook the fish, but Papa usually did this for her. While Mama fished, I'd go and sit with Papa while he painted or cleaned. It was a wonderful time. All we had was our little skiff. The other keeper took the big Lighthouse Service boat and went home. I don't know what we would have done if something had happened while we were out there alone."

The Croatan Lighthouse was located in Mashoes Creek near Manns Harbor, west of Manteo. During the Civil War Confederate forces destroyed it in October 1864 in an effort to keep the Union from using it to move supplies through the Croatan Sound to ports north and south including Plymouth, Elizabeth City, New Bern, Washington, North Carolina, and Norfolk, Virginia. Still an important aid to navigation, the Croatan Light was rebuilt after the Civil War as a typical river and sound lighthouse in the form of a 1,000-foot-square cottage on pilings. It was a true "lighthouse," housing a light while providing living quarters for its keepers.

"We weren't supposed to be at the lighthouse; families were not supposed to stay out there," Ophelia continued. If the tender *Holly* went by, we hid. Sometimes they did not stop. And there was only one bedroom. I had a quilt for a pallet and a pillow and slept on the floor. I was young and didn't mind because it was sort of different. You do what you [have to] do!

"We all three went home to Baumtown where our house was and there were only Baums living there then. Papa and my brother, Wayland, I called him 'Bud,' who was a young man then, would set their nets from our fishing boat down at the creek. I loved to take our little skiff and while they worked with the fish or on the boat, and I was a tomboy, an outdoor person, I would row and row. I could row as good as my brothers! Papa and Bud took the fish off the boat and put them in boxes and then packed them with ice at the 'fish camp' down the creek at a landing where the boats pulled up. Then they took the boxes to be sold to big boats like the *Hattie Creef* at the Wanchese ice plant and then the fish was taken to places like Elizabeth City."

Ophelia let the memories pour forth about her family. "We took the mailboat from Manteo to Buxton to visit my grandfather. Mother's daddy was Christopher C. Miller, he was a keeper at Hatteras also. And he was postmaster. There were no roads, you walked in the sand. There wasn't grass, just sand. I loved most of all to visit with Mama's brother, Baxter. They had a big, lovely home near his and Mama's father. They were all good people. Papa loved the church, in fact, he was superintendent of the Sunday School of the Wanchese Methodist Church. It was so beautiful where I grew up. My cousin had a big peach orchard and in the spring when the trees bloomed, people would come just to see them."

I grew up in a time when we had no electricity. We used lamps, and when you went from room, you took your lamp with you. We had no running water, either. The toilets were outside and it was miserable when it was cold! But at night, we'd run from the warmth of the wood stove in the kitchen or living room and jump into our feather bed. I'd sink down into that big feather bed and it was warm. Quilts that Mama made kept us warm. I think about Papa - and though both Mama and he cooked, Papa could make the best cornbread I ever did have. And the sweet potatoes! How did they cook them when there was no temperature control? Mama or Papa would scrub the sweet potatoes, put wood in the stove and get it hot, and then throw them in the oven."

In closing, Ophelia went over the family members. Her parents, Thomas and Lillie (1883-1936) married in 1900. Their children were: Thomas T. (1903-1903); Wayland W. (1904), who is the oldest living Cape Hatteras keeper's descendant; Somers (1913-1980), and Ophelia (1918).

"Families were so close then," Ophelia stated with emphasis. "They were it, the focus, the most important thing in the lives of people in those times."

The Croatan screwpile lighthouse was situated at Caroon's Point, at the north end of Croatan Sound between the Outer Banks and the mainland of North Carolina where shoaling sand was a potential danger for passing vessels. This light was destroyed by Confederates during the Civil War and rebuilt afterwards. At the end of the pilings were screw caps to help anchor the pilings into the soft bottom of the sound, thus giving its descriptive name as a "screwpile" lighthouse. The typical style provided keepers with about 1,000 square feet of living space; the tin roof was surmounted with a lantern room that rose from the center of the structure. A fog bell was rung by a wind-up mechanism, or rung for hours by hand if the mechanism failed. A privy can be seen on the left side of the house. Fresh water and fuel were stored in tanks below the house. These buildings were prone to sway in gale-force winds and ice floes presented another hazard. Several keepers transferred to the sound lights later in their careers when climbing many stairs became too physically demanding. But as reported by Keeper Baum, the duties were challenging and time consuming at these stations. *Photo courtesy U.S. Coast Guard*

(Opposite page) Seated is Thomas Hardy Baum, first assistant keeper at Cape Hatteras, and his wife, Lillie Columbus (Miller), a daughter of Christopher Columbus Miller who had been an assistant keeper at Cape Hatteras 1887-1902. Ophelia (1918), daughter of Thomas and Lillie, commented, "Mama was epileptic and we had to keep a watch on her... Papa would try to always be around for her. Families were so close then. They were it, the focus, the most important thing in the lives of people in those times." 1905
Photo courtesy Faye (Baum) White

(Right) Wayland Baum, Keeper Thomas H. Baum's son, proved himself to be a valued substitute keeper at many light stations including Bodie Island Light Station, and the Croatan and Long Shoal screwpile lights during the 1920s. He was a natural for this work, for he had been an apprentice to his father from the time he could accompany him. As a substitute keeper, Wayland was called upon to fill in at a moment's notice. This meant he had to know how to tend a first-order Fresnel lens as well as the seven-day burning post lanterns, which Wayland called "beacon lights." He explained that, "The oil was delivered to the sound lights in five-gallon, square cans. We had to take care of the sound light, like Croatan, and any beacon lights in the area. We would take a few of the cans with us in the Lighthouse Service boat and go 'round to the small beacons on posts along the inland waterway. Each one had a reservoir that held about two gallons of 'k-oil' [kerosene] and we'd fill them and they'd burn about seven days unless a gale of wind blew them out. In that case, we had to go out and tend the light right away, no matter what time of night."
Photo courtesy Bruce Roberts

Information is from interviews with Wayland Baum 1996-97 and with Ophelia (Baum) Smith February 2001.
For a complete story on Keeper Baum, *Lighthouse Families* by Cheryl Shelton-Roberts and Bruce Roberts, Crane Hill Publishers, 1997.

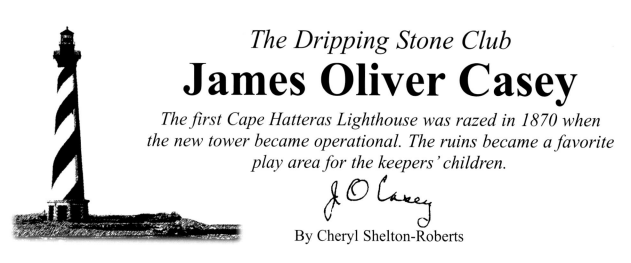

The Dripping Stone Club
James Oliver Casey

The first Cape Hatteras Lighthouse was razed in 1870 when the new tower became operational. The ruins became a favorite play area for the keepers' children.

J O Casey

By Cheryl Shelton-Roberts

Childish squeals of delight, occasionally hushed by seriousness, emanated from the tower ruins where Edna Casey was being initiated into the "dripping stone club."

"I dare you, I dare you!" challenged the veterans of the keeper's circle, children who had lived at the light station and already had declined the dare. Here, a newcomer would be tested, determining who was the bravest of the keepers' kids. Would the skinny girl from James Oliver Casey's family, new assistant keeper at Cape Hatteras, take the dare?

"Sure I did!" Edna answered with a mischievous smile. "Those kids found out that if they dared me, I'd do it!"

"The other kids told me that nobody had ever put their finger on that dripping stone and they bet me I wouldn't do it. There was a stone on the old tower hill [ruins of the 1803 tower] that had water in it. It constantly dripped water. They said I wouldn't do it, and I couldn't stand it. From the time we moved to the lighthouse, the kids had said, 'Whatever you do, don't put your finger under the dripping stone- you're finger will turn to stone!' Well, they dared me, and I put my finger under it and let the water drip on it. They were astonished! All night for several nights, I'd lay in the dark and do this in the light as it went around my room!" Edna laughed big and then gestured with a crooked finger, flexing it like she did as a young girl, just to make sure it hadn't turned to stone as ominously predicted.

I entered the nursing home room to visit with Edna, daughter of James Oliver Casey, Cape Hatteras assistant keeper from 1920-28. She sat in her wheelchair facing away from the door, looking up at a picture of the Cape Hatteras Lighthouse on a small bulletin board by her hospital bed. She was quiet and leaned forward just a bit. Her daughter, Sybil, walked around to face her, bent down, and said, "Hello, 'Ednie'," Sybil's family nickname for the much-loved keeper's daughter.

"Hello! Darlin'," Edna answered with a mother's warmth.

"There's someone here to see you, Ednie," Sybil offered. Edna stiffly craned her neck around to look me over, head to toe.

"Do you think you can talk with me for a while? I asked. I've been told you have wonderful stories."

"Yes! Sure!" Edna said with a warm smile. This keeper's daughter's memories were a pot of gold to this interviewer. All I had to do was listen.

She wanted to get back in bed, but the bed had no sheets on it even though Edna insisted it did. Sybil promised to get someone to make it up for her...later. "You don't know how this old body hurts," Edna complained.

Sybil answered in her most compassionate way, "Yes, I do."

"I'm ninety-three, you know," Edna reminded me in a voice that slid up and down as if playing notes on a musical scale.

"Yes, Edna," I nodded, "and as Keeper Casey's only surviving child, your memories are the last direct access we have to memories of him as keeper and when you lived at Cape Hatteras."

I showed her a picture. "Hello there, Mr. Jim," Edna spoke with love. "My daddy. Awww, he was such a sweet daddy."

"That was when he was at Bloody Point Bar Lighthouse," I pointed out.

Edna didn't care where he was, she was more concerned that it looked as if he'd lost a button on his uniform. The buttons looked larger than the standard Lighthouse Service buttons, but Edna insisted they were the right ones. She should know- she saw him in his uniform for many years. And she knows what a stickler he was for "everything in its place and everything fixed properly."

Still looking at a picture of Keeper Casey, Edna commented, "Daddy called me 'Ed.' I called them 'Dad' and her 'Mother,' and sometimes 'Mr. Jim' and 'Miss Cora.'"

Children were taught to respectfully call adults either "Miss" or "Mr." followed by the person's first name. If your parents were close friends with them, then it was "Aunt" or "Uncle" and the person's first name. Edna confirmed, as many do who grew up on Hatteras Island, that she never knew

> *"The lighthouse would tremble, sometimes the wind would be blowing so hard...I'd fight my way to the lighthouse and climb the stairs with my little lamp. Dad would be waiting for me so...he'd have both hands free and could see to get the mantle lit right."*

TIMELINE

JAMES OLIVER CASEY (1873-1937)
ASSISTANT KEEPER 1920-1928:

While Keeper Casey was tending the light at Cape Hatteras, the "Roaring Twenties" were bringing America prosperity. New roads, airmail, and telephones were connecting towns on the mainland, but on Hatteras Island, life changed little. The first two cars on Hatteras Island, it has been reported, managed to collide head-on. Kerosene continued to provide the illumination for the Fresnel lens and the keepers' homes.

many islanders' last names, or learned them only as an adult.

Edna then began to guide me through her memories.

"I was born in Buxton on February the 21st, 1908. Daddy went to Lowland [Pamlico Point Screwpile] and different places including Ocracoke, and when he was stationed at Cape Hatteras, the family lived there at the light station. When he retired he was at Bloody Point Bar, near Clayburn, Maryland. Dad got tired and left Cape Hatteras. It wasn't long after he went to Bloody Pt. Bar that he had a stroke. He retired after the stroke.

"But of all the places we went, Cape Hatteras is my home. Oh my gosh, I use to take visitors up and Dad would already be up there or he'd send us. We'd just go up there and get out on the deck and holler and carry on! We loved to watch things float all-l-l-l-l the way down. It's about 200 feet high. I went up by myself. Some nights when it was stormy, he'd have trouble lighting the light because the tower would tremble and the lamp would be hard to light. He'd have to hold the lantern steady to get it to burn so Mother would say, 'Edna, you'd better get your lamp ready.' I'd get my little lantern and sometimes the wind would be blowing so hard, it'd almost knock me down. I'd fight my way to the lighthouse and climb the stairs with my little lamp. Dad would be waiting for me so I could hold the lamp and he'd have both hands free and could see to get the mantle lit right. Mother would send me or my brother Ruland with a lantern, but sometimes Ruland was scared. Once we both went up there and heard a cat meow and we searched that tower from top to bottom." She chuckled at the memory. "He could've gotten to an open window and gotten blown out."

Not a very pleasant thought, but reality for a lighthouse keeper's daughter where harsh elements were simply part of everyday life. Sybil said, "That may have been one of the first flying cats on Cape Hatteras!"

The old stones from the 1803 Cape Hatteras tower base provided a favorite play area for the keepers' children and their friends. One stone was always wet and dripped "enchanted" water. The old foundation could be seen until a spring blizzard erased all signs of the ruins in the early 1980s. Circa 1960
Photo courtesy Outer Banks History Center

"We never found that cat in the tower or outside on the grass," said Edna, still wondering at the eighty-year-old memory.

The mantle lamp Edna mentioned is an incandescent oil vapor or "I.O.V." lamp. An I.O.V. lamp was installed in the Cape Hatteras tower in 1913 and significantly increased the intensity of the beam emitted from the Fresnel lens to hundreds of thousands of candlepower. The mantle was made of a delicate material that would disintegrate if not handled gingerly. Under stormy conditions when a great deal of wind shook the tower, the keeper needed three or four hands to warm the mantle and get all parts of the lamp in order to light it with a special water-resistant match.

"I remember poor mother, she'd be wringing her hands almost when he was up there. The lamp was very delicate and the keeper had to be very careful how he handled it. A mistake could mean the light would be off for a while. This meant mariners in peril," Edna recalled from her duty as the keeper's helper.

Each lighthouse was charted in a "Light List," a book carried by every mariner. If Cape Hatteras were not exhibiting its two and one-half seconds flash every seven and one-half seconds, it would have been as critical as a malfunctioning traffic light at a busy intersection. Cape Hatteras was a guide for the mariner to make his way around the dangerous mountains of illusive sand known as Diamond Shoals.

"He had to carry a five-gallon can of kerosene up all those steps...and that was heavy." Edna continued her tour. "It got cold up there but there wasn't a stove or anything up there. They just wore lots of clothes.

"After lighting the lamp, he'd wait for a while and see if the lamp was working well. Sometimes he'd come down to the house for a while and then go back and check on the light again and do any other jobs he needed to. Then he'd call the other man to go on duty. If he had what they called the 'first watch' he would go up just before sundown to light the lamp and stay until 12 o'clock [at night]. Sometimes he had the second and third watch. They rotated each day on a different watch. Only two men were on duty at a time.

Edna continued, "Mother had a bunch of kids. All her time was taken raising kids."

"She had her hands full," Keeper Casey's granddaughter, Sybil, added with a laugh.

"There were six of nine kids living at home at one time, a tenth died," Edna continued as she described the full-house accommodations. "When I was living at the lighthouse, I had two sisters that had married and had left home, so seven of us lived at the double keepers quarters at Cape Hatteras. At the keepers quarters, there wasn't any electricity. Dad was first assistant and we lived on the side closest to the brick primary keeper's house. When we first went there, Mr. Mace [Quidley] was there and Mr. Unaka [Jennette] was primary keeper. Mr. Quidley left and Mr. Bill Quidley came- he was such a sweet man."

Sybil explained, "We called him 'Uncle Bill,' and since he was married to my daddy's cousin and she was older than Daddy, I didn't call her 'Cousin Lenora,' I called her 'Aunt Lenora.'"

Sybil is speaking of Bill Quidley's second wife, Lenora (Williams) Quidley. These keepers' families were not only living and working closely with one another, many of them were related directly or through marriage.

"I didn't have many playmates at the lighthouse, most of my friends were at school in Buxton," Edna recalled. "But we did play a lot at the lighthouse. We played dolls and 'Hoop 'n Hide.' [Hide 'n Seek]. We played in the ocean a lot and there was a big pond right where we lived in the keepers house and Dad bought us a little boat and we could go around in the pond. The ponds were full of water lilies and they smelled so good," Edna says. "And we had a lot of snakes!" This statement is followed by laughter as if she'd cracked a big joke. Of course, this is a tomboy speaking. Edna was known as the "daredevil." The kids knew they could dare her to do anything, and she would with temerity!

"We had mosquitoes galore!" Edna recalled.

"They built up an immunity," Sybil explained.

"No, they loved us," Edna laughed again. "There wasn't anything we could put on to keep them from biting."

"There wasn't any way to keep the mosquitoes from biting?" I asked with an incredulous look.

Edna said almost with sympathy, "No honey, they'd bite you regardless."

These island children were in their element in the great outdoors. These kids played in the ponds barefooted all the time. "It's a wonder we didn't get bitten by a snake!" Edna stated with astonishment. "We'd be in the boat in the pond and that old 'moccasin would poke his head out of the water," this daring girl laughed. "Dad told us to never bother them. And never chase [a snake]. We had a few rattlesnakes, but not many."

Edna explained how "Mr. Jim" kept everything in order with such a large family. "My daddy was strict. We dare not do anything he said not to do. When we were at the lighthouse, sometimes on Saturday we'd want to walk into the village and be with the young folk. We'd ask Mother but we couldn't go unless we got Dad's consent. We were not to stay out late! We could stay out until 9:30 P.M. or so on the weekend, but school nights, we had to be in by 9:00 P.M. Punishment included not allowing the kids to go to the village. If my dad told me, 'No,' I didn't argue. I was never struck a lick in my life. I was threatened plenty of times!"

Sybil kidded her mother, "No wonder, you were such a brat!"

Edna paused for a few moments and looked around her hospital room as if she were somewhere familiar in her past. The she expressed her thoughts. "Thanksgiving and Christmas were so special. I helped with the cooking as soon as I could reach the counter. We had a wild goose cooked on a wood stove when we couldn't get a turkey. Ummmm good!" Edna imagined those delicacies.

"We had about the prettiest Christmas trees anybody would ever want. Daddy would go into the woods and get us

While Keeper Casey was assigned to the Pamlico Point Lighthouse, the Casey family lived in Lowland, N.C. From left to right, back row: Cora Edna, Cora Lee (Spencer), Murray Ross Goodwin, Nancy Margaret (Casey) Goodwin, Hilda Mae, and Nora Lee. In front, left to right, Abbot Ruland, Keeper James Oliver Casey holding Murray Ross Goodwin, Jr., and Linda Celeste. 1915
Photo courtesy Mike Goodwin

a cedar and it would be thick on the bottom with a perfect shape. We never had to buy one. We'd decorate it with glass balls and tensile and icicles. The trees that we fixed were beautiful, just beautiful. My sister and family kept a supply of decorations; they loved the decorations. They'd wrap the balls with tinsel and the light would catch and just sparkle."

Sybil added, "They always had the hand-blown ornaments from Germany."

Edna continued, "Sometimes Mother would allow us to put candles in those little holders that you could snap onto the tree and put the candles in and then light them just for a few minutes. She was so afraid of fire. She was afraid the tree would catch fire. While they were lit, we'd dance around and sing...a special moment. We always opened our presents on Christmas morning. No matter how many we got, we had to wait for Christmas morning. Except sometimes we were allowed to open just one on Christmas Eve. In fact, we didn't see many of them until Christmas morning because Mother kept them hidden until we went to bed and Santa Claus visited. I got mostly dolls, teasets, doll furniture, things like that. There in the house we had a big bedroom upstairs where my sister [Linda] and I set up our 'house.' My sister had one side of the 'house' and I had the other. I have a lot of fond memories of that time.

"I liked living there so much. In the summer it was so wonderful. We had all that wide-open beach to play on and the ocean to explore and fish in the ponds. It was just great. I also had chores, I had to help with the housework. I washed dishes one day and my sister the next [sic]. We drew water by a pump in the kitchen. We had to help cook and keep the kitchen clean and we had to keep the beds fixed. We'd take turns washing clothes; one week I'd scrub and she rinsed, and the next week, we'd trade off. If it was cold, we'd do the wash in the kitchen or if it was warm, we had benches to put the tubs on. We had a nice kitchen and dining room. In the winter, we'd stay in the dining room where there was a big fireplace. And when it got really cold, Daddy put in the stove [inserted it into the fireplace] and we'd be as warm as toast. So, we had bedrooms, dining room, a living room, and kitchen. But we didn't have a bathroom. We had an outside toilet. It wasn't too much fun going to that outside toilet, especially if it was cold! It was a two-seater."

"So you could take company with you," daughter Sybil quipped. Mother and daughter laughed. They touched hands.

Edna continued the privy's description, "One of the holes was smaller for kids!"

"Mother cooked fresh vegetables because Daddy planted collards, string beans, mixed greens, beets, onions, cabbage. Daddy always had such a beautiful garden, everything he planted prospered. One morning he went to check on the garden and here sat Mr. Big Rabbit- sittin' there and chewin' away on something and Dad took his pocket knife out of his pants and threw it at him and hit him behind the ear and killed it. And we ate him! I never had had rabbit before. Mother said, 'Well, honey, it tastes a lot like chicken.' 'But, Mom,' I said, 'it doesn't look like chicken!' It looked too much like a cat and I loved cats. We had one, my gosh, we kept her for years, Nancy. Anyway she started out the door and the door slammed and cut a piece of her tail off. We cried and carried on and we wanted Daddy to sew it back on. He said it'd heal and it did.

"And then we had cattle. We'd kill one and corned the beef- salt the meat and put it in a barrel. We had beef all along in like a keg. We had hogs, chickens, and horses. The hogs and chickens were penned up. We salted down spots [fish], too. We'd take out the meat or fish and soak it and cook it. Sometimes we'd have it for breakfast. It was too tedious for Mother to ask us how we wanted our eggs, so Mother would just boil up a great big bowl of them!"

"Eat them or else," Sybil said, "Grandmother didn't run a short order kitchen!"

"Grandmother made such fine stews," both mother and daughter started to talk at once.

"Oh my land, yesssss," Edna chimed in. "And pastry- some people call it 'pie bread' down there. It's like when you have chicken and dumplings."

"They called it 'pastry' or 'pie bread,'" Sybil commented.

Edna added, "And Mother made pies a lot, lemon pie, coconut pie, potato pie, I wish I had a chunk right now!"

Sybil commented, "And she made molasses cakes, bread pudding and custard, and rice puddings and put raisins in them."

"The chickens gave us plenty of eggs...Dad had a whole flock of chickens in a pen. I don't ever remember going to the store buying eggs, can you imagine? The freight boat brought in flour. They came in by the water. We didn't expect to get food from the Lighthouse Service, though. We had a case of books that the government changed every so often. I read a lot, like *Land of the Midnight Sun* and *Emma*. We had a medicine chest and the everyday things for the bellyache or headache."

"Plenty of iodine and Mercurochrome," Sybil chuckled.

"We had a pill that looked like an aspirin for a headache. We had to buy anything else like for a cold, and we used lots of Vicks salve. When we had the measles or the whooping cough, Mother would make a tonic that tasted good. She would take sticks and boil water and pour water over them and let them steam."

I asked Edna about what the kids did to entertain themselves at the lighthouse. She answered quickly "Ruland had a goat and Dad made him a cart and we'd set up there and take a ride. We had a lot of fun. We never got lonesome, there was a bunch of us kids out there at the lighthouse. We played ball, 'cat' we called it. We had a pitcher and catcher and run around the bases. In the regular ballgame, we'd play at the old tower hill." [ruins of the 1803 tower]

Edna rested for a few moments, her thoughts wandering back over time and then she resumed narrating. "He was a wonderful dad. Dad was jolly and full of fun, he loved to dance and sing and he could ever play a mouth harp [harmonica]. He'd play one piece that he didn't know the name of. So when he'd play for us, we'd say, 'Now, play the piece you don't know.'"

"Grandpa Jim made up some songs," Sybil reminisced. She sang, "Buckeye Rabbit and Hooooooo Hoooo. Buckey Rabbit, Hooo John. Rabbit Skip, Rabbit Hop, Rabbit hit my turnip top."

And then Edna started to sing, moving her hands in rhythm, "Buckeye Rabbit Hooo Hooo," and she laughed at the fond memory.

"Dad had some horses and he let us ride them and that was fun! Oh my golly, one time he sent us down the beach to get his mare and my little brother went to get her. She was with some more horses and when she started to leave this old stallion came after us. I don't ever remember in my entire life ever being as scared as I was then! He reared on his hind legs and screamed. We'd hide under her and she seemed to know we needed her. She stood right still until we got up to the house. I tell you, we were two worn out little kids when we got to the lighthouse. We told Dad about it and he said, 'Don't worry honey, the next time I'm gonna have a gig for you and if that stallion worries you, you stick that gig in him.' And then Mother said in the kindest, most gentle way, 'No, Jim, you don't have to do that. There's not going to be a next time.' And there wasn't! We couldn't go to get the horse unless we were close enough for them to watch.

"My Dad gave a stallion to my brother and he named him 'Bill Phillips' and what a fancy horse and he taught him all sort of things. They cut notches in the ears to tell whose animals were whose. The notches looked sort of like a puzzle.

"Lots of ships came onto Diamond Shoals. We looked through the spyglass, a short one, and could see the ships wrecked."

There is a story handed down to the island children that Edna said is a famous one. "One ship got stuck on Diamond Shoals that had only a cat on it. The coast guard went out to help the crew, but there wasn't a person on it but the table was set like they were going to have dinner." This is the story of the *Carol Deering*, the "ghost ship," known to all Outer Bankers. In 1921, the five-masted schooner was caught on Diamond Shoals during a stormy winter night and was spotted by a surfman of the Cape Hatteras Coast Guard Station. It was reported that no crew were aboard, only a cat with extra toes.

The Caseys took that cat home and she proved a prolific mother with descendants of the cat abundant on the island yet today.

"Tess of the storm country," the family called Edna in memory of a well-known children's book character. All her life she loved to get out in the storms. "The bigger the better," Edna confirmed. We'd go out by the lighthouse and watch those big billows of waves. They were exciting!" said this brave girl.

"If my Dad had first watch during a storm, he'd go up the tower and look out, and yell, 'Kids, there's a nice piece of timber coming in,' and send us to get it. We'd use it to build something."

Sybil reminded us that houses like the family home built

Keeper Casey stood at the lantern room level of the Bloody Point Bar Lighthouse near Claiborne, Maryland. Casey took this assignment following his eight years at Cape Hatteras. "Dad got tired and left Cape Hatteras. It wasn't long after he went to Bloody Pt. Bar that he had a stroke. He retired after the stroke," daughter Edna commented on the rigorous years of duty at Cape Hatteras. Circa 1933
Photo courtesy Mike Goodwin

by her grandmother's uncle, Pharoah Scarborough, and sold to her "Grandaddy Gray," was built with "beach lumber." It still has pegs from the ships. And there's a couple of walnut cabin doors in that house. Edna recalled that one was a bathroom door.

"We loved to go to the beach after a storm and look for things. We never found anything of any value, but it was great to us kids. We'd find pretty shells and pretty bottles. I guess they drank their booze from fancy bottles! Those were happy days! I don't remember having a care in the world at that time. We always had to go to church in the village. If Dad was on watch and the other men couldn't take us, we'd walk about two and a half miles to church on Sunday mornings and go to Sunday School, we'd put on our Sunday best and we enjoyed it. Sometimes the bulls would scare us...they'd stop and look at us like they were going to come get us. I almost froze once. And one time when I was about sixteen, my sister, Linda, and I started to Buxton and she, my land! could walk the legs right off of you and never feel it. Anyway, there was this horse, and it looked like it was inching toward us- one of those stallions out there. A man came along in his Model T Ford, it didn't have a top on it and he said, 'Do you want a ride?' I said, 'I sure do!' And we hopped on, he never stopped the car, we just kept going!" Edna could hardly tell the story for laughing. "We hopped on the running boards until we got to the village."

Edna added that he ran the car into a sand hill and the motor conked out. "That's the only way he knew how to stop it."

"He [Keeper Casey] was at 'Marshes' [Roanoke Marshes] Light, Pamlico Point, Ocracoke, [Myrtle was born here] and to Hatteras, and finally Bloody Point Bar." Edna's earliest recollection was near Lowland, where Ruland was born.

"Here's my lighthouse," Edna said when I showed her another picture of Cape Hatteras. "Isn't she pretty? Did they get it moved? Can you tell that it's been moved?

"He was at one like this," she said as she looked at the river lights pictures. "It had a cellar underneath. We'd go out there to visit Dad and stay a week with him. You talk about fishing, we did some fishing! That is the lonesomest life those men could have, out there on the water by themselves. They put two men on the river lights and a third was on leave. One time two men got off a bigger boat and got into their lifeboat and came up to the lighthouse. Dad warned them off, but they insisted on coming on the lighthouse." Edna recalled her father talking about the feeling he got they were up to no good. "Dad said, 'You may come up, but you won't go back down. I'll feed you to the fish. Hang around, here comes my Inspector, he'll be glad to see you.'"

Keeper Casey had spotted the smoke of an approaching boat, and pretended to know who it was. Edna ended the story with "There was a man murdered at a nearby lighthouse. The keepers had to be cautious. When the assistant went to relieve him [at the nearby lighthouse], the keeper was just in a tee shirt with a few pennies. Someone had stripped and robbed him. Daddy had to be careful. Those men scrambled down the ladder and got in their boat and took off.

"One time we lived right down to the lake there in Ocracoke. He was at S.W. Royal Point Shoals. The sound froze over in 1918 and mother was worried that he'd run out of food. The coast guard went out finally to check on him and took him some wood and when the ice began to break up, Dad's assistant tried to reach him. But it took several tries and Dad lowered him a bucket and the assistant pulled it to him. Daddy yelled, 'I don't care about a [darn] thing you put in there except some tobacco! Send me some tobacco.' The assistant only had a plug he'd been biting off of, so he sent it up to the keeper. Daddy said he grabbed that plug and took a bit bite and, 'You talk about getting sick! I got so sick I had to crawl up into the tower to light the light!' He hadn't had a chew of tobacco in so long it turned on him. Myrtle was born during the freeze before he got back to Ocracoke. Linda and I'd go and stay for a week while the assistant was home visiting. We played dolls, hide 'n seek, fished. There were closets all around the room and they were so DARK. We'd scare ourselves!

"One time we were in the living room [of the river light] and we had our dolls in the dining room; Dad let us have our dolls in there because we ate in the kitchen. One time the Inspector came and we'd made a paper string of dolls all the way across that room. Daddy said, 'Never mind.' The Inspector never regarded us, and Daddy got a good report."

Casey loved to tease the kids. This keeper who loved life and children often gave nicknames lovingly. "And Daddy loved to argue!" Edna said almost with a boast. "He loved to debate, but Mother wouldn't argue with him."

Sybil also remembered that her Grandmother Cora Lee never showed anger. If one of the grandkids acted up, she'd talk fast, but that was the size of it. "She was an angel," Edna said. "My daddy too. I had a good life. Girls couldn't wear pants, but one time I had a pair of knickers. Someone sent me some money for a gift and I bought a shirt and some knickers. I put them on and when Keeper Casey saw me, he said, 'What in the [heck] you got on?' I told him, 'Dad, these are a lot more comfortable and a lot more decent for girls to play in and the skirt isn't flying up.' But it didn't impress Jim, me and my sisters had to wear our skirts. He kept our everyday shoes mended. He'd put them on shoe lasts and make them like new.

"I helped Dad clean the big lens sometimes. I watched it cross my bed many a time. It put me to sleep. If it were at night and we came down the beach, that light was the first thing we looked for. Sometimes the light would get to blinking, and Daddy sat by the window and watch the light all the time. He'd say 'Uh oh,' and we all knew what *that* meant. The light was acting up. It'd still revolve, but it'd flicker. There was a weight and a crank. It stayed wound up all night. He didn't have to rewind it during the night, I don't think.

"I use to run up those spiral stairs. By gosh, I'd slide down the rails and feel my knees quiver! One time the other kids bet me and I went out on the side of the railing [at the top]. I climbed over the rail and hung on and I'll never do that again! You've got to have nerves of steel! My sister used to say, 'Don't bet her, she'll do it!'"

We returned to the present, surrounded by green hospital walls. I stood up.

"Don't go," Edna said. She gave me a big warm hug despite the restraints of a wheelchair. But Edna's memories were not restrained. She had effortlessly recalled her life at the lighthouse and told delightful stories about a daredevil who never grew old.

"Sometime when you come to Buxton to my home, we'll do some serious sitting on the porch and talk about my neighbors," Edna offered in closing.

I said I'd see her there sometime and that we'd go see that dripping stone. Sounding like a kid, she squinted her eyes and pointed her finger, "I dare you!"

Casey's Granddaughter

Sybil is Edna and John "Raymond" Gray's only daughter but she has raised to adulthood five of her own children and she has researched her family's genealogy. "Cora Edna, my mother, was named after her mother, Cora Lee (Spencer) Casey. The family called her 'Edna' to avoid confusion between the two. I'm named after Doc Folb's wife. He came from the Navy radio station and helped us so much.

"Granddaddy James Oliver Casey was born in Buxton. His mother, Cordelia (Cordie) Casey, had him out of wedlock, so she gave James "Jim" her surname. They tried to keep those things quiet when Mother was a child, they just didn't talk about it. James Dixon William's mother, Achsah Casey, raised my granddaddy and when her husband died, she married Cordelia's brother, Bannister Casey, 'Uncle Bannie' we called him. Cordie and little Jim went to live with them for a while [his uncle and Grandmother Achsah]."

Sybil looked at her grandfather's picture in his uniform at Bloody Point, Maryland, and she didn't think he was missing a button. "He could sew and mend shoes, plus he was a jack of all trades as a keeper. He was careful about his things. He had all those children. I have some of the 'shoe lasts,' and he'd come home and get anyone's shoes that needed mending and he'd fix them and make them 'last.'"

Sybil then named the family, "James Oliver Casey married Cora Lee Spencer and they had ten children: Nancy Margaret, Lionel James, Nora Lee ('Nonie'), Hilda Mae, Linda Celeste, Cora Edna, Catherine Eastwood, Abbott Ruland, Myrtle, and Murray Thaxton. Murray was born at the Cape Hatteras Lighthouse and was Rany Jennette's steadfast buddy. Catherine Eastwood died at about eight or ten months and Nonie loved that baby. Grandmother told the story that when Catherine died, Nonie asked if she could take the baby into the living room, it was cold then Grandmother recalled, and rock her. And she did and then they buried her. After Catherine was gone, Edna became the baby of the family again."

Sybil remarked, "I have a letter from Aunt Myrtle to Granddaddy, she was about eleven years old, telling him

Keeper Casey and his son, Ruland, and his sister, Edna, often helped their father in his keeper duties. Circa 1923
Photo courtesy Warren Spruill

Sybil (Gray) McDaniel, left, posed with her mother, Edna (Casey) Gray, daughter of Keeper James Oliver Casey. Sybil, who was born and raised in Buxton and lived at the Cape Hatteras Light Station, is a tremendous resource for information on her family and Hatteras Island. Sybil helped with the interview and added a great deal of depth to the story on Keeper Casey and his family. 2000
Photo by Cheryl Shelton-Roberts

she'd ordered him and Mama a gift and it was written about December 15 and it hadn't come yet and she wanted him to know there'd be a gift coming. He couldn't come home for Christmas and she was hoping he could come home after Christmas. This is a 'little girl' letter, one from a daughter who worshipped her daddy. You can just tell by reading the letter.

"Aunt Hilda, Edna's sister, was the funniest thing- in every way. She was ninety-six years old or older and went to Florida to spend Christmas with her grandson Tony and Buddy and some of the boys from Buxton who had gone down there and took water to the people after the storm and to work. And she just loved it there with all the young people. She told them she'd been married three times and she said, 'I outlived every one of them and if I could find someone willing, I'd to do it again, I love being married.'

"Mother was an adventurer. Aunt Linda was timid and ladylike. I don't think she ever rode the horses. Ruland was an expert rider and Mother was good also.

"Edna returned to live in Buxton after having moved away for a few years. After the lighthouse closed in 1936, Maude White, the postmistress in Buxton, leased the property out there. We lived in the two end rooms on the first floor of the big keepers house. Mother and Daddy, my daddy was John "Raymond" Gray, ran the two keepers' houses like a lodge, renting to visitors, and we used the kitchen in the big house and Mother cooked for the tenants for a few years."

Sybil remembered living in the big house [double keepers quarters] near the lighthouse and recalled a very special eighth birthday. "I was getting ready to go to Sunday School, and Ednie said, 'Back up here, honey, and let Daddy fix the back of your dress.' Well, he put a locket around my neck and fastened it. I had seen this locket in Mr. Hollaby's Store and asked them and they told me they didn't have enough money. So when I got it, it sure was a surprise. 'Mr. Hollavy' is a nickname the kids used for Mr. Hollowell J. Gray. He had a general store- the neatest, cleanest store- and sold candy, ice cream, meats, bread, and he had a jewelry counter, and toys at Christmastime. We'd go in there and dream about what we wanted for Christmas. He was so kind. If some things didn't sell, he'd give them to the kids after Christmas.

"My genealogy goes back beyond the 1700s in the Buxton area. Mother and Daddy owned a house in Buxton and bought another one and eventually sold it. My granddaddy, John A. Gray, took apart a house in Avon and moved it on a boat around 1899 and built it in Buxton across from Mother and Daddy's house, near where the school is now. They were tired of fighting the tides and surges in Avon.

"Granddaddy Jim was very attentive to his family; he was so lively, everybody loved him. He was a quick wit, a small man, energetic, and he loved children. He must have if he had ten," Sybil quipped.

Casey's Grandson

Jack Spencer Goodwin, grandson of James Oliver Casey wrote: "James Oliver Casey was born 8 November, 1873, at Buxton, Dare County, North Carolina, the son of James Dixon Williams and Cordelia Casey. His grandmother, Achsah Maria (Scarborough) (Farrow) (Williams) Casey, his father's mother, raised him. Nothing is known about his education, but he was a man who had a great respect for knowledge and a love of learning. His handwriting is that of an educated man, but it is safe to assume that he was largely self-educated.

He married on 25 August 1894, Cora Lee Spencer, born in Buxton 9 December 1877, the daughter of Samuel G. Spencer and Nancy Jane Tolson, who was to bear him ten children, nine of whom lived to adulthood, married, and produced offspring, but none of whom matched their father's record of ten.

After having served in the United States Lifesaving Service for a number of years, he entered the United States Lighthouse Service. He was appointed keeper of the S.W. Point Royal Shoals screwpile lighthouse in Pamlico Sound near Ocracoke. The family lived at Ocracoke Village in a house he purchased there and where his youngest daughter (and next-to-last child), Myrtle Augusta (Casey) Braxton was born during the great freeze of 1918, when the sound froze over. The freeze prevented anyone from reaching the lighthouse with supplies, but in later years he said that he had had plenty of reading material and tried not think about his almost completely exhausted store of food and water, often quoting Coleridge's line, 'Water, water, everywhere and not a drop to drink.'

The children, and sometimes his wife, took turns visiting the lighthouse, usually for a week at a time, fishing, swimming, reading, and studying various subjects under his supervision. If any of the children did something to displease him, he 'punished' them by assigning them a topic about which to write an essay. In addition to home-schooling, he and several neighbors hired qualified teachers to assure that the children would be properly educated. There were public schools on the Banks, but often it was difficult to get teachers to come and live in the sparse coastal communities for the length of time needed. Also, the travel between communities was time consuming and weather dependent.

'Cap'n Jim' as everyone called him, was a highly respected and popular member of the various communities he lived in. He held a magistrate's commission for Dare County which, together with his keeper's uniform, made him a figure of authority. He was also a skilled musician and dancer. He could play several instruments and his performances of the 'buck and wing' and soft-shoe tap routines were famous.

After leaving Royal Shoals and Ocracoke, he became keeper of the Pamlico Point Lighthouse and settled his family in a newly purchased home at Lowland in Pamlico County. At some point he also served as keeper at Bloody Point Light in Chesapeake Bay. His heart was always at Cape Hatteras, however, and so he took a demotion to become assistant keeper there in the 1920s. He retired in 1932 and continued to live in his beloved Buxton until his death on December 4, 1937."

"I dare you!" is Edna's favorite line. At ninety-three years of age, she still refers to Cape Hatteras as "my light." Edna was called "Tess of the Storm Country" because she helped her father on stormy nights by braving the harsh Hatteras winds and taking her lantern to the lighthouse, climbing the 268 steps, and holding the light for her dad while he steadied the delicate mantle of the incandescent oil vapor lamp in a trembling tower. An avid reader, Edna was proud of the nickname. 2000 Photo by Cheryl Shelton-Roberts

---

Jack Spencer Goodwin, born 1 October, 1928, is the youngest son of Captain Murray Ross Goodwin and Nancy Margaret (Casey) Goodwin. After graduating from the college of William and Mary in 1950, he attended graduate school, earned a Master's degree in Library Science, and became the first librarian of what is now the Museum of American History at the Smithsonian. Mr. Goodwin is now President of the Carteret County Historical Society, and director of the Society's Research Library.

All stories are taken from interviews with Cora Edna (Casey) Gray and her daughter Sybil (Gray) McDaniel September 8, 2000, at the Lake Taylor Hospital (Nursing Home).

Other information is from interviews with Sybil (Gray) McDaniel from several subsequent phone calls and mailings, Casey's grandsons, Jack, Michael, and Murray Goodwin, Hilda "Hickie" Lewis, Dr. Warren Spruill, and James Casey.

Papa and Mama

Amasa G. Fulcher

In 1903 Amasa Fulcher married and was appointed assistant keeper at Cape Hatteras. He brought his bride to Hatteras Island to live in the assistant's keepers quarters, their first home.

By Fannie Pearl Fulcher

Fannie Pearl Fulcher wrote of the Cape Hatteras Lighthouse prior to its relocation in 1999.

When my father, Amasa Fulcher "Papa," married my mother, Dell Spencer "Mama," in 1903, he took her to Hatteras Island, where he was one of the three keepers of the Cape Hatteras Lighthouse. It is no wonder that my grandfather, Summer Spencer, cried when Papa asked for Mama's hand in marriage. It wasn't that he objected to her marrying Papa. It was that he didn't want her to leave Ocracoke for the Trent Woods. Buxton, as it is called today, is only a short distance from Ocracoke via highway and ferry, but in 1903, it was a day's journey by sailboat.

Once the bridal couple had arrived at their new house, they found beautiful new houses by the U.S. Government. Today these buildings (the keepers quarters), are used as a museum and gift shop

> *"It is no wonder that my grandfather cried when Papa asked for Mama's hand in marriage...from Ocracoke to Buxton in 1903, it was a day's journey by sailboat."*

When the Cape Hatteras Light was built in 1870, it was located nearly a mile from the ocean. Today the waters lap almost to its base and threaten the tower. There is even the possibility that is may fall into the sea if efforts to save it should fail.

The three keepers of the light in 1903 and 1904, Amasa Fulcher, Luther Fulcher, and Mr. Quidley had responsible duties to perform. To sailors at sea the lighthouse was an important warning signal at Diamond Shoals, the Graveyard of the Atlantic, so the light had to shine from dawn to dusk. The keepers' main duty was to see that the lamp was filled each day. To transport a five-gallon can of kerosene to the top of the lighthouse was no mean task.

After a few years at Cape Hatteras Lighthouse, Papa was transferred to Harbor Island light. Here life was quite different from that at Hatteras. The lighthouse, a screwpile, was located in the middle of Core Sound. These lighthouses were located on all sounds along the Atlantic coast. They were built like an ordinary house, on iron pilings fifteen or twenty feet above the water. A cupola on top of the house contained the light. Supply boats visited the lighthouse periodically to leave supplies of food and fuel.

As a young man, Amasa Fulcher took his new bride from her family in Ocracoke to a new home at the Cape Hatteras Lighthouse. He served there for two years 1903-1904 and then continued his career at Harbor Island screwpile light in Core Sound. Circa 1903
Photo courtesy Marie E. Riddick

There were two keepers for each lighthouse. They served a month at a time, and their wives were allowed to spend a month with them each year. Evidently there was a period when both keepers and their wives were at the lighthouse at the same time. Mr. Thomas Grace Willis of Beaufort, North Carolina, served with my father. He and his wife Judith and

In this 1905 photograph of the Cape Hatteras Lighthouse you can see many details. The iron fence surrounded the tower to keep free-range animals out. The brick oil house was built in 1892 to keep flammables stored outside. The hill to the right in the background reveals the ruins of the 1803 sandstone lighthouse. The linen curtains are drawn in the lantern room to protect the prisms of the Fresnel lens from harsh sunlight and to give keepers a cooler area in which to work. Just visible is part of the walkway, which ran from the keepers quarters to the door of the lighthouse.
Photo courtesy Outer Banks History Center

my parents became fast friends through their association at the lighthouse.

In 1907, Papa retired from the Lighthouse Service and returned to Ocracoke to work at the J.W. McWilliams store. He remained there until 1918, when he built the Community Store, which was owned by David Senseney. During the years Papa operated the store, he sold practically everything that was necessary for everyday living on the island. There were groceries, including barrels of flour and corn meal, tubs of lard and butter, hardware, dress materials, shoes, rubber boots, and feed for cattle and chickens, and in later years, caskets. No more homemade coffins after Papa began to stock them.

In 1946, Papa died and was buried in the family graveyard where both his parents, Missouri (O'Neal) (1858-1922) and Benjamin (1847-1887), and his grandparents, Amasa O'Neal and Alice (pronounced /Ail-see/ Wahab O'Neal had been buried. Other graves in the cemetery are those of my mother Dell Spencer including: my two brothers and a sister, who died as infants; Papa's brother, Job, age nineteen; his brother, Ben, and his wife, Annie Simpson; his sister, Susan, and her husband, Isaac O'Neal; their nineteen-year-old daughter, Maud, and an infant. The latest graves to be added to the cemetery are those of Mabel and Christopher Gaskill. Some day my ashes will join those of my ancestors.

Though most Ocracokers today are buried in the new community cemetery, established in more recent years, there are still people on the island who continue to maintain their family graveyards. In my childhood, I liked to explore the old graves, some of which had interesting markers, homemade with original inscriptions carved by hand. Alas, these have long vanished, some to be dragged away by tourists; others have turned to dust. Many family graveyards have disappeared completely. When members of a family move from the island and there is no one left to tend the graves, they are soon taken over by oaks, cedars, and myrtle bushes. Houses today are sometimes built on the sites of old graveyards.

TIMELINE

AMASA G. FULCHER (1876-1946)
ASSISTANT KEEPER 1903-1904

Fannie Pearl Fulcher also wrote *Twice Told Tales of Ocracoke*. It is in the works to be published (1/3/01) Submitted by Marie E. Riddick

Confederates Put Out His Light
Benjamin T. Fulcher

He sired a lighthouse legacy: two daughters married keepers, a grandson became a Cape Hatteras keeper, and his granddaughters married keepers. One great-granddaughter has gathered the family story.

By Ruth Fulcher Rickert

Benjamin T. Fulcher was born 6 January 1810 in the Frisco area (then known as Trent) on Hatteras Island of the Outer Banks of North Carolina. He died there 27 November 1867. He was a son of Joseph and Sabra (Burrus) Fulcher. The census gave his occupation as "mariner" and "boatman." For the most part he was a pilot, as many men were in that area during his time. They transported goods, both domestic and imported, brought by larger ships that could not negotiate the narrow and shallow passages through the inlets, sounds, and rivers that the vessels of light draft were able to do. Benjamin married Lydia Farrow, born 13 January 1805, the daughter of neighbors, Christopher and Nancy Farrow. They lived comfortably at Trent and had several children. They were among the small number of residents who owned a few slaves. In addition to being a pilot, he also served two periods as lighthouse keeper at the 1803 lighthouse at Cape Hatteras.

From a partial list of lighthouse keepers and assistant keepers, Benjamin T. Fulcher was appointed assistant keeper 9 June 1845-60 and became primary keeper on 18 October 1860 until an unrecorded date. This was the beginning of the Civil War, and it is not known what part he played in the struggle between the northern and the southern forces to control the Cape Hatteras Lighthouse. Most people of the Outer Banks did not own slaves and were Federal sympathizers during the Civil War. Benjamin sent his oldest son, George Leffers Fulcher, to North Carolina Normal College, which became Trinity College, and later Duke, to study for the Methodist ministry. His son was against slavery when he returned from college. With the coming of the war, Federal soldiers occupied the island after Fort Hatteras fell. Foraging soldiers soon depleted food supplies on the island, and residents were forced to go across to the mainland to live in order to keep from starving to death. Benjamin's son, George, was said to have gone to Hyde County to live after threats were made on his life. Benjamin and Lydia probably followed. After the end of the war in 1865, residents returned. Some of them had a hard time getting their land back.

> *"A trusted man who kept the lighthouse for fifteen years before the Civil War...it is not known what part he played...in the struggle to control the Cape Hatteras Lighthouse. Most people of the Outer Banks did not own slaves and were Federal sympathizers during the Civil War."*

When Benjamin and Lydia returned, he was about fifty-five years old, and both must have been in poor health and spirits after the hardships of the war. Both died in 1867; Lydia on 1 September and Benjamin on 27 November. Benjamin died intestate, and his son, George, was appointed administrator of his estate. His old pilot boat was listed among his possessions on the inventory of things sold. Also sold were over 500 acres of land that he owned, including "the place where the windmill stands." Benjamin and Lydia were buried on some of that land near the ocean side of the island. In later years a bad storm uncovered their graves. Their grandson, Junius Fulcher (1876-1967), was himself a later employee of the U.S. Lighthouse Service, serving as an engineer on buoy tenders in Portsmouth, Virginia. Junius told of carrying their remains and their tombstones with a horse and wagon to Buxton (or "the Cape," as it was then called). He reburied them in the Miller Family Cemetery where they now rest near their daughter Emma [known as "Dolly"], who had married Christopher Columbus Miller, who became assistant keeper at Cape Hatteras from 1887 until 1892.

TIMELINE

BENJAMIN T. FULCHER (1810-1867)
ASSISTANT KEEPER 1845-1860;
PRINCIPAL KEEPER 1860-1861:

Benjamin T. Fulcher was born two years before the war with the British in 1812 and he lived until two years after the Civil War. While he was a keeper in 1854, major improvements were made to the original lighthouse and the double keepers quarters were built. In 1862, Confederate forces removed the Fresnel lens and darkened the Cape Hatteras Lighthouse, then considered the most important light in North America.

Photography had yet to be invented when Benjamin T. Fulcher was born; images of the Hatteras Island area prior to the Civil War, even prior to the 1890s, are rare. To date, no pictures of Keeper Fulcher have been found. Remarkably there is an extant picture of his daughter, Emma P. "Dolly" (1844-1895). In 1868 she married Christopher Columbus Miller, who became an assistant keeper at Cape Hatteras in 1887. Of her nine children with Miller, two sons, born only ten months apart in 1870-71, were celebrated U.S. Lifesaving Service surfmen, and three of her daughters married Cape Hatteras keepers.
Photo courtesy of Jo Ellen (Jennette) Luscombe.

In 1854, while Benjamin T. Fulcher was assistant keeper, the U.S. Lighthouse Service, then known as the Light-House Board, made significant improvements to the old 1803 tower in an effort to make it more visible to mariners who were nineteen miles at sea. The aging sandstone tower, built by Henry Dearborn, was given a boost from 95 to 150 feet, and a first-order Fresnel lens, the state-of-the-art optic, was installed to replace the antiquated reflector system.
Drawing courtesy Outer Banks History Center

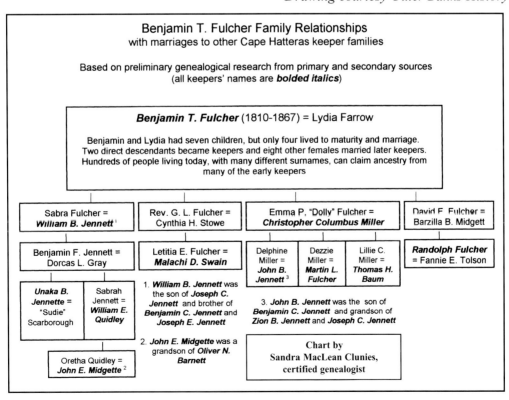

Ruth (Fulcher) Rickert is the great-granddaughter of Benjamin T. Fulcher, and author of this information (1986). This piece was submitted by Beatrice McArthur of the Hatteras Island Genealogical and Historical Society.

Fulcher Family Fabric
Charles Haywood Fulcher

*Jennie, the oldest Fulcher daughter, taught her younger sisters
to help take care of the growing family; Annie, the tomboy,
enjoyed closeness to her keeper father; "Day," the youngest and frail,
was a constant companion to her mother.*

By Cheryl Shelton-Roberts

Keeper Charles Haywood Fulcher transferred from St. Michaels, Maryland, to Cape Hatteras where he served from 1906-1920, becoming one of the longest continuous keepers on record there. Circa 1902 Photo courtesy Aaron Fulcher

Delora (Austin) Fulcher, about twenty years old in this portrait, enjoyed a long, full life as a keeper's wife. She and Charlie worked tirelessly together for his career and their children.
Photo courtesy Annie (Fulcher) Pellegrini

Charles "Charlie" Haywood Fulcher and Delora Austin, "Lorie" as Charlie called her, were the warp and waft of the family fabric. Three surviving sisters of their dozen Fulcher children helped weave the colorful tapestry of this family's story. Jennie, at ninety-four years of age, spent the first fourteen years of her life at the double keepers quarters at the Cape Hatteras Lighthouse in 1906. Sisters Ann, "Annie" and Nevada "Day," continued the family story in the 1920s, quite a different era with school buses and bustling nearby villages.

The Fulcher family was built of strong material: closeness and loyalty. Jennie, eldest daughter and authoritative, worked diligently to help with each baby that came along about every other year while Annie, the tomboy, enjoyed closeness to her keeper father, and Day, youngest and frail, was a constant companion to her mother.

Charlie married Delora, joined the U.S. Lighthouse Service, and began his first keeper's duty in Baltimore, Maryland, in 1903 as keeper of the Hoopers Strait (St. Michaels) Light, a Chesapeake Bay Lighthouse. Their first child, Earl, was born in 1904 in Maryland. In 1906, Keeper Fulcher transferred to Cape Hatteras where he served from 1906-1920, becoming one of the longest continuous keepers on record there. Fulcher also served at various Pamlico Sound screwpile lights, or "water lights," as the girls also call them. Memories of living on Hatteras Island and of spending time with him at Gull Shoal give the sisters a wealth of stories from which to draw.

Not long after Charlie, Delora, and two-year-old Earl moved into the double keepers quarters at Cape Hatteras, Jennie Levinia was born. Jennie spent the first fourteen years of her childhood at the light station and was expected to help with the growing family. "We helped Mother do all that was needed to be done," Jennie stated with a no-nonsense attitude she has possessed since childhood.

> *"During WWI...
> I remember the dropping of depth charges from sub chasers. The water would come as high as the house. We watched as the ships came as close in shore as they dared while the subs would try to run them onto the beach."*

"We used a washboard and the water came from the cistern and was hand-dipped," Jennie continued her memories. "We ate fish that Papa sometimes bought from other fishermen. And we had a garden. Papa planted all kinds of vegetables including potatoes and onions, tomatoes, cucumbers...we ate everything. And I remember climbing all those stairs, and going out on the deck and looking down and everything looked so small. I was allowed to go up with Papa as soon as I could handle the stairs. We kids went up there all the time. And I was there until I was fourteen years old. If visitors came, we'd take them up the lighthouse. We had lots of uncles and aunts and cousins who came to visit.

Timeline

Charles Haywood Fulcher (1878-1942)
Assistant Keeper 1906-1920

While Assistant Keeper Fulcher was tending the Cape Hatteras Lighthouse 1906-20, the Navy radio station picked up the SOS from the Titanic in 1912, and the newest of lamps, the incandescent oil vapor lamp, was installed in 1913, increasing the intensity of the beam to 80,000 candlepower. In 1918, the Diamond Shoals Lightship was sunk by a German submarine. When Keeper Fulcher transferred from Cape Hatteras in 1920, horsepower was still the norm and electricity was not commercially available on Hatteras Island.

"I started school at six years of age at the school in Buxton. In 1910, there were no buses or cars, so we got to school in a horse and cart- a horse and buggy. Papa took us every morning and picked us up every afternoon. I had a wonderful mother and a wonderful father. And yes, they were strict! They taught us right from wrong. If we said we were going to the store and we went beyond the time agreed, Mother would punish us. My Papa was always on guard and kept an eye on us children.

"We were mischievous, really," Jennie admitted. We loved to play on the sandhills and go to the beach and wade in the ocean. Once I picked up a stinging nettle. I picked up one and I had pains up my hands and arms, I had it for a long time and was in bad shape. I never picked up another one after that! I don't recall any medicine being given to me then. In fact, I don't think I went to a doctor when I was young. We used a lot of Vicks salve, and still do. I probably haven't taken two aspirins in my life and I'm still healthy," Jennie said with the confidence of a nonagenarian.

Around the turn of the twentieth century, often the only medical treatment was a lesson well learned in "I won't do THAT again." Medical help on Hatteras Island was often not readily available. The only resident doctor, Dr. Joshua "Josh" Davis had left Hatteras Island after seventeen years on the island in 1910.

Jennie continued her stream of consciousness delivery. "Papa was so dedicated to his job; it was much like the military and [he] expected the same of his kids. During the war [WWI], the submarines would run the ships onshore. We weren't allowed up the tower during the war. Papa kept it going during the war as far as I remember. Us children weren't frightened. I remember the dropping of depth charges from sub chasers. The water would come as high as the house. We watched as the ships came as close in shore as they dared while the subs would try to run them onto the beach."

Menacing German patrols along the North Carolina coast during WWI were a frightening experience for islanders who hadn't experienced the presence of aggressors since the Civil War. Although the patrols were not as fatal as WWII German U-boat action, families feared for those who worked the beachfront, including lighthouse and lifesaving station keepers.

Earl and Day were the only Fulcher children who were not born at the double keepers quarters at the Cape Hatteras

Delora (Austin) and Charlie Fulcher stop for a moment to be captured on film. While Keeper Fulcher was assistant keeper at the Cape Hatteras Lighthouse for fourteen years, his family lived with him in the double keepers quarters. When he served duty at several of the area sound screwpile lighthouses, his family either stayed in the family home in Frisco or visited him for a week at a time. Meanwhile, Delora, mother of Charlie's twelve children, kept the home fires burning. When Charlie returned home, he had supplies to stock, repairs to be made, and lots of family time to catch up on. Two of his daughters, Annie and Nevada, concurred that their parents exemplified the community spirit on Hatteras Island of neighbor helping neighbor. Photo by Earl Fulcher Photo courtesy Annie (Fulcher) Pellegrini

Delora, the keeper's wife and center of the family, carried and delivered twelve Fulcher children between 1906 and 1925. Born in 1882, she saw the transformation of Hatteras Island from lamp to electricity, sailboat and horse and cart to automobile, and experienced family life at the Cape Hatteras Lighthouse and area sound lights and back home in Frisco. She kept her family close to her and, until her last day, she walked among her children's homes nearby on land that Charlie had bought with a little cash and a boat.
Photo by Annie (Fulcher) Pellegrini and courtesy Bobby Pellegrini

Delora Fulcher stands in her living room in 1944. Her friend, coworker, spouse, and keeper, Charles Fulcher, died in 1942, leaving her not alone, but with many caring children. Charlie's plan to buy land and Delora's plan to save it for the children was successful in that several of her children either lived close to her all her life or they came home frequently to visit her.
Photo by Bill Pellegrini and courtesy Annie (Fulcher) Pellegrini

Lighthouse. "We didn't have to help with the new babies when they were born. My Papa had a nurse, 'Miss Rozene' [Rovena Quidley], to come in and help and Papa had to [go and] get her in a buggy. We didn't have to wash diapers, nothing. Papa didn't think a child should take care of a baby brother or sister. The nurse would come back everyday. Mother stayed in bed thirteen days after a child was born and she did no work during that time."

According to other family members, Jennie is very modest in describing her duties. Betty ("Bett") told stories about her beloved sister who was like a mother figure to the rest of the children. Jennie was responsible for teaching the other girls to cook and sew and clean.

"My Papa read lots of library books. He was a fanatic reader. Papa used to always tell us as soon as we got home to get our lessons done. He showed us adding, subtracting, multiplying, and dividing long before we were shown it in school. He had us to read a certain amount each day. When Papa was in school, there were only seven grades. That's as far as you went in school around home. After you passed the seventh grade, you went to Manteo School, and then eighth or ninth grade was as high as they taught back then. What education we got, I think my Papa taught us as much as they taught [us] in school. Mother had so many children that all she did was wash [clothes] and take care of us all. I only had two [children] and I hardly could take care of them!" Jennie said with a big laugh.

"Chores were done in a very organized way. We use to boil clothes in a lard can on the wood stove. That's how we sterilized them."

A lard can held fifty pounds of lard, so the metal container was approximately eighteen by twenty-four inches. Lard was used to make prized biscuits and cakes, fry fresh fish right out of the ocean or sound, and the containers were as prized as the contents. Lard cans were recycled to do jobs from boiling clothes to storing future hog's lard renderings.

Jennie continued, "He [Keeper Fulcher] was on a light across from Hatteras, [all the children pronounced it "Ha'tress"] down that way. It was a screwpile lighthouse, I think it was Oliver's Reef [Hatteras Inlet]. We'd visit with him a week at a time and that's where he did all that reading and educating himself. He read library after library of books. They'd [the Lighthouse Service] take the library away and bring in new books on lighthouse tenders."

The U.S. Lighthouse Service delivered coal, wood, and lamp oil to each American lighthouse on a regular basis, usually twice a year, on a tender specially equipped to carry supplies and offload them. Out of concern for keepers who spent many nights in solitary vigil over a lamp's flame, the Lighthouse Service rotated a "library" of books. The wood case with two doors that folded towards the center held numerous books for all reading levels. Sometimes the library contained educational magazines including *National Geographic*.

"Mother, Papa called her 'Lorie,' was a good cook. We had lots of clams, oysters, fish, scallops, all kinds of seafood. Papa bought most of this; he took the boat across the sound to Englehardt and bought a barrel of flour and fifty pounds of lard in a lard can and a crate of eggs. He only bought large amounts of everything! He had a big family to feed!" With this statement, Jennie's wise eyes opened wide and she leaned forward in earnest to emphasize "large."

"But nobody ever dressed better than we did. We ordered lots of our clothes from a catalog. Mother didn't have much time to sew with all those kids to take care of!"

Jennie was known for her crocheting. She taught many of the keepers' girls as they took up residence at the lighthouse. Today, her home is generously laced with her handiwork and her former "students" have passed this legacy to their girls.

"And oh, lord, we had animals. We had horses, cattle, sheep, pigs, and we had bats, too! They'd [birds] fly into the lighthouse and we'd go in there and gather bushels of birds that had flown into the light. We never ate the birds that I recall, but we did eat chickens and geese. They'd [Papa and Earl and other lighthouse residents] go hunting for birds sometimes.

"The Jennettes were there when we lived there. We knew the Caseys and all the kids use to play with the neighbors. If you wanted to associate with others, okay, and if you didn't, that was okay, too. We had our privacy if we wanted it," Jennie said.

Cape Hatteras Light Station was a unique duty station with three keepers and their families in full-time residence, all living within just feet of one another. Two families occupied the 1854 double keepers quarters, split down the middle with one half of the house exactly like the other half. The primary keeper had a private house east of the double keepers quarters.

"I'm much like my Papa because I'm independent, but people say I look like my mother. I've tried to be good to my family like Papa was to me. My son Paul is alot like him. He devotes so much time to this family."

When Keeper Fulcher transferred from the Cape Hatteras Lighthouse in 1920, he moved his family from the light station back to the family home in Frisco, then Trent, that Charlie had helped his father, Tom, build in Frisco in 1888 as a young lad. Jennie recalled that she often traveled by sailboat with her Grandpa Tom from Frisco to Hatteras village. At other times she walked or ran. "And I remember the old hand-crank ice cream makers that we used big, coarse salt. It was good times when the family gathered." The home would become the hub for the Fulcher family for a century.

Annie was the last Fulcher child to be born in the double keepers quarters in 1920, just prior to Fulcher's transfer from Cape Hatteras. During the 1920s and 30s there were two medical men on the island, Annie remembered. "Dr. Fobb, Pharmacist's Mate at the U.S. Coast Guard Station at the present site of the Fessenden Center, and Dr. McNabb were in Buxton." But Rovena Quidley, a midwife, brought Annie into the world. Rovena assisted in the births of hundreds of babies born on the island during that time.

Annie was sixteen and fourteen years younger than Earl

Early photographs of Cape Hatteras are few and far between. Keepers' families have lost many, and in some cases all, of their personal photographs to the "tides," as the older generations refer to the island overwash from storm-driven tides. This 1935 picture of the lighthouse is still safely stored in a family album by Keeper Fulcher's daughter, Annie, and her son, Bobby Pellegrini.

Hatteras Community Spirit

Annie's son and Keeper Fulcher's grandson, Bobby Pellegrini, sees some of the Hatteras Island community spirit in man's reaction during a recent event. "We see this attitude in neighbor taking care of neighbor today in most pressing times or in the face of natural disasters such as that of hurricanes. I remember Emily (1994), which delivered a direct blow to Hatteras Island where many homes and businesses were flooded and property damaged by winds that were clocked in excess of 100 mph! The sound surge inundated all soundside properties including Highway 12 and flooded back to the Piney Ridge, a high land area where some people experienced water in their homes, and this area never floods! I remember as it were only yesterday, how powerful the sound flooding was from Emily. I had 150 feet of a 250-foot boardwalk out from my soundfront cottage in Frisco swept away in sections by the 8 to 9-foot sound surge. But it was only through the help of local residents of Frisco that contributed their time and toil to help pitch in and help me out when they themselves also experienced damage to their property. With this help, we were able to find each of the sections and put my boardwalk back in place. This passion for your neighbor was exhibited by ALL the islanders. Both my parents, Annie and Frank Pellegrini, were extensions of this attitude manifested in my grandparents, Charlie and Delora Fulcher, and I am proud of this heritage."

Keeper Charles Fulcher plays in the yard of his family home with Paul, Jennie (Fulcher) Sharp's son. Paul commented on this photo, "Pop let me get away with murder on the front porch. He let me play 'mumbly peg' when "Mom" [Grandmother Delora] scolded me. I remember when I was older, we clammed in the sound from the family home and we sailed from Frisco to Hatteras into Fulcher's landing to visit." 1931
Photo courtesy Paul Sharp

When Keeper Fulcher transferred from the Cape Hatteras Lighthouse in 1920, he moved his family from the light station back to the family home in Frisco, then Trent, that Charlie had helped his father, Tom, build in Frisco in 1888 as a young lad. This home was alive with the keeper's twelve Fulcher children, two grandchildren, and a host of friends. Charlie built a park across the road for the kids and there were many "socials" held here with countless hand-cranked ice cream containers shared with all.
Photo by Dorsey Conner and courtesy Annie (Fulcher) Pellegrini

and Jennie, respectively, and reaped some of the benefits. Annie explained, "I was with him [Keeper Fulcher] every minute I could be with him. Pop [sometimes Annie and sister Day referred to their father as 'Daddy,' 'Pop,' or 'Pop Pop'] taught me my ABCs backwards and forwards, and I sat on his knee and he read to me for hours. My Pop was a very smart man. And I loved my mother, don't get me wrong, but with nine children, she didn't have lots of private time. Pop, Bett, and I would go out to the lighthouse at Gull Shoal in the sound and stay for two weeks at a time. I remember we would boat to Stumpy Point for food and other supplies to last us for the two weeks. I loved it out there on the lighthouse."

Charlie's buddy, Annie, distinctly described her daddy's duties on the various sound lighthouses. "Depending on which lighthouse he was on, every Saturday he polished the doorknobs and ALL the brass. And he made all the meals himself when we visited! I was always with my father. In those times, women did those kinds of jobs and I was amazed seeing him clean the way he did. He kept the lighthouse spotless. He had to keep a logbook of the lighthouse every day. His duties were to make sure the lighthouse operated at all times and was clean. He was serious about his duties and was so devoted to being a keeper so that everything he did was thorough. He made mistakes but he was a man of integrity and trust.

"We went out to the lighthouse in a Lighthouse Service boat. The smell of the gas was different from what you get today. It was a LONG trip to me, and the most enjoyable thing was to go and come with him to get the groceries he needed. The most enjoyable thing was to come with him and Bett to get the groceries he needed from Stumpy Point. I remember the salt spray hitting our faces!"

Annie summoned the memory about how extreme cold on the sound would freeze it solid as far out as one could see for at least two weeks. It was so solid that not only would people walk out on it, they drove cars on it. Once the ice thawed, the fish that had been frozen and suspended in the water washed ashore at what the family called "the landing," the shoreline out from their home into the sound.

"We also had our own skiff," Annie explained, "that we used to go fishing and boating in, and we fished off the lighthouse deck everyday no matter the weather! I loved to fish! We caught croakers, spots, trout, flounder, and of course, crabs that would eat away our bait. We didn't always eat what we caught, though.

"I remember Roanoke Marshes [screwpile lighthouse], the last one Pop operated in the late 1930s. He died five years later [1942] after retiring from the Lighthouse Service in 1937. Another lighthouse I also remember is Brant Island; Pop rotated operating the sound lighthouses with other keepers. Two men that Pop rotated shifts with were Julian H. Austin and David Quidley. I just loved being with Pop and my sister, Bett. Having her with me was wonderful. It certainly kept us happy being out there alone with Pop on any of the lighthouses. He was careful with us; Pop wouldn't let us get into the water around the lighthouse until we were older.

"The inside of the lighthouse was plain and very simple. All the rooms were simple. There was a kitchen and eating area and two bedrooms with single beds, not bunk beds. The wood walls were kind of dark, and it had to be kept clean and spotless. I used to dust a lot for Pop. If it got foggy out there, Pop had to operate the bell by winding up the mechanism that struck the fog bell. I can remember there were ferries that went by carrying cars, trucks, and people, and when they got near the lighthouse, the ship would salute Pop with their horn and keep blowing it until they got a ways away and Pop answered by ringing the bell."

Annie described how rainwater was collected from eaves on the lighthouse and stored in large wooden tanks. This was the only fresh water the keeper had for cooking and cleaning at the sound lighthouses. A cistern system was also used at the lighthouse and at their family home. "Pop had built a large cement cistern that also caught rainwater that drained from the house gutters. We would go out to the cistern that was just out from the house with a bucket and ladle water into the bucket, which we dipped from in the house for our water use.

"From the family home in Frisco, we went to school in Buxton on a school bus, but the road wasn't good since it was sand. We also went to school in Hatteras on a school bus but we would have to use the beach on a low tide to avoid getting stuck. From Frisco in the 1920s, it was hard to get to villages like Buxton by the sand road, or to Avon either way [sand road or beach at low tide] in Pop's horse and buggy or sometimes our car. On Sundays we had to go to church at the Little Grove in Frisco twice a day, Sunday School in the mornings and church service at night.

"I remember that our family night was every Wednesday when I was growing up. That was the one night that all the family gathered to enjoy games, parching peanuts, and making fudge candy. We all looked so forward to this time to be together particularly when Pop was home from the sound lighthouse.

"It was during the early '20s that Pop purchased a DELCO plant to supply electricity to our home. Prior to this, we used oil lamps. As I remember, we were the first family to have electricity on the island. Businesses had electricity. The plant was a gasoline-powered motor connected to a series of twelve batteries. Pop would start the motor to charge the batteries. When fully charged, the batteries generated electricity for our lights, radio, refrigerator and stove. This would last three to four days before Pop, and sometimes Sharpe [Jennie's husband], would restart the motor to charge the batteries. The motor was bolted to a cement base which served as the foundation. We lost the plant from sound flooding during the '33 storm. We then had to revert to lamps until electricity was commercially available. The memory of this comes back to me everytime I see that cement base that is still in place in my front yard!"

Reverting to a pre-electrical lifestyle included using the old icebox. "We had an ice box to keep perishable foods," Annie explained. A large block of ice up to fifty pounds was placed in the box for cooling. The blocks had to be replaced every couple of weeks. Ice was delivered to our house from Frazier's ice plant in Hatteras. Pop also had a milk house that was out from our house and sat on pilings. Mom kept her dairy products there like eggs, butter, and meats that she could not keep in the icebox. Since we had a large family, overflow items were kept in the milk house. This was mainly used in the summer months. Of course, we didn't have a cellar because if you dug just a couple of feet into the ground, you hit water!"

Annie revisited some childhood adventures. "My sisters

These three 1942 bathing beauties are three of Charlie's girls. Having fun oceanside in Frisco are left to right, Nevada, Ina, and Annie. Photo by Bill Pellegrini and courtesy Annie (Fulcher) Pellegrini

and I had lots of fun playing and swimming at the sound and climbing trees, and Pop had swings for us in our backyard. Earl had a horse called 'Sterling' that we would ride around Frisco, but we never rode on the beach. Mother would allow us to play in the sound water for as long as we wanted during the summer when the sound water was warm. We also enjoyed walking to Arthur Fulcher's General Store. I would buy hard stick candy there. The orange blossom and peanut butter filled were my favorites."

Bett and Annie were four years apart in age and became best buddies. Bett called Annie the "tomboy" of the family. "I was a tomboy!" Annie admitted with a smile. "I did things that boys did like climbing trees, playing ball, fishing, boating, and tending to animals that I had. My best friend was Sylvia, also from Frisco. Her daddy was in service and died before she was born. We were together a lot since she did not have her daddy growing up, so I palled around with her as much as I could. She was a tomboy as much as I was and we loved to climb trees! We'd climb trees and swing from one tree to another.

"And I was the animal person," Annie continued. "I had a dog, many cats, a crow, a goat, an alligator, and a sea gull.

This five-generation picture of Fulchers includes top row, left to right: Deborah Ann (Sharp) Ives, Jennie's granddaughter, holding Bridgett Ann Ives; Virginia Lee (Bernard) Sharp, wife of Jennie's son, Paul; Jennie Levenia (Fulcher) Sharp, the keeper's daughter; Delora (Austin) Fulcher, the matriarch of the Fulcher family. Circa 1975
Photo by and courtesy of Paul Sharp

You name it, and I had it. I would get an animal when it either was small or was hurt and nurse it back to health. They would stay with me and the family all the time and follow me around. The sea gull would go with me to the sound and come back home with me. The crow that I caught when it was real small, it followed me everywhere! While I washed the dishes, he'd get on the screen door and just CAW at me. At Christmastime there was a bush with red berries on it, yaupon, and I'd put ribbons on it myself and I had a gift for each animal on the tree. Once my little goat tore apart EVERY gift and ate all the paper! Pop always told me that as long as I took care of my animals, he and Mother would never say 'No' to me. He even built me a little house for my animals in our backyard where he had his storage house for keeping our family supplies.

"When I was staying at home and Pop was away at the lighthouse, I looked so forward for his return so he could take Bett and me net fishing. I remember how I set a fish net with him in the evening and we'd check it very early the next morning. We would catch croaker, trout, flounder, shark, jumping mullet, sea bass, channel bass, and crabs. We would bring our bounty home and share with other families. We also clammed at low tide in the sound. We would clean the clams for Mom to prepare. Our favorite seafood that Mom prepared for us included shrimp, oysters- Bett found a pearl one time- Hatteras style clam chowder, fish, and crabs. Mom would cook fish many different ways, but all were good!

"When Pop left to go to Arthur Fulcher's store, or somewhere, I followed him, and sometimes he'd tell me to go back home. But I'd follow and wait for those words. He'd turn around and say, 'I'm willin,' and I knew I could come along! And I was right there with him.

"Daddy was born on Hatteras Island and I was named for his mother, Annie Mozelle Fulcher. I have always loved Hatteras Island and to this day spend my summers here. To say that I was born at Cape Hatteras Lighthouse is an honor. There was danger there for my daddy, but I had good memories, too. But there was terrible danger...the U-boats bombing all those ships during WWI. Mother told me that they had to darken the lights of the windows of the keepers quarters at Buxton because the Germans got so close to the coast. She was very upset and nervous about Pop's safety and being out there during those dangerous times. She had six children at the keepers quarters and she feared for them and their safety. It was scary to be out there on the beachfront during the war. I heard Mom say that he'd take the kerosene can and go up to fill the reservoir of the lamp, regardless of how bad the conditions were...he had to go. Daddy told me many times about the ships that had been torpedoed and he would go into the lighthouse and watch as the ships burned.

"The same thing happened along the coast in 1941-42 during WWII. The light kept burning through the war as far as I can remember.

"My sisters and I liked dancing. We would go to the 'Beacon' in Hatteras because at that time I loved to dance and I liked to party as a young lady. I remember one time that I danced with what turned out to be a German spy. At the time, I did not know his motive or that he was a German officer even though he did have an accent that was different from the other boys. This fella started to talk to me and asking questions about the lighthouse and the lightship, and how far out in the sound was the river lights, but of course, I couldn't tell him anything. I danced with him. Within a couple of days, I heard that he was arrested and that he was a Nazi spy."

The "tomboy" matured into an attractive "young lady." Annie blushed at the suggestion that she was said to be pretty. "I was pretty popular, I'll admit. I was in many plays at school."

Annie changed the subject quickly. "Now, Earl [the oldest of the children] loved it out there at the lighthouse. He caught fish in the ponds around the lighthouse. He walked from Buxton to school, and that was a long way. Earl worked with Pop, doing many of the keeper's duties right along with him. Daddy used to talk about carrying kerosene, those heavy cans of oil, to the lantern at the top of the lighthouse.

"I remember our family Christmases. They were special to all of us. As a child, our family would go to church on Christmas Eve and come back home and gather around our potbelly stove and our tree to sing carols and enjoy the time together. As a teenager, we sisters would go to parties at neighbors' houses after church service. Mom would still be up waiting for our safe return home. Christmas and Easter were the big holidays at home," Annie reminisced.

Nevada agreed. Youngest sister, "Day," as the family calls her, said the important holidays were "Christmas and Easter. They were always made special for the children."

Day, closest to her mother began speaking, "I was born at the family home after Pop had moved to a lighthouse out in the water. But I have the lovely memories of Earl and Mama and Pop talking about living at the lighthouse. My brother was always talking about how he'd go with my dad up all those steps everyday with five gallons of fuel. He'd walk all the way up and help him fix the lamp.

Cars taking the sand road at low tide in 1944 had an unexpected visitor on the beach. This oil tanker had been driven ashore by notorious Cape Hatteras weather. If ships were fortunate enough to beach in good condition, they could be floated again at high tide and continue their journey. During the early part of WWII until late 1942, the route around Cape Hatteras hosted many oil tankers on their way from the southern Atlantic Ocean to northern ports. German U-boats sank many of them off Cape Hatteras to prevent their valuable cargo from reaching Allied troops. Photo courtesy Annie (Fulcher) Pellegrini

"Earl and my sisters talked about how much they loved living at the Cape Hatteras Light Station. If they were near the water, they wanted to fish, and I think, of course, it was because they were born there. I never really understood this, but they loved their birthplace even though the family home wasn't far away in Frisco. They had a special bond with that place." Day said with emotion.

"I used to go with Mom wherever she went. So, if she went out to the sound light to visit Pop, I went along. When I was growing up, he was gone to the sound light so much. I was afraid of the water, but Ann was like a duck at the sound light." Day said with her ever-ready laugh. "I had asthma and all those bad things. There was a powder I had to inhale. But Ann always tried to get me out on the deck at the water light." Day shook with laughter as she said, "But I was terrified of the water; in fact, I never learned to swim. Mom and Pop didn't want me to get my chest wet because of my asthma and all.

"Ann was always such a tease! She'd take me out in our little boat and tell me, 'We're going to sink! We're going to sink!!' And I would scream and scream and Mama would hear me crying and send Charlie to get us. To this day, Ann will call and play tricks with me and I believe her!"

Day returned to the sound light days, "Mama brought books for us to read and we had comics that we could have for a certain time of the day and I fished everyday, but I wouldn't get down next to where the water was."

With a great laugh Day continued about her sister, "Ann was quite the tomboy. Dad fixed a big house for her animals and she even had a talking crow and a mouse and rats and everything. She would threaten me, 'If you don't do so and so, I'm going to get that white rat after you!' I never had anything like that because I'm allergic to animals!

"My dad was such a wonderful, kind, and free-hearted, considerate man," Day said. "No wonder God has bless us so much. He would take any extra money he had and buy groceries for a family in need. And from all around, people who couldn't afford to travel to a dentist would come to Pop and he pulled their teeth! He wanted to be a dentist, but he never got to school. Older people would come to Charlie...he'd sterilize his pullers, and pull the teeth for them. Mother worried that something might have gone wrong and Charlie would be blamed. But the old people calmed his fears when they insisted Pop do the job. And he used no anesthetics!

"Pop was an excellent carpenter and helped his father build our family home in Frisco. Others would come to him," Day said admiringly, "and tell him what kind of house they wanted and he could tell them right away what it'd cost and how much lumber it would take. He told me that he made a skiff and along with a small amount of money, he bought Piney Ridge. The owners couldn't afford to pay the taxes on the land so they wanted to get rid of it. It has been divided among nine children. He couldn't have afforded much money.

"Mother," Day continued, "was a home person. She was always busy preparing food and doing clothes. She did a little sewing, and she had such beautiful flowers and the tide would come and wash them away and she would plant them again.

"Dad never got much formal schooling, but he read books and taught himself and taught us in turn, and his handwriting is beautiful. And education was very important to him. I started school in Buxton, but for the first three years the parents in Frisco hired a teacher around 1928-29 to teach the children. The trip to Buxton was long and the tides would often overwash, and it was dark before we got home many times.

"People knew who my daddy was. They knew he was a keeper and respected him very much. Other parents allowed their daughters to come only to the Fulcher home because they knew they'd be safe there. There'd be eight or nine of us trying to get on one bed! Daddy always arranged for us girls to be at home- that home was for girls. Mama and Daddy were always willing to fix two or three extra things of ice cream. It took all day to fix just the desserts! The Fulcher home was the gathering place for the young people in Frisco and across the road Daddy had even fixed a little park for the kids with a swing and grass.

"We loved our mother and daddy because they gave us so much," Day continued. "For our graduations or special occasions, Daddy would have a man in Manteo, I think his name was Davis, to send four or five evening dresses for us to choose from. Because he knew my dad real, real well, and with changing weather and no good roads, we might never get up the beach. Sometimes Daddy would take us kids in the boat to Manteo to see what was going on if there were any activities. Mama always said she'd be glad when we could afford a car so we didn't have to go over the water, knowing how afraid I was of it!

"Mama continued to walk up and down the road every evening up until her death and see her family. She kept us close," Day said with reverence.

Adding further color to the Fulcher fabric was Grandson Dorsey Conner, Bett's son, who pointed out that "Grandma was the center of the family. Everyone revolved around her. They [family] came to see her and often stayed with her. I can remember the trips down the road through the villages at Avon and Buxton to Frisco. It was completely lined with trees and so beautiful. People today don't realize how beautiful the road coming down the island to here [Frisco] was. Going to Grandma's was always something to look forward to."

Annie and Day confirmed this by recounting the special arrangements they made with their husbands and children for their permissions to travel to Frisco and stay with Delora.

When Day comes back to Hatteras Island and Frisco to stay for the summer, she doesn't bring any phone numbers, radio, or television. Like her Pop, she reads. She loves the quiet that she once enjoyed on the sound light with her family when there was no electricity, no running water, no enter-

At home in 1943 with Annie is her husband, Bill Pellegrini. Keeper Fulcher had a tough duty in addition to being a lighthouse keeper- guarding eight lovely daughters.
Photo by Betty (Fulcher) Conner
Photo courtesy Annie (Fulcher) Pellegrini

At ninety-four years of age, Jennie is one of the oldest known keeper's descendants alive. Born in the double keepers quarters in 1906 just after Keeper Fulcher arrived there, she spent the first fourteen years of her life at the Cape Hatteras Light Station. The oldest Fulcher girl, Jennie had tremendous responsibilities in helping raise her siblings. According to stories that Jennie's sister, Bett, told to her son Dorsey, Jennie is extremely modest in describing her childhood chores. "She taught the other girls how to clean and cook," Dorsey said. "She worked very hard to help Grandmother take care of the rest of the family while a baby came along about every other year." 2000
Photo by Bruce Roberts

Annie Fulcher Pellegrini is Keeper Fulcher's daughter. She still returns to Frisco every summer to a home she established next door to her childhood home. Annie commented, "Daddy was born on Hatteras Island and I was named for his mother, Annie Mozelle Fulcher. I have always loved Hatteras Island and to this day spend my summers here. To say that I was born at Cape Hatteras Lighthouse is an honor." 2000
Photo by Cheryl Shelton-Roberts

tainment for kids. These children of water are children of reflection.

Sisters Annie and Day concurred that their parents exemplified the community spirit on Hatteras Island. Annie and Day both recalled times when Charlie took from his meager stock of food, clothes, and other supplies to share with another family in need; he was keeper of more than just lighthouses. If a home burned, the neighbors combined skills and materials to build another. Though humble about herself, Annie and her husband, Frank, became an extension of Annie's parents throughout their lives together, creating and nurturing an extended family.

"Home is where your heart is, and I can make any place home, but I love Frisco and Hatteras Island. I gained serenity here," Annie said softly while sitting in her home in Frisco, built next to the old family home where she grew up. "Here, I am spiritually at peace."

Nevada, "Day," proudly shows the remainder of a limb that was driven through one side of her storage building and out the door on the other end. The "hurrakin," as islanders pronounce "hurricane," of 1999 caused great damage to the East Coast. Day spends her time in a home near Annie in Frisco each summer simply reading. 2000
Photo by Cheryl Shelton-Roberts

Part of the extended Fulcher family is caught in this group photo. Bottom row, left: Bobby Lee Pellegrini, Annie (Fulcher) and Bill Pellegrini's son; second row, left to right, Unith Rollinson, Charlie's Nephew; Frank William Pellegrini, son of Annie and Bill; Marlene Kumor, Nevada (Fulcher) Palmer's daughter; Deloris Jennette, Linda (Fulcher) Whedbee's daughter; Judy Townsend, Earl Fulcher's daughter; third row left to right, Leonard Rolinson, Hilda (Fulcher) Rollinson's husband; Hilda (Fulcher) Rollinson; Ina (Fulcher) Burris, Linda (Fulcher) Whedbee; Earl Fulcher; Delora Fulcher (rocking chair); Wilma Fulcher, Earl's wife; Annie (Fulcher) Pellegrini; Zach Whedbee, Linda's husband; Nevada (Fulcher) Palmer. Picture taken in 1944 and in family room during a typical Saturday night Fulcher family gathering.
Photo courtesy Annie (Fulcher) Pellegrini

Quotes and stories are taken from: interviews with Annie (Fulcher) Pellegrini and Nevada (Fulcher) Palmer August 11, 2000, and many follow-up phone calls and mailings; interview with Jennie (Fulcher) Sharp and son Paul Sharp September 1, 2000; interview with Dorsey Conner September 30, 2000. Thanks to Bobby Pellegrini for extensive correspondence and assistance with interviewing Annie for added information for the Fulcher family story. Thanks also to Paul Sharp, Wayne Fulcher, and W.L. Whedbee for many communications and help with procuring family photographs and stories.

A Career Lighthouse Keeper
James Wilson Gillikin

"March 7th, 1924: ...Rec'd a letter from Annie saying Ruth had a very fine daughter born on the fourth of this month. Ruth Anne weighed 7 lbs & 2ozs. I sent the baby a $5.00 check wish it was $100..."

By Sandra MacLean Clunies

We can appreciate this touching tribute of a proud and grateful grandfather in the statement above. He celebrates the news of the arrival of his first granddaughter and wishes that his tangible token of welcome could even better match the great joy that he feels. This baby, Ruth Anne, lives today in Huntsville, Alabama, and regrets that she has no strong personal memories of her grandfather, James Wilson Gillikin, who died in her first year of life.

A photograph of him in his keeper's uniform, and words from this journal that he kept at the end of his long career provide us with a portrait of a hard-working and devoted family man. After his death, his widow Annie made her home with daughter Ruth and her family. Granddaughter Ruth Anne was an only child, and she relishes the memories of many happy hours with her mother and grandmother, listening to the stories of life at the lighthouse.

Born on 10 August 1857, the second of six children of Elijah P. and Nancy (Lupton) Gillikin, James' family had been established for several generations in coastal North Carolina, and his family remains an active part of Carteret County communities today. As a young child during the Civil War period, James witnessed many events that disrupted the tranquillity of life along the Outer Banks. While families struggled with the uncertainty and tensions of those times, the lighthouses were darkened and some destroyed.

After the war years, the lighthouse system was rebuilt along the Outer Banks. We do not have records on the early adult life of James Gillikin, but presumably he worked in one of the traditional trades. He met Annie Davis, daughter of Omeda W. and Margaret (Clifton) Davis of Washington County, when she was a young girl and he was eleven years her senior. It may be just a romantic suggestion, as it is not a known fact, but family lore remains that James set his sights on this pretty, young person and decided to wait for her to grow up.

James stated in his journal that he had thirty years of Lighthouse Service in 1924. However, primary records reveal he was appointed an assistant keeper at Roanoke River Lighthouse in June, 1885, at age twenty-seven. Thus it was almost forty years from first service to last, but he likely had some years not employed by the lighthouse system, as there are periods in which his name does not appear on lighthouse registers. He married young Annie Davis at Plymouth in 1889 and their first daughter, Maude, was born in 1890, followed by daughter Ruth in 1891, and daughter Ulva in 1897. Their first son, Leigh Dobson, was born after 1900 but died of whooping cough within his first year of life. Son Alton arrived in 1904, giving James and Annie a family of four surviving children to raise at the various light stations.

The Lighthouse Service was divided into geographical districts. The Fifth District then covered all of the "aids to navigation" of Virginia and North Carolina, plus the entire Chesapeake Bay. Each district employed a large staff of personnel which included superintendents, inspectors, engineers, mechanics, clerks, keepers and laborers for lighthouses, keepers and crew for lightships, captains and crew for tenders, and employees at various supply depots.

> *"Annie Gillikin became well known for her knowledge of medical treatments, and many of the neighbors near the Cape Hatteras Lighthouse relied on her for advice, which came from her own experience and those medical books."*

The lighthouse keepers were often transferred among the various stations to gain experience in different situations. James Gillikin served first at the smaller stations such as Roanoke River, then as keeper at Laurel Point in 1888, and Harbor Island Bar from 1893-1897. In May of 1897, now with over a decade of experience, he was named keeper at Ocracoke, from which he was transferred to the position of keeper at Cape Hatteras in December 1897.

Keepers were required to maintain a written journal of their work and the weather. Some keepers added personal details. James noted various tasks that he and the other keepers performed: "chipping paint in the tower getting ready for painting,"..."finished putting 1200 gals of oil in the tank"..."helped get a boat off the beach"..."painted the frame work of the tank"..."been cleaning boat"..."working on brass

TIMELINE

JAMES WILSON GILLIKIN (1857-1925)
PRIMARY KEEPER 1897-1900:

Keeper Gillikin watched many ships passed Cape Hatteras as they traveled the sea route from Norfolk, Virginia, to fight the Spanish in Cuba in 1898. In 1899, one of the worst hurricanes on record, the "San Ciriaco," (source: David Stick, *Graveyard of the Atlantic*) a term used for the storm since no formal names were given then, hit the East Coast. Strong winds drove the Diamond Shoals Lightship #69 ashore about one and one-half miles southwest of the lighthouse.

work in the tower"... it was an endless round of maintenance and repair to keep the lighthouse in the excellent condition that the Inspectors demanded.

The Lighthouse Service provided many supplies for the keepers and their families. Ruth Anne remembers her grandmother describing the medical books, which were part of these provisions. They were meant to assist families stationed in remote locations with the diagnosis and treatment of simple ailments when they were distant from other medical help. Annie Gillikin became well known for her knowledge of medical treatments, and many of the neighbors near the Cape Hatteras Lighthouse relied on her for advice, which came from her own experience and those medical books.

Ruth Anne recalls the story about a technique to reduce sudden fever in a child: a metal band was attached to the pulse spot on a wrist, from which a band of cloth was suspended in cold water. The cold water chilled the metal band that then was expected to reduce the fever.

Schooling for the keeper's children was often a challenge. When the Gillikin family lived at Cape Hatteras, their children were pre-school age. When James was transferred to Cape Lookout during the school season, the keeper's wife, Annie, and her children lived in Beaufort and James came there on his days off. He took a great interest in their education and Ruth Anne's mother recalled long hours with their father as he "listened to lessons." He was very strict about the schooling and very concerned about the children's safety as they walked to and from school. He devised a walking route through back streets that he ordered the children to use, so they would not walk along the busy main streets. There were many enticements to walk closer to the center of town where there was always something to see and do; some of his children obeyed his orders, and some did not!

This keeper and his family could not swim - a rather surprising fact. Ruth Anne recalls her mother did not learn to swim until she was a young adult, long after her lighthouse years. During heavy storms, the keepers would tie a rope around themselves and attach the end to a secure spot.

When the Gillikin children had grown and left home, the family home in Beaufort was leased out and Annie divided

James Wilson Gillikin (1857-1925) came from a long-established family of Carteret County, North Carolina. His career with the U.S. Lighthouse Service spanned forty years, serving at many Outer Banks lighthouses. He was at Roanoke River, Laurel Point, Harbor Island Bar, and Ocracoke before becoming primary keeper at Cape Hatteras 1897-1900. In 1900, he was transferred to Cape Lookout. While there were some later periods during which he was not on active duty, he was serving there in 1925 when ill health required surgery in Richmond, Virginia. Sadly, he died during that surgery, but he left a journal which remains in the family today and provides a personal memory.
Photo courtesy Ruth Ann Geer-Lloyd

Annie (Davis) Gillikin was born in 1868 in Washington County, North Carolina to Omeda Washington and Margaret (Clifton) Davis. She married James W. Gillikin in 1889 in Plymouth, and had five children, four of whom lived to maturity. During the many years that her husband was stationed at Cape Lookout, she maintained the family home for the children in Beaufort.
Photo courtesy Ruth Ann Geer-Lloyd

her time between visiting her children, who lived as far away as Greensboro, assisting with the arrival of grandchildren, and returning to keep James company at the lighthouse.

"... *Annie seems to be getting along alright down here & she is a great pleasure to me down here...*"

The entire family is listed in the January 1920 census as living in Morehead Township, Greensboro, Guilford Co. with James listed as a lighthouse keeper, although Greensboro is a long way from the ocean! The three daughters, then ages twenty-two through twenty-eight, were all employed there, two as teachers and one as a clerk at an insurance company. Perhaps James was on inactive duty at this time, or had been assigned some other position within the Lighthouse Service, for we know he returned to Cape Lookout where he wrote his journal in 1924 and 1925.

The keepers took turns on shifts and were often separated from their families. When his wife was away, James noted in his journal:

"*...This is a lonely place to spend Xmas. I miss Annie very much. Wish she could stay here all the time ...*"

His health was deteriorating due to a condition he called "the gravel," which was a painful attack of gallstones:

"*April 6th, 1924... I am getting worse all the time...I reason I will have to go to a hospital & be operated on & I hate it so....*"

James postponed that step more than once, but the pain continued. He then submitted a request to the Superintendent of Lights to be excused from duty on a leave of absence to attend to his health. This permission was granted and plans were made to travel to a hospital in Richmond.

February 9th, 1925 "*...Annie & I have been getting ready for going to Bft. [Beaufort] tomorrow & from there will go to Richmond for treatment ... I have given Annie all my possessions in a will...*"

James Wilson Gillikin never returned to his lighthouse, as he died in Richmond during the surgery. He was sixty seven years-old and had been on duty as a keeper for much of forty years. From his four surviving children, there were five grandchildren, seventeen great-grandchildren, and now the great-great grandchildren generation has grown past twenty in number.

In researching this story, a serendipitous contact with an unrelated person in California added a very personal artifact to this account. Decades ago, this person purchased a small leather-bound family record book at a flea market in North Carolina, giving the account of births, marriages, and deaths of members of a family she did not know. She was moved to try and locate the family, but it took twenty years to do so. She placed a message on the Internet, which this writer spotted, and electronic correspondence revealed that the book related to this Gillikin family. Learning of the Hatteras Keepers Descendants Homecoming, she graciously donated the book to be returned to family members who planned to attend.

James and Annie Gillikin would be so happy to have the records and the family at the lighthouse once again.

This 1930s view from the catwalk at the top of the Cape Hatteras Lighthouse is the scene that keepers of the early twentieth century saw each day. Looking north, the Navy radio station towers and a few other structures are the only manmade buildings on the horizon, a far cry from the twenty-first century view. Notice the sand road that ran between the dune line and the lighthouse grounds. This is the sand road that many of the keepers' children talked about while being interviewed for this publication. Rany Jennette, Keeper Unaka Jennette's son, called this the "High Water" Road.
Photo courtesy N.C. Archives and History

The Jennett(e) Family Group

*Eight Jennett(e) keepers held the rein at both the
1803 and 1870 lighthouses at Cape Hatteras.
Joseph Claude Jennett was the first of this family group to serve in 1843.
The last was Unaka Jennette, twenty-year veteran who left in 1939.*

By Sandra MacLean Clunies

The Jennett family was residing in the Outer Banks of North Carolina in the early 18th century. A John Jennett who lived c. 1670-c.1748 is among the earliest mentioned, but we cannot reconstruct his entire family group from remaining records. The first federal census, taken in 1790, shows two Jennett families in the Cape Hatteras area, headed by a Joseph and a Jesse.

Our family history begins with this Joseph Jennett and wife Christian. By 1798, Joseph had died, as Christian was listed as guardian of her four children: William, Jabez, Mary, and Aquilla in a deed providing the first four acres for the Cape Hatteras Lighthouse. In the 1800 census, "Criston" Jennett was listed as the head of a family, which included herself plus four young people, probably her children. Although the census does not specify relationships, two boys and two girls are listed whose names match the names of the children on the deed.

William and Jabez Benjamin both married wives born into Farrow families. William and Naomi (Farrow) Jennett were parents of **Joseph Claude Jennett** (1805-1866) while Jabez Benjamin and Salinda (Farrow) Jennett's children included sons **Zion B. Jennett** (1814-1888) and **Wallace R. Jennett** (1829-1908). Joseph Claude and his first cousins, the brothers Zion and Wallace, all served as Cape Hatteras Lighthouse keepers at different times over a period of thirty-five years from 1843 to 1878. The present Cape Hatteras Lighthouse was first lighted in 1872, so their service spanned the two lighthouses.

Children in lighthouse families observed and learned all the skills needed to perform the many tasks involved. They assisted their fathers and apprenticed from a young age. So it is not surprising that five children of Joseph Claude and Terah (Williams) Jennett then became lighthouse keepers or married other keepers: **William B.** (1829-1862), **Joseph E.** (c.1842-1881), and **Benjamin C.** (1846-1874) were keepers. Their sister, Rhoda, (1831-1884) married her first cousin, once-removed, **Wallace R. Jennett**, while sister Chrissa Naomi (1833-?) married keeper **William B. O'Neal**.

William B. Jennett married Sabra Fulcher, a daughter of keeper **Benjamin T. Fulcher**. Their grandson was **Unaka Benjamin Jennette**, the last keeper at Cape Hatteras Lighthouse.

Zion's daughter, Parley F. Jennett, first married her second cousin, **Benjamin C.**, and after his early death, she married Keeper **Alpheus W. Simpson**. Her son, **John B. Jennett**, was a keeper, and her daughter, Eulalia Jennett, married Keeper **Amasa Jones Simpson**.

This brief outline of relationships, illustrated on the accompanying chart, confirms the strong ties that the generations of lighthouse keepers held by blood and by marriage. It was a close-knit community. Public records remain to reveal much about these early families living and working at Cape Hatteras more than a century ago.

When the Civil War broke out, the Union troops soon established a strong presence on the Outer Banks. In August 1861, in the first combined military operation of the Civil War, the Confederate troops were forced to abandon the two forts under construction at Hatteras Inlet. The victorious Union troops then completed building Fort Clark and Fort Hatteras. Companies H and I of the 1st North Carolina Infantry were recruited from the Outer Banks to assist in protecting the Union position. The lighthouse lens had been removed by Confederate forces in 1862. But the lighthouse families were ready to volunteer for the Union for two simple reasons: the protection afforded by the Federal government, and the recruitment bonus and pay which provided a regular source of income. Three of Joseph Claude Jennett's sons enlisted as privates in 1863: Benjamin C., Joseph E., and Nasa F. Jennett.

Military records remain to describe them in some detail, and we learn that all three brothers had black hair. That two of them later became lighthouse keepers, with arduous duties requiring much physical strength, it is surprising to learn how slight they were in size. Joseph was the tallest at 5'9", while Benjamin was 5'5" and Nasa stood just 5'4" tall.

A tragic accident happened on the night of January 16/17, 1864, when five soldiers in a small boat capsized and drowned near Hatteras Inlet on their way back to Fort Clark. Apparently, they had made the short trip to visit family members without approval to leave, as later applications for military survivor pensions were denied on the basis that the men were not on official duty orders at the time, and were away from their post without permission. One of these victims was Nasa F. Jennett, who left a wife and small son.

Benjamin C. Jennett appears to have had many leadership qualities, which more than compensated for his short physical stature. Born in February 1846, he was not yet eighteen when he mustered into the Army as a Private. One descriptive record notes that his eyes were "firey" [sic] and he was soon promoted to Corporal and then to Sergeant. He was later appointed as primary keeper at Cape Hatteras in 1866 when just twenty-two years of age, and he died at the young age of twenty-eight in 1874. His brief life was filled with accomplishment, and he left two surviving children who remained part of the lighthouse community. His son, John B. Jennett, later became a keeper and daughter Eulalia married keeper Amasa J. Simpson.

Four generations of Jennett keepers served at Cape Hatteras for a period of time over ninety years from 1843 to 1936.

Keepers' names are in bold the first time they appear in the text. At some point, Keeper Jennett added an "e" to the family surname.

Joseph Claude Jennett (1805-1866) sat for a rare photograph with his wife, Terah (Williams) Jennett (1807-1882) Joseph's daughter, Rhoda, married Wallace R. Jennett, son of Jabez who was the brother of Joseph's father, William Jennett. This closely-knit family's offspring had several children who either became keepers or married keepers. Joseph C. served at Cape Hatteras in 1843 and again in 1849.
Photos courtesy J. Charles Jennette, M.D.

Parley and Benjamin C. Jennett posed as man and wife.
Parley F. Jennett (1845-1926), daughter of 1870 Cape Hatteras Assistant Keeper Zion B. Jennett, married Benjamin C. Jennett (1846-1874). Benjamin C. was primary keeper at Cape Hatteras from 1868 until 1871 and was in charge when the old tower was destroyed and the new tower was activated. Their son, John B. Jennett(e) became an assistant keeper at Hatteras 1899-1903. After Parley was widowed, she married Alpheus Simpson (1844-1905), a member of another family group of Cape Hatteras lightkeepers.

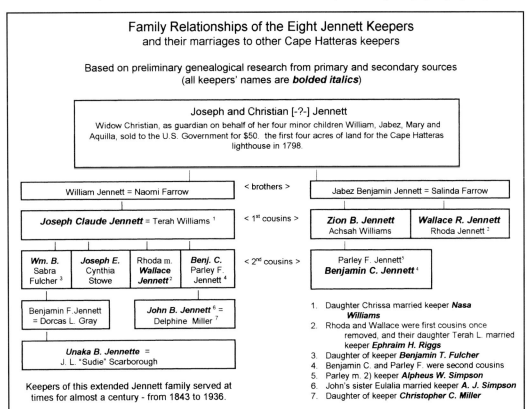

Chart on Jennetts by Sandra MacLean Clunies

John Benjamin Jennette
J. B. Jennette
With Christopher Roy Jennette

John Benjamin Jennett's son, Christopher "Chris" Roy Jennette, prided himself in being a family genealogist and has left great information organized for descendants to learn of their many ties to the Cape Hatteras Lighthouse and the family of Jennett(e) lighthouse keepers.

After a successful career as a retired U.S. Navy Commander, Chris wrote a brief history of his parents and their lives. His father, John B. Jennette, who became a "Sr." in 1901 when his son was born, attended the one-room school with six grades in Buxton. His mother, Delphine, daughter of Cape Hatteras Assistant Keeper Christopher Columbus Miller, attended a school in Elizabeth City. John B. Sr. served as assistant keeper at Cape Hatteras from 1899-1903, and during that time, three children were born: Arthur (1899), John Jr. (1901), and Lorena (1903).

> *"My mother and father were great believers in education and about 1904 gave the land for a new school at Buxton. They also gave land for the Methodist Church."*

Chris wrote, "My father transferred from Cape Hatteras to the Lighthouse Tender *Holly*. This was approximately a 150-foot long sidewheel ship that supplied lighthouses, lightships, repaired and replaced buoys in the sound and river of North Carolina, Virginia, Maryland, and Washington, D.C., including the waters off these states. This was the Fifth Lighthouse District. My father was quartermaster on the *Holly* and he also ran the deck machinery when working buoys and supplying lightships. Around 1908 he was transferred to a lighthouse in the Pamlico Sound. There was also an assistant keeper. They served one week on and one week off. In the summer, my mother, Pearl, Arthur, John, and Lorena would spend time with him at the lighthouse.

"My mother and father were great believers in education and about 1904 gave the land for a new school at Buxton. They also gave land for the Methodist Church.

"In 1911 my father requested and received a transfer to New Bern, as keeper of the New Bern Harbor Lights. There were nine beacons up the Trent River, six up the Neuse River, and six down the Neuse, a total of twenty-one lights. These were kerosene lights that would burn about ten days. Papa would tend the lights once a week and it would take about four hours each way or about twelve hours total. He also had to keep the beacons painted. The lighthouse tender did all the repairs on beacons and took care of all the buoys. Papa remained Keeper of the New Bern Harbor Lights until he retired in 1935 due to a heart attack.

"He loved sports and never missed a ball game on the

A young John B. Jennett (1871-1951), son of Parley F. (Jennett) and Benjamin C. Jennett, is pictured. An aspiring Cape Hatteras Lighthouse keeper, he served at Cape Hatteras 1899-1903. He grew up among many keeper relatives rendering him an experienced apprentice as a youngster. "He was the first to begin adding an 'e' to the Jennett name, and my father, John B. Jennette, Jr. continued this spelling of the name," commented Jo Ellen (Jennette) Luscombe, the pictured man's granddaughter.

Photos for the John B. Jennett chapter have been preserved by Christopher Roy Jennett and furnished for this book by Jo Ellen (Jennette) Luscombe and J. Charles Jennette, and Aaron Fulcher

radio. He had his last, fatal heart attack while listening to a close basketball game between NC State and UNC Chapel Hill in 1951. My mother was a housewife dedicated to the home and the raising of their children.

"All the children, except Christopher, were born in Buxton and brought into this world by the midwife, Mrs. Rovena Quidley. Children, grandchildren, and most of the neighbors called my parents Papa John and Mama Delphine. These names were given to them by their first grandchild Carol Bartling."

John Benjamin Jennette's granddaughter, Jo Ellen (Jennette) Luscombe, also is a keeper of the Jennette family lineage and has preserved the history collected by her Uncle "Kit."

Delphine Miller, daughter of Cape Hatteras Keeper Christopher C. Miller, married a keeper's son, John B. Jennett in 1896. On a government form describing his duties in 1928, John B. Jennett listed his experience: "1891-1897 seaman on Light House Steamer Violet, 1897-1903 Asst. Light House Keeper Hatteras Inlet & Cape Hatteras, 1903-1911 Keeper Hatteras Inlet. Since 1911 in charge of New Bern Harbor Lights." John B. retired in 1935.

TIMELINE
JOHN BENJAMIN JENNETTE (1871-1951)
ASSISTANT KEEPER 1899-1903

The great-grandson of John B. Jennett, J. Charles Jennette, M.D., has identified this photograph as the Jennett's home in Buxton taken circa 1904. The man in the front yard is John Benjamin Jennett. On the porch is his wife, Delphine (Miller) who is holding Lorena Jennett. The children in the yard are left to right: Arthur S. Jennett, Pearl F. Jennett, and John B. Jennett, Jr.

John B. Jennette talks about his duties at the New Bern Harbor Lights

Some details of John B. Jennette's duty are gleaned from a form he completed in 1928. He wrote on the Personnel Board Form No 14- Field Questionnaire that he was in charge of the "Newbern Harbor Lights." He gave his education as seventh grade and his experience as "1891-1897 seaman on Light House Steamer *Violet*. 1897-1903 Asst. Light House Keeper Hattress Inlet & Cape Hateress 1903-1911 Keeper Hatteras Inlet. Since 1911 In Charge of New Bern Harbor Lights."

The New Bern Harbor Lights stretched for twenty miles to guide ships into the harbor safely. Jennett was "required to be available for duty at all times to relight any lamp that had been reported extinguished by storm or collision." He was required to furnish and operate his own motor launch for attendance on the lights; he valued this requirement at $300.00 per annum." Though his hours of duty were "not regular," he estimated that he worked 44 hours per week, year-round.

John B. Jennett described his duties thus: 60% of his workweek, "I have in my charge 21 Beacons. These are arranged that I take three different days in making a complete trip. On each visit each lantern is cleaned, burners and chimneys changed and the lanterns refilled with new oil. Once a month the lamps are changed. 10%: The Government Reservation here consists of a small lot on which is an oil tank and a fireproof oil house. This requires care and attention. The grass has to be cut and the general appearance kept neat. 30%: Occasional Duties consist of
1. Painting Beacons when needed.
2. Trips made to lights after stormy weather.
3. Assistance rendered to officers of Government Boat when here, also helping working party.

I hereby certify that the foregoing was composed by me after reading P.C.B. Form No. 15 and that it is a true statement of my duties,

J. B. Jennette

September 21, 1928, Superintendent of Lighthouses, Harold D. King, inspected Keeper Jennett's report, verifying that he'd been on this duty since 1911 at the yearly pay of $1,740. He commented, "Beacon lights above mentioned are oil burning lanterns on pile structures on marine sites distributed along about 20 miles of river." King and the Lighthouse Service realized the importance of these harbor lights and established the possibility of a small raise, increasing the pay range from $1,500- 1,800. Jennett had faithfully kept these lights in good order for seventeen years.

Special thanks to Jo Ellen Luscombe for sharing photos from her private collection on her grandfather. John B. Jennette Sr.'s parents were Cape Hatteras Keeper Benjamin Claude Jennette and Parley (Jennett). See Sandra Clunies' family chart and article on the eight Jennette keepers.

John Benjamin Jennette, Jr. was born in 1901 at the double keepers quarters to his proud parents, John B. Jennett and Delphine (Miller) Jennett. John Jr. became the descendant of six lighthouse keepers including Joseph C. Jennett, Zion B. Jennett, and Benjamin T. Fulcher. John Jr.'s grandmother was Emmie Fulcher, who was married to Keeper Christopher C. Miller. Finally, John Jr.'s father, John B. Jennett Sr. was also a Cape Hatteras keeper. This healthy youngster went on to play football and basketball on varsity teams for N.C. State University 1922-1925. During his long career as a civil engineer with the N. C. State Highway Commissioner, he supervised building of bridges over the Neuse and Trent Rivers in New Bern, a highway between New Bern and Morehead City, and roads around Beaufort, from Morehead City along the coast to Emerald Isle, and roads around Washington, N. C.

John B. Jennett (left) became a keeper at Cape Hatteras. John's brother-in-law, Horatio Seymore Miller, was a son of Cape Hatteras Keeper Christopher C. Miller and the brother of John's wife, Delphine Louise (Miller). Seymore and his younger brother, Baxter, won Lifesaving Medals. John and Seymore represent the interrelationship of the U.S. Lighthouse and U.S. Lifesaving Service families on Hatteras Island.

He Held the Helm the Longest
Unaka Benjamin Jennette

Keeper Jennette came to the Cape Hatteras Light Station as primary keeper with fifteen years of experience in the U.S. Lighthouse Service. As a Buxton native and respected community member, he supervised an impressive team of assistant keepers over a span of twenty years.

By Lynn Jennette with Rany Jennette and Family

Unaka Benjamin Jennette was the last keeper for two lights at Cape Hatteras. As principal (primary) keeper at the Cape Hatteras Light Station, he served from 1919-1936. When the striped tower was darkened due to the threat of erosion, he then tended the skeleton tower in Buxton Woods 1936-39. His twenty-year tenure as principal keeper was the longest of all keepers on record at Cape Hatteras.

Descended from a long line of Jennett(e) keepers this family's name has always been associated with lighthouse keeping at Cape Hatteras from the beginning. For it was a sixth generation ancestor, Christian Jennett, widow of Joseph, who sold the first four acres of land used for the first lighthouse at Cape Hatteras to the U.S. Government in 1798. She sold the land on behalf of her four minor children for a sum of fifty dollars. The ninety-five-foot-tall sandstone tower was built in 1802 and first lighted in 1803. Additionally, Unaka himself signed a warranty deed in 1936, which ceded to the U.S. government the land for the replacement skeleton tower constructed when the 1872 tower was discontinued. Thus, records of the Jennett family and the Cape Hatteras Lighthouse lands extend for 138 years.

Thirty-seven-year-old Unaka arrived at the light station as a native of Buxton with fifteen years of prior training in the U.S. Lighthouse Service. Since a keeper's duties were second nature to him, he confidently took the reins at the Cape Hatteras Light Station.

Unaka was born in the village of Buxton, November 30, 1882. He was the son of Benjamin Fulcher Jennett and Dorcas (Gray) Jennett. His grandfather, William B. Jennett, and his great-grandfathers, Benjamin T. Fulcher and Joseph Claude Jennett, were the early Hatteras keeper ancestors from which Unaka and his two brothers, Utah C. and Alaska O., lighthouse keepers in Virginia and Maryland, were directly descended. As keeper's kids tended to marry into other keeper families, these three Jennette brothers had a sister Sabrah who married keeper William E. Quidley, whose daughter Oretha married keeper John E. Midgette.

Unaka joined the Lighthouse Service in 1904 as a deckhand on a buoy tender. In 1909 he was promoted to Quarter Master and transferred to Diamond Shoals Lightship. In 1911 he was promoted to Master and served as Captain on the thirty-five-foot Channel Lightship and the Lighthouse Tender *Maple*. In 1913, he became Master of the Diamond Shoals *Relief* Lightship. In 1918, he was Captain of the Tender *Jasmine* and in 1919 he was given the prized assignment as principal keeper at Cape Hatteras.

He married Jennie Louana Scarborough "Miss Sudie" in 1911. She was born in Kinnakeet (Avon) on 7 April 1890, the daughter of Richard and Rebecca Midgett Scarborough. Unaka and Miss Sudie had seven children: Almy (1913-1985), Vivian (1916-1999), Myrtle (1919), Rany (1921), Olive (1923-1996), Dorcas (1927), and Ramona (1929). All but Almy and Vivian were born in the principal keeper's quarters at Cape Hatteras.

Unaka was called "Captain Naka," "Capt. Akey," or "Cap'n." A member of a well-known family to all the community, he was respected by everyone. When asked to describe their father, Vivian, Myrtle, Rany, Dorcas, and Ramona began their comments on the Jennette family with a unanimous, "He was the best Daddy anybody could have."

> *"All of the families had very close ties and on Sundays, relatives from the village would come for picnics and games. We had a croquet set in [the lighthouse yard] and this was a favorite with young and old alike. Competition was very keen, often resulting in arguments and temporary disputes!"*

Miss Sudie, as she was affectionately called, was a wonderful Christian woman. She was very active in the Buxton Methodist Church. About her mother, Myrtle stated, "Mama was a very sweet person. She was very reserved and only saw good in people." Miss Sudie read her Bible every day and often played favorite hymns on the piano. Mornings in the Jennette household started with everyone at the breakfast table with Mama reading a passage from scripture and Daddy praying."

Rany related a delightful memory about his mother's "Lady's Aid" prayer meeting, regularly held at the keepers quarters. Because his mother often served lemonade, he thought that the group's name was the "Lady's Lemonade Society."

Another favorite childhood topic for Rany, the third oldest

TIMELINE

UNAKA BENJAMIN JENNETTE (1882-1965)
PRIMARY KEEPER 1919-1939:

Keeper Jennette witnessed many changes to the Cape Hatteras Light Station while tending the flame. In 1919, the U.S. Lighthouse Service was still a respected civilian-staffed government organization, which was praised for its efficiency. During the late 1920s, the Lighthouse Service developed radio navigation, the technology that began the decline in the need for lighthouses. He witnessed the damage of two hurricanes in 1933, which ended family life at the light station. After electrification in 1934, he turned off the light in 1936 when it was re-established in a nearby steel tower. Jennette saw the war clouds gathering in Europe as Hitler came into power; thus, President Roosevelt merged the Lighthouse Service with the U.S. Coast Guard to help prepare the country for future conflict. Today, Keeper Jennette would be pleased to see his light station coming back to life with interpretive exhibits. One exhibit is the original foundation granite stones, which have been engraved with the names of Cape Hatteras keepers' names.

child, was a visual description of the light station while he lived there during the 1920s and 30s. The beach, he remembered, was usually flat with no dune system, and seldom disturbed since blowing sand could quickly cover an occasional car track or hoof print. Shells were in abundance almost everywhere.

The lighthouse complex was notably different in the early 1900's with several outbuildings and penned areas for animals. Each of three keepers, the principal and two assistants, had a storehouse for feed, paint, and other supplies. There were outdoor privies that were described as "three-holers - large, medium and small just like the three bears." There were also coal bins, which were divided into three compartments and three cisterns, one for each family. Rainwater was collected in the cisterns from runoff into roof eaves, which was then piped into the clean storage tanks as a source of fresh water for the families' consumption. The lawns were green with grass and clover and kept neatly trimmed at all times. There was a large, deep pond surrounded by sedge made up of flags with their long sword-shaped leaves, cattails, and lily pads. The pond and sedge areas were alive with wild life including ducks, turtles, fish, and cottonmouth moccasins. A wire fence supported by reinforced concrete posts surrounded the dwellings. A fence divided the principal and double keepers houses, and a large concrete walk ran from each house to the lighthouse. Just beyond the pond, there were garages, pens for hogs and chickens, and a vegetable garden. A car "track," dotted with small hills, yaupon, and scrub oaks led to Buxton Village and beyond. The area where the Comfort Inn is located today was once called the "Head of the Sedge."

Rany and Myrtle remembered life at the Cape Hatteras Light Station as pleasant. Rany said, "The lighthouse and Coast Guard families were large and visits were frequent between neighbors. All of the families had very close ties and on Sundays, relatives from the village would come for picnics and games. We had a croquet set in our yard and this was a favorite with young and old alike. Competition was very keen, often resulting in arguments and temporary disputes! Other games played were 'Bull in the Pen,' 'Hoop 'n and Hide,' 'Pitching Quoits' (half bricks), and baseball on the beach."

Unaka Jennette was the last primary keeper at the Cape Hatteras Lighthouse. When he stepped into his uniform, he was a Lighthouse Service veteran with fifteen years experience aboard buoy tenders, the Diamond Shoals Lightship, and the tender Maple. *Due to good leadership skills, he kept the position as primary, or principal, keeper for twenty years, the longest on record at this light station. He was the direct descendant of six other Jennett keepers.*
Photo courtesy Rany and Lynn Jennette

Myrtle added, "We would play all over the beach. As kids we were anxious to shed our shoes and go bare foot, but under no circumstance were we allowed to do this until the first day of May, and we could never go to the beach for a swim on a full stomach. There were plenty of pets to play with as well."

Dorcas recalled, "All of the lighthouse families were large and we never wanted for children to play with, and I remember Uncle Bill, Assistant Keeper William E. Quidley, who would dress up on Halloween and scare everyone. We called him 'Old Man Bill Spriggins.'"

Myrtle noted her best friend was Myrtle Casey, Assistant Keeper James O. Casey's daughter. "They called her 'big Myrtle' and me 'little Myrtle.' Olive's best friend was Melita Midgett, Assistant Keeper John E. Midgett's daughter, who was a cousin, and Rany's best friend was Murray Casey."

Rany stated, "Dr. Folb, a young Pharmacist's Mate at the Naval radio station, along with 'Miss Rovena,' a midwife, took care of most of our severe illnesses and performed many miraculous wonders with their limited skills and 'modern' medicines. 'Doc' Folb will always be remembered by folks along the Outer Banks- we always considered him as one of us as long as he lived. He died at age ninety-four."

Dorcas and Ramona were quite young while the Jennettes lived at the lighthouse, but Myrtle recalled vividly the night Ramona was born. "Mother asked Mrs. Edna (Casey) Gray to take us to the movies- I think she knew that the baby was coming. Mr. Gaskill showed movies weekly at the schoolhouse and that night's feature was 'Ramona.' And sure enough, while we were gone, the baby was born. Mama had planned to name the baby Ruby, but Ms. Edna asked if she could name her, and that's how she became Ramona."

"One time," Dorcas added, "Daddy took us to the movies to see '42nd Street' and when we came home, Mama said 'Unaka, forever more, if I had known you were going to take the children to that movie, I would never have allowed it.'" Miss Sudie evidently did not approve of the modern music and dance of this movie set in New York.

Rany, Myrtle, Dorcas "Dot," and Ramona have described Christmas at the lighthouse. They all recalled that it was a happy time and was celebrated about the same as in most homes. They had a fresh Christmas tree, planned presents for giving, and prepared a big dinner. Stockings were hung from the mantel over the fireplace and filled with nuts, fruit, candy, and one small gift.

"Oh those were such happy times," Myrtle commented.

Dot added further detail. "Everyone in the village went to the Methodist Church in Buxton on Christmas Eve. A huge tree was placed in the church and every parent would hang two presents on the tree for each of his or her children, usually toys or doll babies. Sometimes the tree would be so loaded with presents that they would have to be placed underneath. The Sunday School provided a Christmas bag of candy, with an apple and an orange for each person in the village. After the Christmas program of choir and congregational singing and children's speeches, the Sunday School Superintendent, who was dressed like Santa Claus, got up in front of everyone."

Rany Jennette (right) played outside with his sister, Olive. "We painted everything," Rany laughed, "even the rocks we brought back from the beach when they washed up." Children and adults alike loved a good storm. Afterwards, the children stayed together for safety on the beach, but thrilled to the expanses of beach in their front yard, a large holding area for gifts from the sea including timbers, buttons, coins, driftwood, and intricately patterned seashells. Circa 1926
Photo courtesy Rany Jennette

"And then came the exciting part for the kids," Ramona continued. "He would call each of the children up to get their gifts. Laughter would roar through the crowd when he started calling the names of families who had fourteen persons! No one was ever missed and if someone was unable to attend, their church gifts were delivered."

Myrtle, Dorcas, and Ramona chatted about Rany and what a big tease he was and how he nicknamed everyone, some not so complimentary. The girls finally found a good one for him in "Chester Gump." How Rany hated it! Myrtle, Rany's dear sister who others mistook for his twin said, "Chester was a character in the comic strip, 'The Gump Family.' One Christmas Eve when Santa was calling the children's names, he called out for 'Chester Gump.' Rany was so embarrassed, but he knew that if he didn't answer he wouldn't get his Christmas presents!"

Rany remembered when the addition was built on the principal keepers quarters about 1927. The Lighthouse Service sent a work party from Lazzereto Depot in Baltimore on a buoy tender. Behind the tender, they towed a house barge and anchored it in Cape Channel, which became the crew's living quarters. "W. F. Lynch, the foreman lived with us. He and my father had been friends for a long time. He would tell us all about snipe hunting at night, and we just had to go. So one night he said he would take a friend and me. We were about ten-years-old. We took two bags and a flashlight and walked the surf to the old Tower Hill, where the ruins of the 1803 lighthouse were. He said, 'Boys, you lie down one on each side of the bag and hold it open. Place the light beside the bag and let it shine down the beach. I will walk down the beach and scare up some snipe; they will see the light and run toward it. When they get close to the bag, close it real fast.' We waited for hours until we got tired and disgusted and walked back home. The old folks got a big kick out of the joke, but we were too wise to ever go again."

The lighthouse would occasionally need a complete paint job. This was usually supervised by the lighthouse working party with some local help that the keeper could hire. On one occasion, Rany remembered there were three or four local boys in their late teens or early twenties who were working in the paint box, which was hanging from the deck rail on the side of the lighthouse. "My father was using his car to raise and lower the platform by attaching the lead rope in the pulley system to the rear bumper of his car. He noticed the boys were acting in a strange manner and doing pretty sloppy work. He suspected meal tea or white lightening might be the cause, so he took matters into his own hands. He got into his car, released the brake, started the motor, put the car in reverse, and backed up a few feet. The sudden drop had quite a sobering effect on his young workers, and the job was properly done from then on!"

A good friend, Raymond Basnett recalled a time after Unaka Jennette had retired. "The Coast Guard had awarded a contract to paint the lighthouse to a local man, William Finnegan, in 1946. He hired me and Cap'n 'Naka to help him." When asked how they did it, Raymond chuckled and said, "Well we had a box which was about five feet wide and ten or twelve feet long, and we hung that with a block and tackle to the top of the light at the lantern room level. It had lines running down from there to the ground where we had a truck. The right rear wheel of the truck was jacked up, the tire removed, and a hub put on it. That's what we used for a pulley. The rope ran around that and that's how we would pull the box up and down. Cap'n Nakey was the line man on the hub and the rope would run around the hub and he would pull on it and that would raise the tackle to raise the box up or let it down- whichever way we wanted to go. We'd use the guidelines on the sides to pull ourselves around the lighthouse. If we wanted to go to the right, we'd pull to the right. You'd be surprised how far that thing would go. Finnegan and I were in the box doing the painting, and Unaka would let us down and we would go around again. Someway, somehow, we finally painted it and did a good job! It took about two weeks. As I recall, we painted the white first and then the black."

Continuing, Raymond can laugh today about this dangerous job. "We were painting one day, and I would say we were about half way down, and we had to move up or down, I forget which way we were going now. Cap'n Unaka was down on the ground and he missed the turn on the hub and lost it- he lost control of it, and here we started to fall, and we were hollerin' at him! And he was hollerin' at us! And he was hanging on the line and burned his hands all up and he finally had to turn her loose as he was going up in the air as we were coming down. I suppose he got off the ground maybe six or seven feet, something like that, and he decided to turn loose. When he turned loose, he fell, and so did we, box and all. We came on down the side of the lighthouse and hit the stone ring, you know that thing that goes around the bottom of the lighthouse and bounced around for a while. The box turned on its side and threw us out on the ground. We finally regained our senses and knew we were all right, but that Unaka had burned his hands right bad. That was quite an experience and nobody was hurt seriously. After it was all over we laughed, but coming down there I didn't laugh! I think we called it a day after that, then come back the next day and fixed the locks and fixed the rope and everything and got started again."

In later years when Rany was a National Park Service ranger at the lighthouse he loved for visitors to ask him a favorite question, "How did they paint the lighthouse?" Rany replied with a straight face, "Oh it was real easy, first they would paint the whole tower white. Next, after it dried, they would paint one vertical black stripe down the middle. Then my father would go to the top, take a large wrench and give it a three-quarter twist." Rany got a big charge out of that story and continued to tell it often. The best part was that many of the people would actually believe him!

Rany resumed his childhood memories. "'Grubbing up' once a month at one of the general stores in the village was a big event for the young folks. Our main supplies came by buoy tender, but other items would be purchased from one of the local merchants.

"We went to school in Buxton for grades one through eleven, the highest grade offered at the local school. Sometimes we would walk to school, but usually a keeper or someone from the Coast Guard would take us. My Uncle Charlie Gray was the school principal for a long time. At recess, morning and afternoon, we played ball, marbles, and basketball, just a hoop nailed to a pine tree. We also had skis made from barrel staves that we used to slide down a steep pine straw covered hill. The girls skipped rope a lot and made pine straw houses. I still remember when the school burned down in 1928. We had to go to various places nearby for classes until the school was rebuilt.

"A trip to the mainland was a rare occasion and a big event in our lives. There were three routes we could take to go up the beach to Oregon Inlet to get the car ferry: 'Dead

Cap'n Unaka's car carried lots of things including five youngsters. Left to right front: Ramona, Myrtle, Cousin Earl Midgett, Dorcas. At the wheel is Rany Jennette. Always willing to help a neighbor, Keeper Jennette took sick islanders to see a doctor. One time a friend had made a large catch and in order to get the fish to market quickly, Unaka offered the use of his new car. "Miss Sudie was NOT pleased, " Rany commented, "the car smelled forever."
Photo courtesy Dorcas (Jennette) Anderson

Miss Sudie and Unaka Jennette, a much-loved couple on Hatteras Island, were both natives and lived and worked near their family home all their lives. They devoted twenty years to the Cape Hatteras Lighthouse 1919-1939. All children were welcomed in their home, the principal keepers house, and Miss Sudie taught new brides of assistant keepers how to cook.
Photo courtesy Rany and Lynn Jennette

Family gatherings were a frequent activity for the Jennette family. In front of the principal keepers quarters at Cape Hatteras, front row, left to right are: Ollve, Myrtle, and Rany. "We were so close that most people thought we were twins," Myrtle said. In the back row are: Cousin Goldie Midgett, Aunt Minnie Jennett [Miss Sudie's sister], Vivian, Rebecca Midgette (Scarborough) [Miss Sudie's and Minnie's mother], Dorcas, Keeper Jennette, Ramona, and Miss Sudie.
Circa 1930
Photo courtesy Dorcas (Jennette) Anderson

Low Water' was when we took the path closest to the surf and could make it almost as quickly as now; 'High Water' was when we took the inside road, or 'car track' winding east and west and full of ruts and sometimes full of water. This was a very slow way to go, taking three or four hours. The other alternative was the 'Bank of the Beach' when we made our own tracks. We would drop the tire pressure to around ten to twelve pounds for better traction. Getting a head start and just keeping on going was the key. Getting stuck was a regular occurrence and usually a rough trip."

The memories continued to be recalled by Rany. "Mail time each day was quite an event. People didn't wait for the mail to arrive at the Buxton Post Office, but went to the mail landing, which was located where the Pilot House Restaurant stands today, and would wait for the mail boat to arrive from Manteo, usually around 4:00 p.m each day. A local man had the responsibility of getting the mail to the post office. He would carry those large bags on his back and start walking up the road. Sometimes all you could see was sacks of mail piled on two legs. Occasionally a passenger would arrive on the mail boat who was either a local person returning home or a visitor new to the island. It was easy to tell a visitor. They talked 'different' and were very careful not to get sand in their shoes. A native would pull off his shoes, roll up his pants, and wade ashore before the skiff landed."

Rany shared a favorite tale, which has been told over and over on the island about an incident in which a man, hired to carry the mailbags from the mail boat to the post office, was loaded down with all he could carry. "When one of the bags fell to the ground, about half the way to the post office, he heard a tiny voice say 'ma-ma.' He was so scared that he picked up the bag and ran all the way to the post office. When he arrived, the postmaster wanted to know why he was in such a hurry. He said, 'Unlock this bag quick, there is a baby inside!' It was just before Christmas and someone had ordered one of those new talking doll babies from the Sears and Roebuck catalogue."

Recalling the time spent with his father, Rany said, "Many times I climbed the lighthouse with my father and helped with the routine maintenance, I shined lots of brass. My fondest memory at the top of the lighthouse was going out on deck, looking through the huge spyglasses, or binoculars, and observing ships passing - so close you could see crew members on the ships."

The good times and further memories of life for the Jennettes at the Cape Hatteras Lighthouse came to an abrupt end during August 1933. Rany sadly recalled, "My family left this home, never to return again. My father moved us into Buxton to my grandfather's house after a severe hurricane hit the island. You will understand this when you see the report written by my father on August 25, 1933."

Two days after a huge hurricane hit Hatteras Island, indeed the entire East Coast, and caused extreme damage, Keeper Jennette urgently requested the help of the U.S. Lighthouse Service for the second time.

Dorcas, Keeper Jennette's daughter, and Roger Reid Farrow play in front of the double keepers quarters. Roger is the son of Keeper Bill Quidley's daughter, Esther Quidley and her husband, Connie Farrow. The sidewalks that weaved in and out of the keepers quarters gave the children lots of roller skating room. Norma Gray Rhoden, Bill Quidley's granddaughter and frequent visitor/playmate of these children chuckled, "I had more skinned knees than anybody in the world. It was the best place for a child to grow up."
Photo courtesy Dorcas (Jennette) Anderson

"Report to Superintendent of Light Houses, Baltimore, Maryland

Subject: Report of damage done by storm of August 22.

Sir:

I beg leave to submit herewith detailed report of the damage done by the recent storm of the 22nd inst. I wired you hastily on the morning of the 23rd, but have heard nothing from the office since that time. This was by far the highest sea tide recorded since I have been at Cape Hatteras. Two store houses and garages were washed down. Three toilets washed down. Floor bursted up in one room of 2nd asst. quarters. Screening on keepers dwelling destroyed. Furniture in keepers dwelling badly damaged. Sand banked around oil house up to oil tank. Tide came through windows recently cut in oil house and flooded the house with water and sand. Sea water at present is standing even with porch floor. All cisterns filled with sea water, a crew having to bring water from neighborhood. Beach changed and wasted badly, bank of beach extending on a level from keepers fence. Plaster in 1st. asst. parlor fallen in. I advise that some one from the office be sent down to look over the situation and make a general survey of the damages and changes made by the storm. The entire reservation is completely submerged, and I have been forced to move my family away from the station. Respectfully, *Unaka B. Jennette*

Keeper Jennette received the following reply:

"Response from Office, Superintendent of Lighthouses, Baltimore, Maryland, August 28, 1933.

1. Copy to Commissioner of Lighthouses, Washington, D.C., with information that party with equipment will arrive at this station on the 29th to electrify tower. Condition of station will be inspected and report submitted as soon as practicable. Signed Superintendent of Lighthouses, Luther Hopkins [sic]"

Source: Personal letter from Supt. Light Houses Dept. of Commerce Lighthouse Service Fifth District Cape Hatteras

Recalling this trying time, Rany stated, "A second, more severe storm hit Hatteras Island three week later and brought even larger seas ashore. The area was still flooded from the first storm and was unable to handle any more. The torrents of waters, which flooded into the house, uprighted the large oak dining table my father had nailed to the front door. The entire first floor of the house was flooded. Anything that had not been damaged by the first hurricane was now completely destroyed since there was virtually no recovery time between the two. Since the houses were deemed uninhabitable, even after electrification of the houses in 1934, the keepers and their families never returned to this complex."

In 1939, the U.S. Lighthouse Service was merged with the U.S. Coast Guard. All personnel of the old Lighthouse Service were given a choice to join the Coast Guard or to remain a civilian employee until they retired. Neither choice was to the benefit of the older keepers with many years of

A few of Cap'n Naka's and Miss Sudie's family gathered at a reunion in front of the principal keeper's house on November 30, 1962, to celebrate Unaka's eightieth birthday. This was the first time that all of the family had returned to the keepers quarters since they had abandoned their home after the damaging hurricanes in 1933. Miss Sudie had wanted to return, but never had the opportunity before her death in 1960.

Pictured are front row, left to right: Jimmy Anderson, Rebecca (Gibbs) Abrams, Valerie (Jennette)Wolverton, Patricia (Provo) Lee, Timothy E. Jennette, Teresa (Jennette) Ponton, Lori (Jennette) Jonkers.

Second row, left to right: Betty (Brite) Jennette, Myrtle (Jennette) Gibbs, Dorcas (Jennette) Anderson, Keeper Unaka B. Jennette, Ramona (Jennette) Provo, Olive (Jennette) Peek, Josephine (Miller) Jennette

Third row, left to right: Maleta (Williams) Jennette, Almy B. Jennette, B. Errol Jennette, Vivian (Jennette) Frontis, Tia (Provo) Cheek, Jacque Anderson, Eyvonne (Frontis) Oden, Rany B. Jennette

Fourth row, back center, left to right: James Anderson, Wesley Provo.
Photo courtesy Rany and Lynn Jennette

experience. Joining the Coast Guard meant loss of seniority in rank and lower pay; however, the only alternative was for a keeper to remain with the old Lighthouse Service and be subject to a transfer to a more remote and less important lighthouse. In North Carolina, many keepers were transferred to the sound lights; although these lights were once important to vessels carrying passengers and cargo to ports of business, they were beyond their heyday in 1939. Like approximately half of the veteran keepers, Unaka chose to remain with the old Lighthouse Service and he was transferred to Roanoke Marshes screwpile lighthouse near Wanchese. He remained there until he retired in 1943. Unaka's children Rany and Myrtle remembered their father as a very proud man and that he refused to put on a sailor suit.

Rany concluded, "My father enjoyed twenty-two years of retirement before he passed away in 1965 at the age of eighty-three. He was never in ill health. He was highly respected by everyone on Hatteras Island. He was a kind-hearted and mild-mannered man and always gave a hand wherever needed. He was a good husband, father and neighbor. One of his old shipmates, in his eighties, came up to me after my father's funeral and said, 'That was the finest man and shipmate I ever knew.' What more can be said?"

The Jennette family dog, Nero, stands watch over the flooded compound. Behind him is the unoccupied principal keepers quarters, severely flooded during two back-to-back hurricanes in August 1933. Keeper Jennette moved his family to the home of his father, Benjamin Fulcher Jennett, in Buxton and filed this report with the USLHS: "This was by far the highest sea tide recorded since I have been at Cape Hatteras. Two store houses and garages were washed down. Three toilets washed down. Floor bursted up in one room of 2nd asst. quarters. Screening on keepers dwelling destroyed. Furniture in keepers dwelling badly damaged... Sea water at present is standing even with porch floor."

(Left) Rany Jennette, son of Keeper Unaka Jennette returned to Cape Hatteras and his home in Buxton to resume the presence of his family at the lighthouse. Rany then became a National Park Service ranger for fourteen years, sharing stories with visitors about growing up at the Cape Hatteras Lighthouse. Rany stated, "During my work history, I've worn with pride six different uniforms for the United States government. However, none have I worn so proudly as the green and grey of the National Park Service."
Photos courtesy Rany and Lynn Jennette

(Opposite page) Fortunately a photographer, Clifton Adams for National Geographic, *climbed the 268 steps in 1933, just months before two hurricanes would do great damage to the light station, to capture what has become a nationally famous image of a keeper at work. Unaka B. Jennette carefully polished the first-order Fresnel lens with soft chamois cloth and jewelers rouge. The incandescent oil vapor lamp, which sat in the center of the Fresnel lens, and the lens itself were two of the most important pieces of equipment at a light station, for they produced the intense beam for mariners - the reason for all else at a light station. Erosion threatened the brick lighthouse; therefore, a skeleton tower was built nearby in Buxton Woods from which to exhibit the light emitted from a modern optic. An era ended with Unaka Jennette when he darkened the Cape Hatteras Lighthouse for the final time May 12, 1936. He descended the steps alone that morning and walked past the deserted keepers quarters to go home. In 1939, he remained a civilian with the U.S. Lighthouse Service when the service merged with the U.S. Coast Guard. Keeper Jennette transferred to the Roanoke Marshes screwpile lighthouse and retired in 1943.*

The majority of this story was taken from excerpts from a manuscript, *Cape Hatteras Lighthouse, As I Knew It*, written by Rany B. Jennette, a proud son, and transcribed by his wife Lynn Jennette. Unable to join the United States Lighthouse Service, Rany kept alive the Jennett(e) lighthouse legacy by telling his stories "Life at the Lighthouse" as a National Park Service ranger for fourteen years. Unaka and Miss Sudie would have been proud of his contribution.

Also contributing were Rany's sisters, Myrtle (Jennette) Gibbs, Dorcas (Jennette) Anderson, Ramona (Jennette) Provo, and Mr. Raymond Basnett.

For more reading on Keeper Jennette and his family, see *Lighthouse Families* by Cheryl Shelton-Roberts and Bruce Roberts. Crane Hill Publishers, 1997.

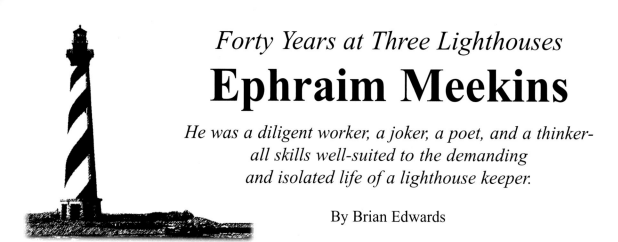

Forty Years at Three Lighthouses
Ephraim Meekins

He was a diligent worker, a joker, a poet, and a thinker- all skills well-suited to the demanding and isolated life of a lighthouse keeper.

By Brian Edwards

By the time Ephraim Meekins reported for duty at the Cape Hatteras Lighthouse in 1900, he was already a tested veteran of the Lighthouse Service. This Roanoke Island native served with distinction for the next six years. But this was only one part of an impressive career that spanned forty years, all but three of which as principal keeper. Even more remarkable, he served at just three stations during this period. In many ways, Meekins was the proverbial man of many talents. He was a diligent worker, a joker, a poet, and a thinker-all skills well suited to the demanding and isolated life of a lighthouse keeper.

Ephraim was born on Roanoke Island to Daniel W. and Sarah "Sally" Etheridge Meekins in December 1861. Although Meekins served at various lights throughout Dare County, the island remained his home for the rest of his life. Little is known of his early life, but some information can be culled from the census records. His parents owned a farm midway between present-day Manteo and the north end of Roanoke Island where they lived with their four sons, William L., Ephraim, Isaac Chauncey, Johnson Marchant, and daughter, Delaria. Nearby lived the Etheridges, including Richard Etheridge of Pea Island Life-Saving Station fame. Presumably, Ephraim helped with chores around the farm and attended school. By 1880, when he was nineteen, his formal education had ended and he had begun working with his father farming and fishing. According to one of his early exploits preserved in an 1897 article in Elizabeth City's *Daily Economist*, "the bluefish were so thick on the coast of Dare [in 1876] that he rowed his boat into a school of them while they were pegging away at the fat backs [menhaden] that were trying to escape them, . . . took out his rudder, laid it on their backs in mid ocean, stood up on it and gave three cheers for Sam. J. Tilden." Since Tilden was the Democratic candidate in the 1876 presidential election, it seems that Meekins was as yellow dog as they came, especially since he was not old enough to vote. The story also illustrates the well-defined sense of humor he was known for throughout his life. In December 1885 he married Margaret "Mag" Dough, also an island native, and settled into wedded life. Their first child, Arretta "Rett" Cecella was born in September 1887.

Capt. Eph, pronounced by friends as "Cap'n Eef," as he came to be known, entered the Lighthouse Service in June of the same year as the assistant keeper of Croatan Light. Located off Caroon's Point in northern Dare County, this screwpile lighthouse marked the confluence of the Albemarle and Croatan Sounds. He remained there for the next thirteen years, becoming keeper in March 1890. Meekins became principal keeper of Cape Hatteras Lighthouse on 1 June 1900 and remained in charge until 30 September 1906. His tenure seems to have been fairly typical. The light had survived the infamous San Ciriaco hurricane a year before his arrival, and not until 1904 did a similar storm affect the coast. His primary duty, like the keepers before and after him, was to keep the light burning. As principal keeper, he would most likely have had some administrative duties as well. A number of assistant keepers served with Meekins, including his brother, Isaac. The first and second assistant helped with tending the main light; the third assistant was in charge of the Cape Point Beacon. In January 1906, this last position was eliminated, suggesting that the beacon, mainly used by coasting vessels, had been decommissioned. It was also during this period that Capt. Albert F. Eells attempted unsuccessfully to construct a light tower on Diamond Shoals. Unfortunately, Meekins' thoughts about this endeavor are not preserved.

> *"Capt. Eph, pronounced by friends as 'Cap'n Eef,' as he came to be known, entered the Lighthouse Service in June [1887] as the assistant keeper of Croatan Light."*

With Eph gone much of the time, home life revolved around Mag. Separation, though, did not affect the size of their family. Rett was joined by four sisters, roughly four years apart: Martha Jane in 1892, Mary Stewart (later known as Mary Tom after her husband, Tom Basnight) in 1896, Lucille Pulitzer in 1900, and Rebecca Isabell "Beck" in 1903. The baby of the family, Margaret "Blackie," did not arrive until March 1912 - some twenty-seven years into the marriage. Meekins built his own house on the family's land. It, like most country houses of the time, had a dairy or springhouse, a washhouse, playhouse, and swings surrounded by fruit trees. Mag kept busy as a homemaker and was active in

Timeline

Ephraim Meekins (1861-1940)
Assistant Keeper 1900-1906:

Keeper Meekins arrived at the Cape Hatteras Light Station on June 1, 1900, a few months before the Wright Brothers arrived to begin their glider flights at Kill Devil Hills. Three years later, Henry Ford founded the Ford Motor Company and the Wright Brothers made their first successful motorized flight. The year Meekins transferred from Cape Hatteras, Einstein shared his theory of relativity with the world. Also, the Navy radio station at Buxton was in operation and had tied the lighthouse to the rest of the world with instant communication.

Capt. Ephraim Meekins, principal keeper of Cape Hatteras Lighthouse (1900-1906) stands in his U.S. Lighthouse Service jacket and work pants. Circa 1902
Photo courtesy Carlisle Davis Collection, Outer Banks History Center, Manteo

the North End Baptist Church. She always seemed to have lots of energy for her family. As the children grew and started families of their own, some would occasionally return to live at home, but, as one grandchild puts it, there was only one boss, Granny Mag.

The growing family lived with, or at least visited, their father occasionally. Most likely, this was during the summer months when the girls were not attending school. Life was spartan at the stations, but the children could have found plenty to entertain them. One visit though was shortened when Blackie cut her hand. Meekins bandaged the wound with apparently the only bandage available, cobwebs, and sent her back to Roanoke Island to the doctor.

Meekins was transferred to Bodie Island Lighthouse in October 1906 where he remained thirteen years until being transferred back to Croatan Light. Finally, after forty years of service, he retired in 1927. He did not stay home long, however. He soon took the job as bridge tender of the recently completed span over Roanoke Sound connecting Roanoke Island and Nags Head. He stayed for ten years.

The Lighthouse Service, like its contemporary, the Lifesaving Service, formed a tight-knit community as well as profession. The Meekins family was no exception. Rett's husband, W.H. Etheridge, for instance, served at Bluff Shoal Light in the Pamlico Sound. In an interview after his retirement, Meekins said that he hated to leave Croatan Light since it meant leaving one of his best friends, Assistant Keeper Christopher Columbus "Lum" Midgett. Midgett was no stranger to the Service himself, having served at Wade's Point and Bodie Island, in addition to Croatan. Capt. Lum, though, was more than a friend; he was family. His son Charlie had married Eph's daughter, Lucille. A possibility also exists that Ephraim was related to, or at least the namesake of, earlier lighthouse families since he is referred to in several places, mainly listing of keepers, as Ephraim Meekins, Jr. Interestingly, an E. Meekins is listed as keeper of the second Bodie Light in 1860. If this were the case, it would follow that the government bureaucrats appended the Jr. to distinguish between the two. The name however, does not appear among any of his immediate ancestors.

Meekins' humor and good-natured personality won him many friends among the visitors to Dare County's waters. One acquaintance, noted North Carolina painter, Clement Strudwick, had him sit for a portrait in 1933 with his omnipresent pipe. Like many on Roanoke Island in the 1930s, the Meekins took in tourists since there were not many public facilities. The guests, though, were not spared his wit. A family story has a guest asking if the house had running water. Eph's answer was "yeah, grab a bucket and run like hell." Another anecdote, this time recorded in the *Dare County Times*, recounts an episode out at Croatan Light between Eph and Lum Midgett. Capt. Lum was particularly fond of beef hash, while Meekins had tired of it. Thinking to have some fun with his friend, he took a large white button like that found on the underwear of the time and put it in his plate of hash. During the meal, he pulled it from the food. When asked where he found the object, he said, "It was in this here beef." Not to be fazed, Capt. Lum replied. "I'd thought they'd a took the clothes off the darn fellow before they ground him up," and he kept right on eating.

The keeper, though, also enjoyed his solitude, a trait especially useful when at the stations. It gave him time to reflect, frequently while cleaning or doing other chores, and observe his beautiful surroundings. Meekins loved literature, songs, and words. One way he occupied the lonely hours on duty was by writing poetry, a journal of which remains in the family. Music was also an important part of family life; his daughters, Mary Tom and Beck are featured on an oral history recording singing songs they learned while growing up around the stations.

The years of service, or perhaps the harshness of Outer Banks life, gave Meekins an especially strong constitution. He reported to the *Times* in 1936 that he had "no aches or pains, nor body afflictions so far as he knows." He still plowed, dug potatoes, labored hard every day, and could, by his own admission, keep up with the rest of the boys - all at age seventy-five. The same article reports that he had just recently removed two of his own teeth with common pliers. Even in rest, he took few luxuries. His granddaughter, Camille Podolski, vividly remembers him taking front porch naps on a wooden bench with a special piece of wood for a pillow.

He retired permanently in 1938, about the same time his wife Mag died. Meekins spent his remaining years at his home tended by his youngest daughter, Blackie. He died of a heart attack at the United States Public Health Service Hospital in Norfolk on Friday, 12 January 1940. Several months earlier, President Roosevelt merged the Lighthouse Service with the Coast Guard, just a month before its own sesquicentennial.

"Capt. Eph" posed with his family at Cape Hatteras Lighthouse. The only identified individuals in this photo are the Meekins family: Front row, left to right: Maggie, Beck, Ephraim, Lucille, and Mary Meekins. The others, presumably, are the assistant keepers (1st Sanders Smith, 2nd Martin Fulcher, and 3rd John Jennett, although one keeper may be Amasa Fulcher) and their wives, but further identification is needed. Circa 1902.
Photo courtesy Carlisle Davis Collection, Outer Banks History Center, Manteo

His Job Was Defined as "Watchman, ranger, doorman, curator, custodian, preserver, and supporter," but Most Important, As Keeper of the Light, He Cared.

John Evans Midgette

"On a dark night, it was the most beautiful sight," recalling the aesthetics of that light beam that bound men, land, and ship at sea together in a form of dependency that only a seafarer can understand."

The Coastland Times *Oct 29, 1981*

John E. Midgette

By Norma Deane Skinner

John Evans Midgette was born May 5, 1895, in Avon, North Carolina, to Edward James Midgett and Alice Barnett. He was the sixth great grandson of the progenitor, Matthew Midyett, of which much has been written. The name "Midgette" or "Midyette" is of French origin. The Midgettes have been a miraculous family whose reputation for lifesaving is noted in Coast Guard records and indigenous to the Outer Banks. John is one of many amongst family members who were lighthouse keepers, assistant keepers, surfmen, and fishermen, or oystermen.

John's father, Edward James Midgett was a surfman at Cape Hatteras Lifesaving Station from 1891 to 1914, and at Big Kinnekeet Lifesaving Station in 1912. He helped with the rescue of the *Ephraim Williams* and also received a Second Class Silver Medal for the rescue of the *Brewster*, a German steamship that washed up on the Outer Diamond on November 28, 1909. Several of John's uncles were surfmen at Big and Little Kinnekeet Stations, Creeds Hill Station, and his mother's father, was Oliver Neal Barnett, assistant keeper at Cape Hatteras.

It must have been inevitable to follow in their footsteps, but not before serving in the Navy during World War I as an Oiler on U.S. Submarine Chaser #122, for which he was issued a Victory Medal Button and clasp. After celebrating the signing of the armistice, which ended the war in 1917, John would later serve again in World War II and another branch of the service. During his career with the Lighthouse Service, he served on several buoy tenders, the Cape Henry and Diamond Shoals lightships, and several lighthouses or light stations along the Chesapeake Bay in Maryland and in North Carolina.

John's most difficult and isolated duty was as assistant keeper at Cape Hatteras Lighthouse under principal keeper, Unaka Jennette. He admired Unaka and remembered him as calm and a good person to work for. John was there for two years. He was with his family, but remembered only having a few days liberty and being very isolated there. The families of the keepers played croquet and there was even a baseball diamond between the lighthouse and the ocean. The beauty of that light shining at night left quite an impression on him.

He and his wife, Oretha (Williams) Quidley, whom he married in 1921, and his family lived in one side of the keeper's quarters and another keeper's family lived on the other side. Miss Oretha was the niece of Unaka Jennette. Her father, William E. Quidley, or Bill, as he was known, was also an assistant keeper at Cape Hatteras and later at Bodie Island Light.

> *"The families of the keepers played croquet and there was even a baseball diamond between the lighthouse and the ocean. The beauty of that light shining at night left quite an impression on him."*

Their children were Clifton Evans (died eight months of age), Melita Lovell, and Ronald Evans Midgette. After John was transferred to Pamlico River, Oretha was gravely ill, so they returned home to Buxton, where she died of tuberculosis. The children were transferred to the sanatorium, as a sort of quarantine for several months until it was determined they had not been infected. The children then remained with relatives while John was transferred to Smith Point Lighthouse in the channel of the Chesapeake Bay.

Another duty station was at Janes Island in the Tangier Sound. He and another crewman had to abandon the tower during a severe freeze. John had to tie the lens in the tower to keep it from tumbling over. They were rescued by a Coast Guard cutter and returned home for 30 days leave. They later heard over the radio that the lighthouse had toppled over into the sound.

TIMELINE

JOHN EVANS MIDGETTE (1895-1982)
ASSISTANT KEEPER 1929-1930:

As a career lighthouse keeper, Cape Hatteras was just one of many stations at which Midgette served. During his two years at Hatteras, the nation witnessed the start of the Great Depression and the stock market crash of '29. Keeper Midgette's job was secure while millions of Americans lost their jobs and found themselves penniless.

When John left Buxton for his next appointment as assistant keeper in Belhaven, he didn't go alone. His second wife, Blanche, whom he married in 1937, and his two children by Oretha, accompanied him.

Miss Blanche Burrus Farrow, of Frisco, had been hired to care for John's children while he was away. She was the daughter of George Washington Farrow and Angeline Reid. George was a preacher and ship's carpenter, while Angeline's father, Warren, a sailor from Maine, was shipwrecked upon the Outer Banks. John enjoyed this duty most of all because he could be with his family more often. John and Blanche later had a daughter, Alice Rebecca "Becky," who was born in Washington, N.C., in 1944. After twenty-two years with the Lighthouse Service, nine years and nine months with the Coast Guard, John retired at age fifty-two and the family returned home to Buxton in 1947.

John turned to carpentry and boat building. He helped to build several homes as well as the Buxton and the Avon Assembly of God Churches. Blanche was a substitute schoolteacher, local seamstress, and worked at a dress shop in Buxton called "Ormonds." She later wrote the personals for *The Coastland Times*.

John passed away at age eighty-seven, in August of 1982, and is buried in the family plot in Quidley Cemetery in Buxton. Blanche lives in Virginia Beach, Virginia, near her daughter, Becky.

In 1960, Rebecca married Charles Dean Matson, a Navy man stationed at Cape Hatteras, and then moved to his home in California. The couple had four daughters, Norma Deane, Sherri Lynn, Michelle Marie, and Nicole Leah Matson. Most of their families now reside in Virginia Beach, Virginia. Rebecca later remarried Alan Mastros in August 1985.

Ronald Midgette has two children and lives in Springfield, Virginia, with his wife, Kay. Melita married Troy Harris and has a son, Bruce, and a daughter, Tamara Gail, who currently live in Buxton with their families. John and Blanche now have seven grandchildren and nine great grandchildren who reside in Buxton and Virginia Beach.

In 1976, John's granddaughter, Michelle Matson had a career day at school and invited him to talk about his service in the Navy, Coast Guard and Lighthouse Service. The children asked questions and did an audio recording as he relat-

Keeper John Evans Midgette wore his summer Lighthouse Service cap with the United States Lighthouse Service insignia (then also known as Bureau of Lighthouses) and wool keeper's uniform pants. He has on his same leather jacket and pocket watch chain as appeared in a photo taken earlier with Vivian (Jennette) Frontis.
Photo courtesy Norma Skinner and Rebecca (Midgette) Mastros

ed many stories about his duties and experiences. The family has been delighted to have such a wonderful keepsake of grandfather John and it is rare these days to hear the "old Hatteras accent," which many think was derived from the "old Elizabethan" dialect.

At the end of the interview, John was asked "If you had to do it all over again...?" to which he responded, "Yes, I don't think there was anything else I was meant to do." He was always very proud of his lighthouse career and although somewhat camera shy, loved to talk about the old days.

Many a day was passed sitting on the front porch with friends trading stories. One such friend, Ben Dixon MacNeill, who wrote the book, *The Hatterasman*, used to visit John often and reminisce. Ben was also a photographer, and one picture was included in the October 1955 issue of *National Geographic* magazine, for an article about Cape Hatteras and the Outer Banks. It depicted John and his youngest daughter, Becky, in their front yard, painting a large red buoy.

Tucked safely in the Midgette family photograph album is a picture of the Cape Hatteras Lighthouse from the time when John E. Midgette served as assistant keeper. The curtains are drawn during the day to protect the valuable Fresnel lens from the sun, just as Keeper Midgette described in his Coastland Times *interview in 1981. The small, brick oil house was built in 1892 when the Lighthouse Service required that all fuel must be stored outside the tower to lessen the risk of fire. Circa 1930*
Photo courtesy Norma Skinner and Rebecca (Midgette) Mastros

John's granddaughter, Norma Deane, a genealogist, lighthouse enthusiast, and member of the Outer Banks Lighthouse Society, has many records, pictures, and keepsakes of her family's background. She thinks that preserving her family's history is a wonderful hobby and hopes her family will treasure her work as it grows. "There aren't many folks left to tell the stories of generations of seaman, surfmen, and light keepers, a heritage of which we are very proud," Norma stated.

Interview with a Keeper's Daughter, Melita Lovell Midgette

By Lynn Jennette

"My father, John E. Midgette, and my mother, Oretha (Williams) Quidley, had three children: Clifton Evans, Melita Lovell (me), and Ronald Evans Midgette. My father and stepmother, Blanche Burrus (Farrow), had one child, Alice Rebecca," began Melita (Midgette) Harris, Keeper John E. Midgette's daughter.

"I remember playing in a skiff in the pond behind the double keepers quarters with my cousins and brother.

"My mother, Oretha, had tuberculosis when we lived at the lighthouse [1929-30]. My brother was about three and I was about seven. After she died, we were sent off to a sanatorium in the western part of North Carolina around Asheville, I think. We were there for about a year. She died shortly after we left the lighthouse and I remember her funeral being held in the double keepers quarters in 1932. She was the daughter of Bill Quidley who was stationed on the lighthouse.

"My maternal grandfather, Bill Quidley, was assistant lighthouse keeper and he lived with his family in the double keepers quarters at the same time that we lived there. They lived on one side and we lived on the other.

"My best friend was Olive Jennette whose father was principal keeper. I remember going around the lighthouse complex arm and arm. We often played up on the dunes behind the lighthouse, but we were forbidden to go out on the beach alone.

"On Sundays, members of the family would come out to the lighthouse and we would have big dinners. My step-grandmother, Leonora Williams, Bill Quidley's second wife, would cook. One time the children were playing on the base surrounding the lighthouse and one of my cousins (I think that was the relationship), Boyce Midgette, pushed me off and I broke my arm. He didn't mean to hurt me, it was an accident.

"I remember climbing to the top of the lighthouse when my father was on duty and he was carrying oil up to the top to light the light. Once when I was at the top with my father and we were on the way down, I tripped and fell down the steps but he caught me between his legs, I think it was only three or four steps.

"Another time my mother's sister, Esther, was visiting and her little son, Larry, four or five years old, wandered out to the pond. We found him floating face down on the pond. Her niece, Norma, took off her shoes and socks and jumped into the pond and saved him. Norma said, 'They were brand new shoes!'

"One vivid memory I have was the sound of the wind. There were screens on the porch or on the ends of the building and when the wind would blow hard it would create a horrible moaning sound that really frightened me. To this day the sound of wind often scares me. Also, you could hardly

These best friends are (right) Olive Jennette, Keeper Unaka Jennette's daughter, and (left) Melita Midgette, Keeper John E. Midgette's daughter. Melita said that she and her friend spent much of their time at the light station playing and walking "arm in arm." Circa 1930
Photo courtesy Melita (Midgette) Harris and Rebecca (Midgette) Mastros

John Evans Midgette and his wife, Oretha (Quidley) Midgette, sit on the running board of Midgette's car, one of the first cars on Hatteras Island. Oretha was the daughter of Keeper Bill Quidley. She died at a young age in 1932 of tuberculosis, a deadly disease that claimed many Hatteras islanders, young and old alike.
Photo courtesy Melita (Midgette) Harris

hear anything- there were so many frogs in the ponds and they were so loud!

"My father was assigned to Pamlico Point screwpile light before we went to the Hatteras Lighthouse. My father went underneath to cut some wood and while he was down there, my little brother, Ronald, closed the hatch and laid down on it and fell asleep. My father had to lift them both up to get back into the building.

"My father was also assigned to Smith Point Lighthouse, Maryland, after he left Hatteras. We did not go there with him because we were at that sanatorium at the time. After the coast guard took over, my father joined the coast guard, and we went to live in Belhaven. Eventually we moved back to Buxton."

Information taken from an interview with Melita (Midgette) Harris July 6, 2000.

The handsome John Midgette posed with Vivian Jennette (1916-1999), primary keeper Unaka Jennette's daughter. Midgette and his family lived at the light station while Vivian was there also. She later married Shelley Frontis (1902-1973) who dashed up the lighthouse tower in record time to ask Keeper Jennette for the hand of his daughter in 1935. Circa 1930
Photo courtesy Norma Skinner and Rebecca (Midgette) Mastros

Keeper Midgette tells in his own words about Hatteras...

Keeper Midgette spoke of his days at Cape Hatteras as assistant keeper: "...It was the most beautiful place with a broad beach and nice ponds. Unaka [Jennette] had a large garden and we kept horses, milk cows, and beef cows. There were hogs in the woods. You could get all the fowl you wanted and plenty of deer.

"Ducks were really unlimited in those days. The light attracted fowl and sometimes ducks would fly against the tower. The next morning, the lighthouse crew could pick up the dead or stunned fowl from the tower base."

The families of the keepers played croquet and there was a baseball diamond between the lighthouse and the ocean. Midgette pitched for a team captained by Dr. Folb.

"Before sunrise," recalled Midgette, "I would climb the lighthouse and put the light out at the top by turning the valve of the mantle lamp. The storm curtains were put up to keep the sun off the lens.

"The lamp burner was filled with pure alcohol and the weights which turned the table on which the lens rested had to be wound. The amazing part of that lens," said Midgette, "was that it was so big. You had to have a ladder to go inside and you polished the inside and the outside. We also had to keep the dust off...and during stormy weather, someone had to stay in the tower."

John E. Midgette's quotes from Coastland Times *article October 29, 1981 in interview with Diane Ransom*

Ronald Evans (left) and sister Melita, about four and eight-years-old respectively, were taken to a Tuberculosis sanatorium after the death of their mother. Circa 1932
Photo preserved by Melita (Midgette) Harris and submitted by Norma Skinner and Rebecca (Midgette) Mastros

Blanche Burrus (Farrow) Midgette was Keeper John E. Midgette's second wife. Keeper Midgette, son of Edward James Midgette (1861-1944) and Alice (Barnett) (1871-1898), became a widower when his first wife, Oretha (Quidley) died in September 1932, leaving him with two young children to care for: Melita (Midgette) Harris (1925), and Ronald Evans Midgette (1929). He married Blanche in 1937 and had one child, Alice Rebecca "Becky" Midgette. Becky's daughter, Norma Deane Skinner, wrote of her grandfather and his Lighthouse Service career from family oral histories and documents that she has preserved.
Photo courtesy Norma Skinner and Rebecca (Midgette) Mastros

Keeper John E. Midgette's daughter, Melita Lovell (Midgette) Harris, posed for this picture as a young woman. Though faced with her mother's death when only seven-years-old and separation from her father, she became a lovely young woman. At right is her brother, Ronald Evans Midgette, a grown and successful man.
Photo courtesy Melita (Midgette) Harris and family

Keeper, Postmaster, and Family Man

Christopher Columbus Miller

C.C. Miller's two sons, Horatio Seymore and Baxter Benjamin, became famous as U.S. Lifesaving Service surfmen, winning Lifesaving Medals for their rescue of men from the shipwrecked Brewster *in 1909. Three of the Miller daughters married Cape Hatteras Lighthouse keepers.*

By Sandra MacLean Clunies

Christopher Columbus Miller (1844-1927) lived a long and illustrious life. The son of Tilmon F. and Amelia (Scarborough) Miller, he was a veteran of the Civil War. He mustered into the 1st NC Infantry January 3, 1863 and was discharged as a Sergeant of Company I on August 15, 1865. He was later awarded a pension for his military service.

Within a year of returning home, he married within the year to Emma "Dolly" Fulcher (1844-1895), the daughter of Keeper Benjamin T. Fulcher, a trusted man who kept the Cape Hatteras Lighthouse for fifteen years prior to the Civil War. Of the nine children born to C.C. and Dolly, three daughters died in their early years. Three of their four surviving daughters married later lighthouse keepers, while both sons were noted members of the U.S. Lifesaving Service.

Baxter Benjamin Miller (1871-1940) won two Lifesaving Medals: a Gold Medal for his role as acting keeper ("keeper" also indicates the highest-ranking surfman at a lifesaving station) of the Cape Hatteras Lifesaving Station during the 1909 rescue of the crew from the German steamer *Brewster*. He was also awarded a Silver Medal in 1911 for saving the life of Joshua H. Dailey, son of venerable U.S. Lifesaving Service surfman Benjamin Dailey, after Josh was knocked unconscious by a shifting boom aboard the *Defender* in 1911. Older brother Horatio Seymour Miller (1870-1917), together with other members of the Cape Hatteras Lifesaving Station crew, won Silver Lifesaving Medals for the 1909 *Brewster* rescue. Baxter Miller is credited with over 300 rescues during his career from 1890 until 1921.

Christopher Miller was appointed assistant keeper at Cape Hatteras in 1887, when the family consisted of six children aged four to seventeen years. Daughter Permelia, born the next year in 1888, died shortly after her first birthday. C.C.'s service at the lighthouse continued for five years, until 1892. In 1893, three of the older children, Horatio, Baxter, and Lorena, all married. Two years later, in 1895, wife Dolly died at age fifty, leaving Christopher with his youngest three surviving daughters - then ages twelve to seventeen, all of whom would later marry lighthouse keepers.

1896 brought two more family weddings. In June, Christopher took a second wife, an accomplished young woman named Mary Ormond "Mamie" Tyer, who had recently moved to Hatteras from Bath, North Carolina to be the principal of the local school. In July, daughter Delphine married John B. Jennett, who would become an assistant keeper in 1899. John was the son of keeper Benjamin Claude Jennett, and grandson of keepers Joseph C. Jennett and Zion B. Jennett. The lighthouse legacy would continue.

> *"While the lighthouse keeping days of Christopher Columbus Miller had ended, and he was approaching sixty years of age, his life, with three sons-in-law as keepers, and a second family with a quartet of growing young daughters, was anything but 'retired.'"*

The three years from 1897 to 1900 were especially productive for C.C. Miller. His new wife Mamie gave birth to four baby girls: twins Mamie (1897-1982) and Annie (1897-1986), Lucy Stowe (1898-1994), and Maude Leigh (1900-1987). This was a hale and hearty group of girls, all living well into their eighties!

In 1897, daughter Dezzie (1880-1950) married Martin Luther Fulcher, who would serve as assistant keeper at Cape Hatteras 1900-1905. And in 1900, the year of the birth of C.C. and Mamie's last daughter, his youngest surviving daughter with Dolly, Lillie Columbus Miller (1883-1936), married Thomas Hardy Baum, who would serve as an assistant keeper in 1905.

While the lighthouse keeping days of Christopher Columbus Miller had ended, and he was approaching sixty years of age, his life, with three sons-in-law as keepers, and a second family with a quartet of growing young daughters, was anything but "retired."

The 1910 federal census reported much of this large extended Miller family living near one another. Listed that year as a retail merchant in the grocery business, C.C. and Mamie's home held their four daughters, ages ten to thirteen.

Timeline

Christopher Columbus Miller (1844-1927)
Assistant Keeper 1887-1892:

The last tall coastal lighthouse in North Carolina, the Currituck Beach Lighthouse, had been finished only twelve years before C.C. Miller took his watch at Cape Hatteras. In 1891, Keeper Miller would have observed the unfolding drama through his spyglasses on Diamond Shoals as the marine contractor, Anderson and Barr, tried to sink a caisson in an attempt to build a half-million dollar, brick-lined lighthouse similar to the famous French icon, La Jument. The caisson was swept away by rough seas and no other attempt was made to tame Diamond Shoals, the troublemaker of the Graveyard of the Atlantic, which is credited for approximately 600 shipwrecks.

Looking the distinguished couple, Christopher C. Miller and his new bride and second wife, Mary Ormond "Mamie" (Tyer) pose for their wedding portrait in 1896. He and Mamie produced four healthy, long-lived girls in three years, 1897-1900.
Photo courtesy Annie Miller (Parker) Hodges

(Below) Christopher C. Miller and his first wife, Emma P. "Dolly" (Fulcher) Miller, appear in this portrait. Miller's shocks of white hair and beard and his ice-blue eyes added to his intriguing appearance. Both he and Dolly were born in 1844, married in 1866, and had their first child in 1867. Together, they had nine children over a period of twenty-one years.
Photo courtesy Jo Ellen (Jennette) Luscombe

Around 1905, the Buxton School could have been called the "Miller's School." Emma, Hilton, Donald, and Agnes are children of Horatio Seymore Miller. Edison and Cantwell are sons of Baxter Miller. These six children are grandchildren of Keeper C.C. Miller from his marriage to Dolly (Fulcher) Miller. Twins Mamie and Annie, Lucy, and Maude are C.C. Miller's four girls from his marriage to Mary Ormond "Mamie" (Tyer) Miller. Keeper Miller had three grandchildren older than his twins, Annie and Mamie, at this time.
Photo courtesy Annie Miller (Parker) Hodges, Keeper Miller's granddaughter

Next door was son H. Seymour, wife Mollie and their growing brood of six children, followed by the house of his younger brother Baxter, wife Josephine, and their six youngsters. In 1910, John and Delphine (Miller) Jennett had five children living with them at the keepers' quarters. With seventeen grandchildren nearby, some older than his own four young daughters of the second marriage, we can know that daily life was rarely quiet or dull! All told, C.C. Miller had over forty-five grandchildren, and for many years to come the Miller home on Rocky Rollinson Road in Buxton was the scene for many family gatherings when the other family members returned home for visits.

C.C. Miller was a trusted community citizen, and received other local and federal appointments. Serving as a Notary Public and a Justice of the Peace, he witnessed many events and signed countless documents for his colleagues and neighbors. Many of these signatures remain in papers filed with Civil War pension applications at the National Archives. In 1896, he was appointed Postmaster at Buxton, and then the position was transferred to wife Mamie, who served for nine years as Postmistress. Daughter Maude, who served for almost thirty years, followed her mother's tenure as Postmistress. In a small community like Buxton, the Post Office - then and now - was the center of town. And the Miller family was prominently centered in the life of Hatteras Island.

There are few living descendants who can share personal recollections of Christopher C. Miller, who died in 1929. Granddaughter Annie Miller (Parker) Hodges told, "Concerning that postmaster job, I'll tell you how that happened. Between the terms that Grover Cleveland served as President, he visited Hatteras Island. C.C. Miller took him fishing and the story goes that the President was so impressed with Miller that he looked favorably upon his appointment as Postmaster."

A great-granddaughter, Evelyn Strickland, grew up learning that "he was a loving and family man. He took care of all his children and grandchildren." Evelyn recalled her grandfather, Baxter, with respect and adoration. She still has Baxter's rolltop desk salvaged from the Brewster rescue. "It has a secret latch that sometimes catches and we think we cannot unlock it; sometimes by accident we'll do something 'right' with it and it will unlock. That desk will always stay where it is on the island."

Over four hundred descendants of Christopher Columbus Miller were identified this year, and surely many more remain scattered around the country, and perhaps around the world - still connected by heritage and history to this memorable keeper of Cape Hatteras.

Thanks to Annie Miller (Parker) Hodges for sharing of rare photographs and information.

Keeper C.C. Miller's son, Baxter Benjamin, stands in his U.S. Lifesaving Service uniform. He is with his wife, Josephine (Gray) Miller, and one of his nine children. Baxter is renowned for his participation in the rescue of the Brewster in 1909. He was awarded a gold Congressional Medal of Honor and his brother, Horatio Seymour, was awarded a silver medal. Baxter is credited with saving over 300 lives; two of his duty stations were the Cape Hatteras and Kinnekeet Lifesaving Stations. Photo courtesy Annie Miller (Parker) Hodges

> From the book, *Old Coast Guard Stations-Volume Two* by Richard L. Chenery III, p.54, a description of the Cape Hatteras Lifesaving crew who were awarded congressional medals of honor for the rescue of the *Brewster* in 1909. "... The Gold Lifesaving Medal was awarded to Surfman (Acting Keeper) Baxter B. Miller from this station for the 1909 *Brewster* rescue on the Outer Diamonds off Cape Hatteras. Silver Lifesaving Medals were awarded to Surfmen H.S. Miller, O.O. Midgett, I.L. Jennett, E.J. Midgett, U.B. Williams, and W.L. Barnett from this station for the 1909 *Brewster* rescue. In 1911 the Silver Lifesaving Medal was awarded to Surfman Baxter B. Miller from this station for saving John [sic - it was Joshua who later served on LV Diamond Shoals] H. Dailey (Son of Captain B.B. Dailey) who was swept overboard in heavy weather....."

This illustrates the close inter-relationships between the U.S. Lifesaving and U.S. Lighthouse Services; for example, look at the surfmen's names:
Baxter B. Miller and **Horatio S. Miller** were the sons of Cape Hatteras Keeper C.C. Miller;
Oliver O. Midgett's great-granddaughter, Beatrice McArthur, co-founded the Hatteras Island Genealogical and Historical Society in Buxton; Beatie is a direct descendant of six Cape Hatteras Lighthouse keepers;
Isaac L. Jennett was a son of Cape Hatteras Keeper William B. Jennett;
Edward J. Midgett was a brother of Cape Hatteras Keeper John E. Midgett;
Urias B. Williams was a son of Cape Hatteras Keeper Bateman A. Williams;
Walter Loran Barnett was a son of Cape Hatteras Keeper Oliver N. Barnett.
Photo courtesy Outer Banks History Center

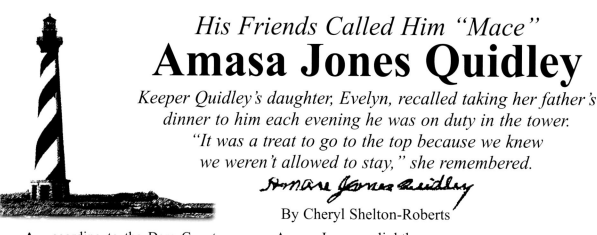

His Friends Called Him "Mace"
Amasa Jones Quidley

Keeper Quidley's daughter, Evelyn, recalled taking her father's dinner to him each evening he was on duty in the tower. "It was a treat to go to the top because we knew we weren't allowed to stay," she remembered.

By Cheryl Shelton-Roberts

According to the Dare County census, Amasa Jones Quidley was born in 1877. His first assignment was as an "additional assistant keeper" during February through April of 1917 at the Croatan Light Station. After being listed "at large" for the next several weeks, he assumed the position as second assistant keeper at the Cape Hatteras Lighthouse 20 August 1917. He signed an oath of office August 30, 1917, which is notarized by former keeper and then notary public, Christopher C. Miller.

Keeper Quidley transferred 30 September 1923 with an increase in pay to Bluff Shoal Light Station, a screwpile lighthouse similar to the Croatan Light. In September 1924, he moved with another increase in salary to the Deep Water Shoal Light Station in Virginia. Records indicate that he stayed there until a brief duty during July and August of 1929 at the Currituck Beach Light Station. Quidley continued to be promoted with an increase in pay each time he moved, proving that he was a valued employee. For about one year, he served at the Thimble Shoal screwpile light in Virginia. During August of 1930, he was again given a salary increase to serve at the Roanoke River Lighthouse (screwpile), and finally in January 1931, he retired with partial paralysis on his right side and drew a pension for his hard work during fourteen years in the Lighthouse Service.

Friends and relatives called Keeper Quidley "Mace." His parents died when he was a young boy, and he was raised and nurtured within Rovena and David Quidley's household that included four other boys who became lighthouse keepers (see story on Rovena Quidley).

Keeper Quidley's daughter, Evelyn Quidley Cullipher, was born October 2, 1915. It is from her that we gain more knowledge of her father, someone she said was a "quiet man." Evelyn offered a picture of her father to be copied for this book and as she looked upon his image, she commented, "He was raised in a house that was in back of where the school is now. He was much self-taught and was a smart man."

Evelyn lived at Cape Hatteras while her dad was there as keeper and she had to wash dishes and help cook. In a personal interview, she shared that, at age fourteen, she was expected to do much of the cooking. She often took her father's meals up to him while he was on duty in the lighthouse.

She recalled clearly being sent by her mother to get Keeper Quidley. "If it was time to eat, I had to tell my dad the food was ready or take it to him. We ran up the steps." She can only dream of that now. "We went up to the top, but we weren't allowed to stay. The trip to get him for dinner was a treat because we knew we weren't allowed to stay.

"I didn't particularly care for the beach. No, I wasn't afraid of the water, I just didn't like all the sand. And I still don't." She chuckled at the thought that she lives with it all the time.

> *"His parents died when he was a young boy, and he was raised ...in a household that included four other boys who became lighthouse keepers."*

"Pop served at 'water lights' and one was Gull Shoal." She would visit her dad when her mother, Evelena Stowe "Miss Lena," went at certain times of the year. "She [Mother] was strict. Sometimes too strict in my opinion, but we just played out there and I played with my younger brother Mace [Jr.]. We played on our own. There were three or four other kids other than Mace that went, I think, including Taylor, Mahonie "Monie," and sister Vanie. There were about ten children 'all toll' in the family.

"The family home was on the Back Road. Pop died at eighty-five years of age of a stroke." Evelyn paused for a few minutes with sadness in her eyes. She continued to look at his picture and returned to her comments. "Pop never seemed worried about his job. If he did, none of us knew about it. He was a confident man. He retired after the stroke. He was at home where I grew up that he had it built."

Evelyn looked at the picture of her dad. "Bless his heart," she whispered. Her tears fell on the kitchen table. "I sure do miss Pop. I remember seeing the flash of the light - and I can still see it flash." A quick smile returned to her face; Evelyn put a double meaning on this last statement. The light had been comforting to her as a child because her Pop kept the light working, and she can still see the flash today from her home on Hatteras Island.

All quotes are taken from a personal interview with Amasa Quidley's daughter, Evelyn (Quidley) Cullipher on October 2, 2000. Source for Amasa J. Qudley's career: National Personnel Records Center, Civilian Records Facility, St. Louis, MO.

TIMELINE
AMASA JONES QUIDLEY (1877-1962)
ASSISTANT KEEPER 1917-1923:

According to correspondence from the U.S. Lighthouse Service, Keeper Quidley served at Cape Hatteras from 20 August 1917 until 30 September 1923. When he took over his duties at Cape Hatteras, WWI was raging in Europe. Families in Buxton, as well as all over the nation, feared for loved ones in a war that was meant to "end all wars" while German submarines prowled the East Coast. America was headed into the good times of the "Roaring Twenties." Kerosene continued as the source of fuel for the beacon as it swept over the unpredictable Graveyard of the Atlantic and a serene Hatteras Island.

Evelyn (Quidley) Cullipher, Amasa J. Quidley's daughter, laughed when she was told that she had to smile for the picture. "I have to?" She grinned. And in spite of her failing health at the time of this picture, she did. She got emotional each time she was shown a picture of the Cape Hatteras Lighthouse. "There we are," she would say each time in a manner like that of a grateful person who had found something lost.

Amasa J. Quidley looked handsome in his U.S. Lighthouse Service uniform. "He was a quiet...confident man," said his daughter, Evelyn.
Photo courtesy Evelyn (Quidley) Cullipher

Keeper at the Tall Lights
John Bunion Quidley

John Quidley and his new bride were, Emma Midgette, on their honeymoon in Manteo when the Wright Brothers were attempting their first powered flight in Kill Devil Hills. He served at Bodie Island, Cape Hatteras, Cape Lookout, and Cape Charles. He loved the big lights.

My Dad

By William L. Quidley

When the Wright Brothers flew their first flight, my dad was on his honeymoon in Manteo. Around this time, Dad was stationed at the Cape Hatteras Lighthouse for the U.S. Lighthouse Service.

My oldest sister, Celia Marie (Quidley), was born in the keepers quarters in 1905. My sister, Mary, and brother, Jethro, were born in Buxton, North Carolina. Marie was always telling stories of how she had been born there at the keepers quarters at the Cape Hatteras Lighthouse. She told many stories about how she and friends would go oystering and enjoy them with one another and other friends.

I heard stories told about dad about how he would break out his violin and play for dances and parties while at Cape Hatteras. How everyone loved to hear John play while they would dance to a square dancing tune. I can hear it now- "Turkey in the Straw"!

When Dad and Emma moved to Beaufort, his mother-in-law, Celia Anne (Rolinson) Midgette lived with them. She was determined to make that century mark, but missed it by only three months. I remember her so well. She was a sweet old soul- a sweet lady who liked to dress. Her husband was John Allen Midgette who won a gold Lifesaving Medal.

Dad began at the Pamlico Sound lights, including Harbor Island, transferred to Bodie Island and, after leaving Cape Hatteras, Dad was stationed at the Cape Lookout Lighthouse and finally at Cape Charles until he retired. And he was a very fit man. They use to say that he got his exercise each morning by picking up two-five gallon cans full of kerosene and running up the steps!

Information is from family records, William L. Quidley's correspondence, and an interview March 2, 2001. Family information also has been shared by Jim Lewis, Ronnie Quidley, and Dallas Quidley.

> *"And he was a very fit man. They use to say that he got his exercise each morning by picking up two five-gallon cans full of kerosene and running up the steps!"*

John B. Quidley looked dapper in his suit and side-lace shoes with his mother-in-law, Celia Anne (Rolinson) Midgette. John was born in 1877 and died in 1936. "Dad liked to carve model ships and play the fiddle," son William said.
Circa 1910
Photo courtesy William L. Quidley

Timeline
John Bunion Quidley (1877-1936)
Assistant Keeper 1904-1905 and 1909-1911

John B. Quidley was a keeper at Cape Hatteras 1904-1905. He served again 1909-1911. In 1903, John B. married Emma (Midgette) (1885-1951) and they had seven children: Celia Marie (1905-1997) who was born at the double keepers quarters at the Cape Hatteras Lighthouse, Mary Zane (1907-1996), Jethro Hooper (1909-1997), James I. (1918-1999), John Howard (1912-1913), John Desmond (1922-1924), and William Lewis (1925).
Photo courtesy William L. Quidley

Cape Hatteras: A Family Affair

William Edward Quidley

*William E. Quidley was "Grandpa Bill" to Norma and Sabra Gray
For them and their brother, Glenn, Cape Hatteras was home away from home
while they and their mother visited frequently at the lighthouse to see
her father and two uncles.*

By Cheryl Shelton-Roberts

For those who think that an assignment at Cape Hatteras was isolated and lonely, you may want to reconsider after reading this family's story. If we could step back to the years during the mid-1920s and 30s and eavesdrop for a while, we'd hear the giggles of a dozen or more kids. Each of the three keepers' households welcomed one and all, especially children. While mothers were at the hub of the busy activity, each in her center stage in the kitchen, fathers were reaching great heights atop the lighthouse, tending the light: the sole purpose for all the other activity on the light station. Contentment for a keeper and his family was a working beacon.

The daily ritual of extinguishing the light, cleaning every part of the light station until it sparkled, and the lighting of the evening's fiery warning to mariners were enhanced by growing, active families. Mothers' daughters were trained to take over the dishwashing and clothes scrubbing and keepers' sons were taught to help with polishing brass and gently cleaning the prisms of the Fresnel lens. But when the children's chores and homework were done, all other time belonged to them. There were holes to dig, fish to catch, turtles to hook through the privy seats, ponds to traverse, beaches to explore, dunes to capture, winds to lean into, endless imaginations to be unleashed after a storm abated, and treasures to be claimed.

Two granddaughters, Norma Gray Rhoden and Sabra Gray Jennette, recreated a portrait of Keeper William E. Quidley and life at the Cape Hatteras Light Station. Addenda by two of his great granddaughters, Connie Rhoden Manley, and Jacqueline "Jackie" Jennette, daughters of Norma and Sabra respectively, further enhance the image of this keeper and the Quidley heritage.

Izetta (Quidley) Gray and Christopher "Kit" Columbus Gray had three children, Glenn (1914-1950), Norma (1919), and Sabra (1920). Izetta was Keeper William Edward Quidley's daughter and often took her children with her to visit at the lighthouse. Ranging over several years, from preschool age through high school, the three Gray children were seen at the light station about as regularly as the keepers' own children.

The Gray children loved visiting their Jennette cousins since Keeper Unaka Jennette was their grandmother Sabrah's brother. Also at the lighthouse were "Grandpa Bill" [William E.Quidley] and Uncle John [John E. Midgette]. Midgette was married to their mother's sister, Oretha, making it one big family at Cape Hatteras for many years. As the big sweep of the Fresnel lens began its nightly journey out over Diamond Shoals, a dozen youngsters piled onto a couple of beds in one of the keepers quarters bedrooms and enjoyed a night of security among friends and family.

"We kids had fun at the lighthouse," Norma began. "We had practically nothing to play with, but we enjoyed being together. While my father was in the Navy and away on duty, sometimes on Diamond Shoals, we'd go out to the lighthouse and stay with friends and relatives."

Norma remembered the nights of childish laughter with her friends and relatives in the keepers quarters at Cape Hatteras. "While Uncle Unaka was the main keeper, I'd go and stay with Myrtle Jennette, my cousin. I fit right in their house.

"I was small at the time, and we had roller skates and there were cement walks that went from the lighthouse all the way around the keepers houses and all around the yard and we had a time with the roller skates! I had more skinned knees than anybody in the world. These were the old ones [style of roller skates], some of the first around here [Buxton]. We ordered them from a catalog. We ordered anything from Sears and Montgomery Ward-clothes, shoes, everything. There were some exciting times waiting for the mailboat at the mail landing on the sound near where the Pilot House restaurant on the sound in Buxton is now, I believe.

"I've been up that lighthouse many a time. But they wouldn't let us go up without our shoes on. I'm not sure why, but it may have been because of the sand we carried in on our feet and that was bad for the paint. We went barefoot a lot elsewhere. Some of us were up there one time and we wanted to see how long it took us to run down. We went from the top to the bottom in three minutes!" Norma stated with a smug smile.

Norma remembered seeing her granddaddy and other

> *"As the big sweep of the Fresnel lens began its nightly journey out over Diamond Shoals, a dozen youngsters piled onto a couple of beds in one of the keepers quarters bedrooms and enjoyed a night of security among friends and family."*

Timeline

William Edward Quidley (1874-1961)
Assistant Keeper 1928-1934:

In his final years at Cape Hatteras, William E. Quidley saw our nation gripped in the Great Depression. In 1933, two hurricanes, one following on the heels of the other, battered Hatteras Island, causing much flooding and damage to homes. Erosion threatened the lighthouse and the Lighthouse Service sought a new location to exhibit the light. The automobile began to replace horses as the primary source of transportation on the island.

Keeper Quidley sits with his great-granddaughter, Linda (Jennette) Caudill, daughter of Sabra (Gray) Jennette. Just visible above them on a shelf is a boat model that he carved and built. Like many Hatteras Islanders, Bill Quidley was multi-talented, self-sufficient, and devoted to family.

William Edward "Bill" Quidley posed in partial U.S. Lighthouse uniform. He was known as a gentleman and he always smoked his pipe. Granddaughter Norma described Grandpa Bill as a "roly-poly, short man. He was only about five- foot-four." Keeper Quidley's face reveals his kind nature. "Even when Grandpa Bill was in his 80s and in a wheelchair, he had an unsinkable sense of humor," Norma said with sincerity. Sabra noted her grandpa's large hands. "They had to be strong in those days."
Photos courtesy Sabra (Gray) Jennette

Left to right are William E. Quidley, Joe O'neal, Beatrice O'neal and Rovena R. Quidley. Some O'neal families of Hatteras Island spell their name with the small letter "n" following the capital "O." Rovena was mother to Miranda Quidley and Miranda was mother to Beatrice O'neal; Beatrice is mother to Darlene (O'neal) Willis, who shared this photo. Melita (Midgette)Harris also submitted this photo.

keepers carry the big brass can of kerosene up to the light each evening. "Sometimes they'd carry a smaller can and take some up each time they went up."

Izetta, Norma's mother, planned many of the visits so she could be with family and friends, especially her father, Keeper Bill Quidley and his second wife, Leonora. Norma stated, "Leonora had no children and Bill was older than she was, and she was probably too old when they married to have children. So, she didn't want to be called "grandma" so the kids just called her Leonora. They [Bill and Leonora] got along so good together," Norma commented of someone she loved as her grandmother. "She called him 'Mr. Bill' every time she spoke to him."

These keeper families were closely tied both as relatives and friends. For example, Norma remembered Edna (Casey) Gray. "She's a card, isn't she? She had a small house across the street from where we lived [in Buxton]. Edna would let us come in and play records and dance and enjoy ourselves. It was Edna's sister, Myrtle Casey, that I was such good friends with- she and I were about the same age- she was one grade ahead of me in school in Buxton. She was 'big Myrtle' and Myrtle Jennette was 'little Myrtle.'"

When not visiting at the lighthouse, Norma and her family lived in the home her father bought, just a short distance away from Grandpa Bill's home on the "Back Road" in Buxton. Norma resides in her childhood home today.

William E. Quidley's mother, Miranda Farrow (1854-1879), died when he was only four or five years old. William's father, Dave, married again and his stepmother, Rovena Quidley, raised him. Rovena is best known as the midwife who birthed over 300 babies on Hatteras Island and the person everyone called when someone fell ill. "She wore lots of clothes with a big wool wrap-around skirt," Norma described.

Norma's sister, Sabra, agreed that there are so few "old ones," as she refers to the older generation of Hatteras Island natives, left to remember life at the light station. Born in 1920, this granddaughter also remembered well "Miss Rovena." Children from other families pronounced her name differently, but all the names referred to exactly one woman. One can call her anything, but "love" is a fitting term, based on the descriptions of children who were helped into this world by the midwife.

"We all called Rovena 'Grandma,'" Sabra began. "She delivered me. She delivered all three of us, Glenn, the oldest, Norma, and me. She delivered 300 that I know of, but she delivered more after that."

Sabra also remembered well that Rowena kept vigil over the Buxton community's health and raised a fine group of boys. She became mother to husband Dave's first son, William, and her own three sons, Dave, Thomas D., and Guy. Another cousin, Amasa J. Quidley, was taken into the group when his parents died at an early age. Of these five boys, three would become keepers, two at Hatteras, William and Amasa J. Quidley. Thomas D. was a substitute for Keeper Gillikin at the turn of the twentieth century at Hatteras; although it was not a formal federal appointment for "T.D." Quidley at Cape Hatteras, he went on to a full and respected career as lighthouse keeper for the U.S. Lighthouse Service.

"There were no doctors around then," Sabra continued speaking of Rovena. "She tended my mother when she was sick and she'd stay overnight. Mama had TB [tuberculosis] and somebody had to be right with her. She was like a local doctor. She was a midwife, but anyone who had complaints, she tended to. She made up her own potions. She'd give them [patients] a dose of this or that, I'm not sure that would be called medical, but she did the best she could. No one ever paid her that I know of. They just did a lot of work for each other around here then. It wasn't like it is now. People helped you, if you had anything [to be done] they'd help you. People that weren't her family might have paid her a little something, but she had a big family around here then. Grandma Rovene had her own house, down on the shore, back of the school [where the present Cape Hatteras School is located]. She had all kinds of animals like cows. I don't know exactly what she is to me. But we all called her 'Grandma' and she seemed to like it. I'll tell you that she was good to the people."

Tuberculosis was rampant in the country during the 1920s and 30s. This disease claimed several Quidley family members including their Grandmother Sabrah, Mother Izetta, and brother, Glenn.

Sabra, Norma's younger sister by fifteen months, was named for her grandmother, Sabrah (Jennette) Quidley, William E. Quidley's first wife. "Grandmother Sabrah was thirty-five when she died and Mother Izetta was thirty-six.

"We went out to the lighthouse a lot, sometimes staying a week at a time. We use to have some BIG Easter egg hunts out there in the yard at the lighthouse. The families at the lighthouse would get together." Sabra spoke with a distinct Hatteras Island accent. "We didn't decorate the Easter eggs. They were the candy ones that were made of sugar and they'd hide them around the lighthouse yard. I remember one time I found the most - thirteen! And I probably ate them all!

"And at Christmas," Sabra added, "there weren't many trees in the homes then. The Methodist had a big tree and we

Dressed for church, Norma (Gray) Rhoden, about ten years old, sat for this picture in her backyard at the family home in Buxton. Circa 1929
Photo courtesy Connie (Rhoden) Manley

"This is my mother Izetta Quidley (1898-1934) who married Christopher Columbus Gray (1886-1952). Izetta's parents were Grandpa Bill and Grandma Sabrah. They had Oretha, Rogers, Norman, Esther, and Izetta," Sabra (Gray) Jennette commented upon this picture of her parents. Christopher Columbus "Kit" Gray worked on LV #80 called Relief, *which served off Diamond Shoals from 1927-31 when the lightship regularly stationed there went into port for repairs. Izetta died in 1934 of tuberculosis, a nemesis of many Hatteras Island families.*
Photo courtesy Sabra (Gray) Jennette

got one present maybe. They'd give a bag of candy and oranges, all mixed together, with one apple and two oranges. They made these up at Rany's [Jennette] uncle's store. His Aunt Odessa's husband, we called it 'Mr. Charlie's store,' had a store and they'd gather there to make the Christmas bags. We'd hang our stockings and get raisins and maybe a little something. You didn't get a lot of gifts then."

"Uncle Unaka [Jennette] and Grandpa Bill [Quidley] and Uncle John [E. Midgette] were all there when I used to go visit," Sabra also remembered. "And Mr. James Casey, Edna's father, was there also. Edna's a 'bird.'" This comment brought a big laugh from her and daughter Jackie who was with her mother while she reminisced.

"She'd be proud of that," Jackie chuckled, referring to her mother's calling Edna a "bird."

Sabra continued, "I remember one time Edna cut my hair out there [at the lighthouse] in a small room in the double keepers house. She stood me up on a chair and cut my hair and I vomited." Sabra and Jackie exchanged glances and then laughed at the image.

"How many kids were there at one time at the lighthouse?" Sabra repeated the question I posed to her. "Well, there were all Unaka's kids, Rany, Almy, Vivian, Myrtle, Olive, but Dorcus and Ramona, I don't think they were old enough to be there with us. Olive and Melita [Harris- John Midgette's daughter] were same the age and they played together. There were others like Ronald and Clifton. The children had scooters and all those walks out there and we used them! We played croquet out in Unaka's yard where they had all that stuff for us young'uns. We loved the scooters, you know, you put one foot on it and pushed along with the other.

"We went down to go swimming and play down on the beach. There was always a crowd of us children together, some older than others, so we were allowed to go down by ourselves. Not everyone could swim, and I still can't. We were always surrounded by water but I never learned to swim. And I'm scared to death of it! I wasn't scared of it when I was young, I guess I didn't know any better, not knowing the danger. We didn't get far in the surf, we'd just wade. We had to make up our own games because we didn't buy them like they do now."

Sabra reminisced about her childhood and visits to the Cape Hatteras Lighthouse. "We got plenty of castor oil," Sabra chuckled and then drew up her face in disapproval. "They'd give it to you in the spring, I think it was, sort of like spring cleaning! And I remember the first dip of snuff I had was out there at the lighthouse. And it was the last dip. I didn't have the sense not to take it. Our folks were going out someplace and Norma and Vivian and myself, we were going to take a dip of snuff while they were gone. That was at Leonora's place [double keepers quarters]. We all got down over a coal bucket because we thought we were going to be sick," Sabra confessed with a mischievous smile. "When we

Christopher C. Gray joined the Navy in 1905 as a Water Tender and earned promotion to Chief Water Tender. His granddaughter, Connie Rhoden Manley, discovered these facts from her grandfather's records, which state that he left the Navy with fourteen years of service in November 1919. He then continued a career in the U.S. Lighthouse Service in 1923 on the tender Maple and on lightship duty. Circa 1916
Photo courtesy Sabra (Gray) Jennette

Leonora Williams married Bill Quidley after his first wife, Sabrah, died in 1912. Leonora helped to raise Bill's five children as her own. "They [Bill and Leonora] got along so good together," granddaughter, Norma (Gray) Rhoden commented of someone she loved as her grandmother. "She called him 'Mr. Bill' every time she spoke to him."
Photo courtesy Sabra (Gray) Jennette

said it was time to take our dip, they all slapped theirs in my mouth along with mine. And that's why I didn't forget it! It was the dry kind - Leonora's snuff we went into. I reckon she found out what we'd done, as sick as I was! That was a dirty trick cause that stuff was awful!" Jackie and Sabra both convulsed with laughter.

"When we were at the lighthouse, Grandpa Bill never took me out of the group to spend time with me separately. They [keepers] didn't have time," Sabra said matter-of-factly, yet with understanding. "He was working."

While Sabra's and Norma's father, Kit Gray, was away, he would make things while on the lightship, like the wooden boat with incredible detail and a wooden life preserver Sabra and daughter Jackie cherish. "He loved to do stuff like that," Sabra stated. The life ring is painted "Relief." Sabra's Pop also worked on tenders that serviced the lightships.

Sabra continued, "I remember one time my mother made a pineapple cake and sent to Pop while he was on the lightship. She said she'd never do that again," Sabra laughed softly. "It was nothing but crumbs when he got it. She didn't know better, I don't think. She was real young when she got married I think. About fifteen. She had to learn to do things like to bake a cake because she was the oldest when her mother died. They had to live different lives, you know. Girls learned to do things at an earlier age back then."

Sabra and Norma realized what their Grandpa Bill and Mother Izetta had learned as they also had lost their mothers at an early age. "We didn't have to do some of those things like that until we were about fifteen. We always had a girl hired to help with things like cooking when we were younger. I was fourteen when Mom died. When I was fifteen, Norma and I took turns doing cooking and cleaning and such," Sabra told.

Sabra and Norma were born in a home by Sonny's Motor Court. The closest neighbor was up by the Fish House Restaurant. "And then Frisco was the closest down that way," Sabra continued her description. "We were off to ourselves. I went to the school in Buxton. We walked...had to."

Jackie explained, "The old school used to be at the end of Light Plant Road. Where there's a highway state shed now is where the old school was. Children from as far as Kinnakeet [Avon] came to this school."

Sabra explained, "When a bus was around, we were faced with maybe having to go to 'Hat'tres,' and that was probably when the school burned down, but when the time came, I wasn't forced to go. I've always loved being close to home. I went for a few days in the eleventh grade, and that's all the grades they had then, but I was sick, so I dropped out."

Sabra and Norma married and raised children of their own but have stayed close to Hatteras Island where they both live today as octogenarians. Since the island has become a favorite destination for visitors from all around the nation, Sabra and Norma stick close to home. "Crowds are not for me," Sabra explained. "I haven't even been to church in many years."

And what would Izetta say about Sabra not going out? "She probably wouldn't either," Sabra said with complete seriousness and then smiled. She looked at pictures of Grandpa Bill and his grandchildren, including her daughters Jackie and Linda. "He has some new great-great-great grandchildren now. Mama was crazy about babies. I wonder what it'd be like to have her- and him- around to enjoy their grandchildren? Angie (Caudill) Draper is the great-great granddaughter of William E. Quidley. And she has a two-year-old, David Clay Draper, and a three-month old, Margaret Gayle Draper who are his great-great-great grandchildren."

Norma and Sabra quickly stepped back in time to allow a glimpse of life at Cape Hatteras and their island neighbors during the early part of the twentieth century. It was not the lonely outpost that many make it out to be while keepers tended a flame atop the spiral giant.

"When all of us kids were there at night," Norma remembered, "and we piled together at Uncle Unaka's, Almy would say 'Good night' to everyone. But he didn't say it just once. He'd say, "Good night, Myrtle, good night, Vivian, good night, Rany, good night, Norma...until he'd said everyone's name. He was so sweet."

Living on government property where stringent rules were followed had its benefits because the coal bin was always full, abundant fish was available even during the Depression, and children were within the protection of their families. Once chores and homework were completed, the kids were allowed to explore at will, and as Norma succinctly expressed, "It was the best place for a child to grow up."

"This is the three of us, Norma, Glenn, and myself," Sabra smiled as she looked at this picture. "Isn't that a sight?!" Sabra asked incredulously. "That suit of clothes [Glenn has on] is something! Leonora made everything we had, everything we wore from our underwear on up." Cape Hatteras Keeper Bill Quidley's grandchildren were frequent visitors to the lighthouse. Circa 1928
Photo courtesy Sabra (Gray) Jennette

A passel of keepers' children are in this picture in front of the double keepers quarters, and this is just part of the group of kids at the Cape Hatteras Lighthouse around 1930. They were not only playmates but also "family." Back row, left to right: Myrtle (Jennette) Gibbs, (Keeper Unaka Jennette's daughter; Sabra (Gray) Jennette, Norma's sister; Norma (Gray) Rhoden, Keeper Quidley's granddaughter. Second row, left to right: Melita (Midgett) Harris, Keeper John E. Midgette's daughter; Olive (Jennette) Peek, Myrtle's sister. Front row: Dorcas (Jennette) Anderson, Myrtle and Olive's sister; Ronald Evans Midgette, Melita's brother; Roger Reid Farrow, Keeper Bill Quidley's grandson.
Photo courtesy Dorcas (Jennette) Anderson

Quotes and stories are from interviews with granddaughters Norma (Gray) Rhoden and Sabra (Gray) Jennette September 30, 2000, and subsequent phone conversations and visits. Thanks go to Connie (Rhoden) Manley, Sabra (Gray) Jennette, and Jackie Jennette for helping proof this story.

Details are taken from information gathered by Jackie Jennette, complemented by a letter dated October 2, 2000, by Connie (Rhoden) Manley, great-granddaughters of William E. Quidley, and a phone interview September 19, 2000 and several subsequent interviews during January 2001. The Quidley cemetery from which Jackie Jennette recorded information is located behind the Catholic Church in Buxton. Connie noted, "Everyone is there, Grandpa Bill, Grandma Sabrah, Grandma Rovena, Glenn, Kit, Izetta- all the children. All are there except for Leonora. It is a tiny cemetery and she is with her family."

Quidley Family Legacy

Jackie Jennette, Sabra (Gray) Jennette's daughter, and Connie Manley, Norma (Gray) Rhoden's daughter, add further depth to our knowledge of their great-grandfather, Keeper William Quidley. From information gathered from cemetery tombstones and other family-archived information, Jackie and Connie have recorded that their great-grandfather Bill married Sabrah (Jennette) Quidley and together they had three daughters and two sons:

William E. Quidley (8 July 1874-24 May 1961) married 13 June 1897 Sabrah (Jennette) Quidley (18 June 1877-13 August 1912)

Children of William E. Quidley and Sabrah:

Izetta Lee (Quidley) Gray (6 April 1898-2 December 1934)

Oreatha (Quidley) Midgett (17 June 1901-27 September 1932)

Rogers Quidley (16 August 1903-5 December 1926)

Norman Quidley (2 July 1906-14 February 1925)

Esther (Quidley) Farrow (8 February 1908-31 July 1977)

Keeper Quidley's daughter, Izetta, married Christopher C. "Kit" Gray (12 April 1886-5 February 1952) and had three children:

Glenn Gray (23 December 1914-1 March 1950) who married Mary Bell Farrow and had six children: Jerry, Debbie, Verna, Izetta, Glenn, and Judy.

Norma (Gray) Rhoden (25 February 1919) who married Oliver Charles Rhoden. Norma's daughter Connie (Rhoden) Manley had one son, Christopher E. Cannon.

Sabra (Gray) Jennette (1920) married Harry L. Jennette. Sabra's daughters are Jacqueline "Jackie" Jennette and Linda (Jennette) Caudill.

After Keeper Quidley's wife Sabrah died in 1912, leaving him with five young children, he married Leonora Williams (4 August 1892-1983). They had no children, but Leonora raised William's children as her own.

Connie further shared information on her Grandfather Christopher C. Gray working career. From documents she possesses, he joined the Navy in 1905 as a Water Tender and earned promotion to Chief Water Tender. Kit Gray left the Navy with fourteen years of service in November 1919. He served part of this time in a special Naval fleet in which all ships were painted white around 1907. The ships and crews traveled extensively under President Teddy Roosevelt's directive, and prominently displayed the American flag to the world as a symbol of pride and power. Gray earned an honorable discharge but sometime during his service he suffered an injury that would haunt him the rest of his life.

A card from the U.S. Department of Commerce and U.S. Lighthouse Service documents that Gray served on the tender *Maple* in 1923, which serviced the lighthouses of the fifth district, including Cape Hatteras. By 1927 he was serving on LV #80 *Relief* Lightship as a fireman. The *Relief* switched off with other lightships in Virginia and North Carolina, putting Gray off of Diamond Shoals while his wife and children stayed with relatives at the lighthouse.

A letter from a supervisor reported that Gray was incapable of doing lightship duty due to his health. An injury left him with neural damage, later diagnosed as Bulbar's Palsy, which caused Gray to suffer mini-facial strokes and weakness in the hands. Under what must have been stressful conditions, he left the lightship and the Lighthouse Service around 1932.

Though she expressed great respect for her great-grandmother Sabrah, Connie has vivid memories of Leonora, William's second wife, who married Keeper Quidley when she was thirty years old, about nineteen years younger than her husband. "She [Leonora] was an excellent seamstress and did dressmaking for many years. She raised William E. Quidley's five children," Connie went on to say, indicating her source of great respect.

"Leonora was his wife through all the years he was a Lighthouse Keeper. Her parents were Rev. George Williams and Clara Bonner Williams. Her father was a Methodist minister and her grandparents were Mr. and Mrs. Merchant Williams."

Connie noted humbly, "I am so proud to be a small part of all this history. Just seeing the Lighthouse when we come home, makes me so proud of all my relatives who gave so much time to the Lighthouse. Not just Grandpa Bill, but all of them. I am so please that they will all be remembered.

"When I was a small child we would visit Grandpa Bill and Leonora many nights. I can remember sitting there listening to the grownups telling and retelling stories. When I had my son Christopher, I wanted him to be a part of my grandparents and great-grandfather. Although he was very young when Grandpa Bill died, Chris was taken to see him and was held by him on many visits. And though he can not say he really remembers him, he has in his heart the knowledge that he was and still is a part of Grandpa Bill. And the many stories and photos we have, Chris has come to be proud of his great-great-grandfather. Chris, too, is very excited about this Lighthouse ceremony. And he is proud to be a descendant of a Lighthouse Keeper," Connie closed.

Norma (Gray) Rhoden is part of a family grouping of pictures. There are three generations represented: Norma and Sabra are grandchildren, Connie is a great-grandchild, and Chris is a great-great-grandchild of Cape Hatteras Keeper William E. Quidley.
Photo courtesy Connie (Rhoden) Manley

Kit Gray's daughter, Sabra, holds a wooden life preserver that he carved and painted "Relief," the name of the lightship on which he served for four years [1927-31]. "He loved to do stuff like that," Sabra stated. Her Pop also served on the tender Maple in 1923.
Photo by Jackie Jennette

Connie (Rhoden) Manley's grandfather was a U.S. Lighthouse Service employee on lightships for many years. Part of his duty was off Diamond Shoals during late 1920s. Of this picture, Connie said, "I'm holding my favorite picture of Grandpa Bill, my great-grandfather. He was always ready to have his picture taken by my father, Oliver C. Rhoden."
Photo courtesy Christopher Cannon

While Sabra's and Norma's father, Christopher Columbus "Kit" Gray, was away, he would make carvings while on the lightship, like the wooden boat with incredible detail that his granddaughter Jackie Jennette holds.
Photo by Sabra (Gray) Jennette

Christopher Cannon was named for his great-grandfather, Christopher "Kit" Gray. Chris has several artifacts that Kit collected during his Navy and U.S. Lighthouse careers. A brass ship's bell, a brass telescope, brass locks, and a shot mold are among the items he treasures from his great-grandfather's lightship service years during the early 1900s. Chris is the great-great-grandson of Keeper William E. Quidley.
Photo courtesy
Connie (Rhoden) Manley

A Large and Lively Lighthouse Dynasty

Simpson Family of Keepers

By Sandra MacLean Clunies

A large and lively lighthouse keeper dynasty began with Amasa W. Simpson, Sr. who was born in 1800. He first married Barbara Ballance, and had four children prior to her death in on 25 April 1842:

- Henry C. Simpson (1833-?)
- Merchant Simpson (1835-1860)
- Virginia Simpson (1837-?)
- Sarah M. Simpson (1840-1895)

As he was left to care for several small children, it is not surprising that Amasa soon married again. Exactly three months after Barbara's death, on 25 July 1842, he wed Parmelia Dailey (1818-1885) and they had nine children, five of whom were deeply involved with Cape Hatteras Lighthouse:

- Amasa W. Simpson, Jr. (a twin b. 1844, and died young
- **Alpheus W. Simpson**, keeper, (1844-1905), who
    married Parley (Jennett) Jennett, daughter of keeper **Zion B. Jennett**, widow of keeper **Benjamin C. Jennett**, and mother of keeper **John B. Jennett**.
- Rowena Simpson, b. 1845, who married George T. Willis and were parents of keeper **Alpheus B. Willis**.
- John C. Simpson (1846-1910) who married Amelia Parker Stowe
- Desdamona Simpson (1847-?) who married George Onslow
- Sunny A. Simpson (1848-1860)
- Sabra E. Simpson (1852-?) who married keeper **Tilman F. Smith**
- **Amasa Jones Simpson**, keeper, (1856-1919) who married Eulalia Jennett, daughter of keeper **Benjamin C. Jennett**
- **Fabius E. Simpson**, keeper, (1858-?)

The handwritten lighthouse registers, still preserved on microfilm at the National Archives, record that the first of this family to serve as keeper at Cape Hatteras was young **Alpheus W. Simpson**, who served two years from 1866-1868 as primary keeper at an annual salary of $600, later increased to $820. Alpheus had distinguished himself with Union military service as a Sergeant in the 1st NC Infantry during the Civil War, when the majority of Hatteras Island men joined the Union forces rather than the Confederate. This was understandable since the federal troops had occupied the coastal area since early in the war. After the war ended, and for many years thereafter, only those men with documented loyalty to the federal government were appointed to federal positions such as lighthouse keepers and postmasters.

Patriarch **Amasa W. Simpson, Sr.** was appointed an assistant keeper 29 March 1869 at a salary of $400, but the position was listed as vacated on 13 April, as the register notes he "declined" the permanent job. That he was then nearly seventy years old may be the reason, for the tasks at the lighthouse were strenuous. The principal keeper at that time was **Benjamin C. Jennett**, whose daughter Eulalia was born on 18 March 1869, just days before Amasa W. Simpson's appointment. Twenty-one years later, in 1890, Eulalia would marry Amasa W.'s son **Amasa Jones Simpson**.

In 1873, **Alpheus W. Simpson** was returned to Cape Hatteras as an assistant keeper and served this time until 1876. Records show that he also served at many other lighthouse stations during his lifetime. He was elected to a term in the North Carolina State Legislature in 1880 and also served as a Justice of the Peace and a U.S. Commissioner in Dare County.

Tilman F. Smith, who had married into the family, to Sabra Simpson, about 1877, was named first assistant keeper at Cape Hatteras in May 1881, and was promoted to primary keeper in January 1887 where he served for ten years. In 1883, Amasa Jones Simpson, brother-in-law to Keeper Smith, was named third assistant keeper at Cape Hatteras, a position that included care of the beacon light. In 1884, Amasa J. was transferred to another station and replaced by his younger brother **Fabius E. Simpson** as third assistant at Cape Hatteras on 9 June 1884. Fabius served one year at this assignment, and was then transferred to another station.

Alpheus W. Simpson was a Sergeant in the Union Army during the Civil War and the loyalty to the government enabled him to be a keeper, no Confederates could hold Federal appointments to post offices or lighthouses after the war. This sketch, from an 1861 Harper's Weekly, shows Union troops camped around the base of the 1803 tower at Cape Hatteras. Drawing courtesy Outer Banks History Center

J. B. Jennette

Over at the nearby Hatteras Inlet screwpile lighthouse, Amasa J. served as primary keeper 1888-1899, where his wife **Eulalia Jennett Simpson** was named an official assistant 1894-1897, when she was replaced by her brother, **John B. Jennett**, who served 1897-1899 and returned as primary keeper at the Inlet in 1903.

Further entwining these lighthouse families were the marriages of the widowed mother of Eulalia Jennett Simpson and John B. Jennett. She was born Parley Jennett in 1845, daughter of Cape Hatteras assistant keeper of 1870 **Zion B. Jennett** and she had married **Benjamin C. Jennett**, primary keeper 1868-1871, himself the son of former keeper **Joseph C. Jennett**. Benjamin Jennett died in 1874 at the age of twenty-eight, leaving widow Parley with two surviving young children, Eulalia and John. She remarried in 1876 to Alpheus W. Simpson, with whom she had two more children.

During this decade when brother-in-law Tilman Smith was primary keeper at Cape Hatteras, Fabius E. Simpson returned as first assistant keeper in 1891 and served there for nine years until 1900, when he requested a transfer to Bodie Island Lighthouse. In 1894, Alpheus W. Simpson returned for a brief tour of duty as an assistant keeper, but records show he was in poor health at this time, and was replaced after two months.

A. B. Willis

In 1906, Fabius E. Simpson came back to Cape Hatteras as primary keeper, where his nephew **Alpheus B. Willis** had been serving as an assistant keeper since 1905. While the records of the end of Fabius' service do not remain, he served until 1919, when Unaka Jennette was appointed and became the last keeper at Cape Hatteras.

Under the Act of 1890, Alpheus W. Simpson applied for a Civil War Pension and was awarded one in September, 1891 for $12 per month. The pension was challenged by two political adversaries of Simpson including **Wallace R. Jennett,** who had served with Alpheus at the Cape Hatteras Lighthouse in earlier years, and was then postmaster at Buxton.

Their opposing political views were strongly held - Alpheus Simpson was a dedicated Democrat and Wallace Jennett was a very vocal Republican. Jennett's son-in-law, **Ephraim H. Riggs,** who was also a Cape Hatteras assistant keeper 1889-1892, had defeated Alpheus in a State Legislature election back in 1882, and their political differences damaged their personal and professional relationships. A volley of letters to Washington, D.C. in 1893 resulted in Simpson's pension being temporarily suspended and then reduced to $8.00 per month from 1894. For the next several years, he protested the reduction with requests for reinstatement, and appeals, and many fellow lighthouse keepers submitted testimony both for and against his case, including:

Christopher C. Miller, then a Justice of the Peace in Dare County
Miles F. Whedbee
Sanders B. Smith,
James W. Gillikin
nephew Alpheus B. Willis
William G. Rollinson
and his brothers, Amasa J. and Fabius E. Simpson

These reports and letters, still on file at the National Archives in Washington, D.C., preserve the memories, the passionate politics, and the signatures of these keepers.

Even before the pension was awarded, Alpheus had suffered poor health, according to many witnesses. He was a tall and slender man, reported as 6'2" and 170 pounds during a physical examination. A letter from Benjamin B. Dailey, keeper of the Cape Hatteras Life Saving Station in

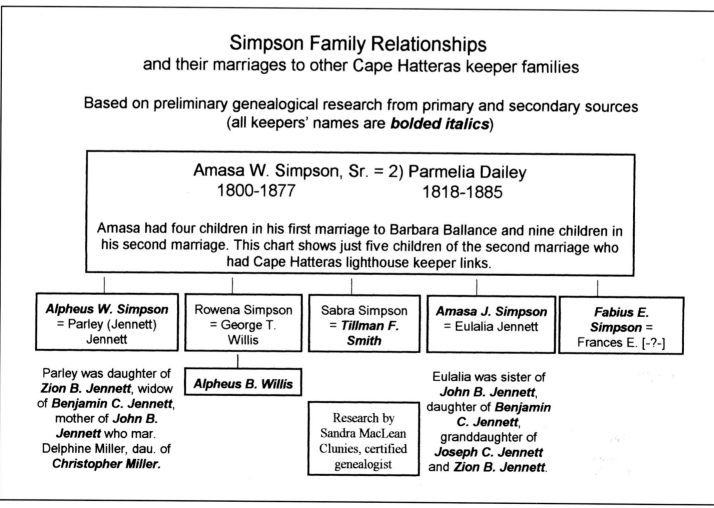

Simpson Family Relationships
and their marriages to other Cape Hatteras keeper families

Based on preliminary genealogical research from primary and secondary sources
(all keepers' names are **bolded italics**)

Amasa W. Simpson, Sr. = 2) Parmelia Dailey
1800-1877   1818-1885

Amasa had four children in his first marriage to Barbara Ballance and nine children in his second marriage. This chart shows just five children of the second marriage who had Cape Hatteras lighthouse keeper links.

Alpheus W. Simpson = Parley (Jennett) Jennett

Rowena Simpson = George T. Willis
  — **Alpheus B. Willis**

Sabra Simpson = **Tillman F. Smith**

Amasa J. Simpson = Eulalia Jennett

Fabius E. Simpson = Frances E. [-?-]

Parley was daughter of **Zion B. Jennett**, widow of **Benjamin C. Jennett**, mother of **John B. Jennett** who mar. Delphine Miller, dau. of **Christopher Miller.**

Eulalia was sister of **John B. Jennett**, daughter of **Benjamin C. Jennett**, granddaughter of **Joseph C. Jennett** and **Zion B. Jennett**.

Research by Sandra MacLean Clunies, certified genealogist

1890, reported that he had "hired Mr. Simpson to cook for me and my crew of six men and in less than three weeks he broke down under the work and had to be carted home. I do not think that he is able to perform any ordinary labor..." Justice of the Peace A.G.B. Salter witnessed this affidavit, and had himself been an assistant keeper at Cape Hatteras lighthouse in 1888.

Amasa J. Simpson's letter of 19 June 1893, on behalf of his older brother, reported that Alpheus was indigent and in poor health, when describing a period over the holidays of 1891 when he hired Alpheus to substitute for him as a keeper:

"I am keeper of Hatteras Inlet Screwpile Light House. It is located ... five miles from any land and ten miles from Buxton... I made a trip to Rocky Mount and Washington, N.C. to obtain medical treatment ... I am his brother and gave him the job on account of the work being easy for him to do, and he needed the money

I paid him one dollar per day from the 20th of Dec 1891 to Jany 5th 1892. I have many years been assisting him being physically unable many times to provide necessary family supplies..."

Amasa J. Simpson

James W. Gillikin, then keeper at Cape Lookout, and a prior Cape Hatteras keeper, gave a deposition on 7 Sep 1903 that provides insight into perceived hazards of lighthouse duties at that time:

"..On the 1st of Jan 1897 he assumed charge of the Cape Hatteras lighthouse and the said Alpheus W. Simpson was one of the Ass't Keepers of that station and he remained there ... until... May 1899 when he was promoted + transferred keeper of North River Light House...

That the rule + custom of keeping Cape Hatteras L. House was that one keeper had to watch the light half of two nights out of three nights; that the dimensions of said light are five inches in diameter and eight inches in height and of 460 candle power, and the affiant believes from self experiences that his eyesight is very much injured by watching these very powerful lights..."

As housing for keepers was often included at the station to which they were assigned, lighthouse keepers sometimes did not own personal real estate, as was the case with Alpheus Simpson. In his testimony of 1904, just a year prior to his death, he claimed he did not "own a penny's value of property" and had no income other than the $8 monthly pension and relied on the kindness of friends and family for support. Former Cape Hatteras keepers Alpheus B. Willis and William G. Rollinson both testified that they "have contributed to his relief." The Lighthouse Service had not instituted any pension system for former employees at that time.

After Alpheus' death in 1905, his widow Parley applied for a continuance of the small pension, which she was granted and received until her death in 1926, when she was living with her son John B. Jennette in New Bern.

The Simpson brothers, their brother-in-law, nephew, and other relatives served at various times as keepers at the Cape Hatteras Lighthouse as well as other light stations. They worked long hours for low wages, and some experienced political problems, poor health, and financial distress. However, it was a large family group whose members always supported one another, and they served the Hatteras community as lighthouse keepers for generations.

These three Simpson brothers served as keepers over a period of time extending more than a half century from 1868 to 1919.

Keepers' names are in bold the first time they appear in the text.

He Lit the Hatteras Beacon for the Last Time
Tilman F. Smith

Keeper Tilman F. Smith, born in 1852, was an assistant keeper from 1878-1887 and primary keeper 1887-1897, making him, with nineteen consecutive years, the second-longest keeper at the light station During Smith's tenure at Cape Hatteras, he served with over a dozen other men. Around 1877, he married Sabra Simpson who was the sister of three of Smith's fellow keepers. All three of these assistants had large families, but Tilman and Sabra had no children themselves.

Keeper Tilman F. Smith sent a letter to the Fifth District Inspector, informing him of the demise of the Hatteras Beacon at Cape Point. Because the light was critical to coasting vessels and local fishermen, Smith wanted to assure the U.S. Lighthouse Service that the light was still functioning as a post lantern.

Dec 1, 1898
Comdr. B.P. Lamberton, U.S.N.
L.H. Inspector, 5th District
Baltimore, Md.
Sir:

The beach had cut away from the Beacon so that the whole structure was in the sea at high water with a dead smooth sea. On the 25th of November I light [sic] the lamp on the pole, and on the 28th, I took the lens and other property except the tank and storm panes out of the beacon. The sea got rough and has been high ever since with only a nominal high wind so I cannot get them out until it gets smooth. Anything like an ordinary gale will demolish the structure. The Light on the pole is by far superior to the light in the Beacon - it is a larger and brighter light and is higher - and out of the way of the spray - but it takes two men to hoist it up.
Very respectfully,
Tilman F. Smith
T.F. Smith, Keeper
I hope this meets with your approval

What is enigmatic about this event is that Keeper Smith is recorded to have transferred to Ocracoke Light Station January 1, 1898, months before the date of this letter. As long-time keeper at Cape Hatteras, had Smith returned to help with the final closing of the Hatteras Beacon and the re-establishment of the light on a pole nearby? In 1898, the trip from Ocracoke to Cape Point was several hours by sailboat. If the letter had been misdated as 1898 instead of 1893, the pieces fit; however, the other letters in the same volume are also dated 1898.

Source: RG26, E24 Letters Received by the Lighthouse Board - 5th District, Vol. 1173, Box 197, p. 256, National Archives, Washington, D.C.

Hatteras Beacon Light
(Lost Light- established 1855)

This tough little light known as the Hatteras Beacon Light was established in 1855 on Cape Point, located about one and one-half miles to the south of the Cape Hatteras Light Station. The beacon light guided coasting (local boats) until around 1906. It marked the turning point on a route from the Atlantic Ocean to the Pamlico Sound through a channel that served as a shortcut from Diamond Shoals. Its sixth order Fresnel lens was tended by the third assistant keeper under the supervision of the principal keeper at the primary light station at Cape Hatteras, though the Beacon's keeper was required to provide his own housing.

The beacon light was a wooden frame building that was painted red, and it exhibited a fixed white light twenty-five feet above mean high water. In the beacon light's half-century of service it was rebuilt and moved in 1857 due to erosion, moved 500 feet inland in 1858, darkened by Confederates in 1861, discontinued in 1879 due to erosion, re-established in 1883, and then moved another 200 feet inland in 1890. On November 24, 1898, Keeper Tilman Smith lit the Hatteras Beacon for the last time and moved the light to a post nearby the next day because erosion untiringly dogged it. The post light was discontinued sometime around 1906, and the third assistant keeper's position ended at the Cape Hatteras Light Station.

Source: North Carolina Lights *by Cheryl Shelton-Roberts and Bruce Roberts 2000*

TIMELINE
TILMAN F. SMITH (1852-?)
ASSISTANT KEEPER 1878-1887
PRINCIPAL KEEPER 1887-1897

The Cape Hatteras "Beacon Light" was photographed in 1893 by Henry Bamber, the official U.S. Lighthouse Service photographer, on a trip to the Outer Banks. His two views of the Beacon Light may be the only surviving photographs of this light located at Cape Point. Built in 1855, it endured the full force of storms sweeping in off the Atlantic, demanding that the light be moved a little further away from the shoreline several times. It was lit for the last time in November 1898 and a light was displayed on a pole nearby. The light guided coasting vessels, or local travelers and fishermen, around Cape Point. Photo courtesy Outer Banks History Center

Recognition At Last

Thomas Levi Wallace

Born on Hatteras Island, Wallace followed in the footsteps of many who had gone before him and became an able seaman, surfman, and lighthouse keeper.

By Agnes (Wallace) Haddaway and Marie (Wallace) Mulvaney

By Agnes (Wallace) Haddaway

Agnes Wallace Haddaway is proud of her father's lighthouse keeper career. So much in fact, it urged her to write to a Hatteras Island publication to express her disappointment that any information on her father's duty at the Cape Hatteras Lighthouse and other lighthouse career records cannot be found.

Like many keepers, Wallace earned experience as a seaman and surfman aboard light vessels and served at various light stations. Records indicate that he joined the U.S. Coast Guard in 1919 and later entered the U.S. Lighthouse Service in 1928, working at various lighthouses including Cape Hatteras, Hog Island, and Sharps Island. In 1959 he tended the Bloody Point Lighthouse in Claiborne and retired in 1960 after more than thirty-eight years with the U.S. Lighthouse Service. Wallace was awarded the Gallatin Award for his outstanding work. There are two other factors that make Thomas Wallace a unique keeper: according to available records, he was the only Cape Hatteras keeper to have been born in the twentieth century on 18 March 1900; and he was the last keeper to be appointed to Cape Hatteras in 1931 when he joined Primary Keeper Unaka Jennette and Assistant Keeper William E. Quidley.

Agnes wrote the *Island Breeze* and stated, "I was given a copy of the special edition of the paper, '*Historic Journey*,' by a relative who visited last autumn, and I found Daniel Couch's article, 'Islanders Share Their Lighthouse Memories' very interesting and enjoyable.

"...The names Jennette, Gray, Barnett, and Midgette are all familiar to me. Though I didn't know any of them, they were always in the stories that my parents related to us of their life 'down home' in Buxton.

"The thing that puzzles me is why my father is never mentioned in stories about the history of the lighthouse."

This situation is changing because caring family members submitted information and photographs on the Wallace family.

Agnes was born in the double keepers quarters October 29, 1932. Thomas Wallace was an area native who became assistant keeper at Cape Hatteras in 1931, serving with Primary Keeper Unaka Jennette. A favorite memory for Agnes is when she talked with Keeper Jennette's son, Rany, in 1992. Rany was then serving as park ranger, greeting visitors and telling stories of life on a light station. Agnes was thrilled to be standing on the step of her birthplace while Rany told her that he remembered when she had been born.

Her brother and sisters, Maurice, Marie, and Melvina, also lived at the double keepers quarters at Cape Hatteras.

Agnes journaled, "Dad was transferred from there in 1933 to the lighthouse on Hog Island, off the Virginia coast, since consumed by the ocean, and from there to Sharps Island, off the tip of Tilghman Island in the Chesapeake Bay in 1937. This is how I came to be a Marylander instead of a North Carolinian."

Agnes continued in her correspondence, "My memories of Dad and Mom are that they were the best of parents who always put the needs of their children ahead of their own, as all good parents do. Sunday School and Church were important parts of my life, as well as family games, story telling and outings.

> *According to available records, Wallace was the only Cape Hatteras keeper to have been born in the twentieth century on 18 March 1900, and he was the last keeper to be appointed to Cape Hatteras in 1931, serving with Primary Keeper Unaka Jennette and Assistant Keeper William E. Quidley.*

"In summer, when Dad came home with the boat, Mom would fix a fried chicken dinner, and we would go in the boat to a sand beach for a picnic, crabbing, and swimming.

"When he was 'on leave' he and Mom worked together at whatever needed to be done while he usually whistled one of their favorite hymns. It never seemed unusual to find him washing windows, cooking, or scrubbing floors as well as cutting grass, raking the yard, or gardening.

"Dad was a big man- over six feet tall. He had a great sense of humor, and usually a joke or a funny story to tell. Sometimes his jokes were a little on the 'bold' side, which would cause Mom to exclaim, 'Oh, Dear!'

"Mom died in 1959 and Dad lived alone as long as he was able, and then he went into a nursing home where he died in 1987.

TIMELINE

THOMAS LEVI WALLACE (1900-1987)
ASSISTANT KEEPER 1931-1933:

President Roosevelt was elected by a landslide vote in 1932 to help lead the nation by putting economic recovery programs in motion. The Civilian Conservation Corps was one of these programs, setting up a camp at Cape Hatteras later in the 1930s to plant sea oats and build a protective line of dunes. During the 1930s, no matter how meager a keeper's pay, it helped to provide monetary stability and support his extended family during the Depression.

(Below) This picture is taken thirty-one years and eight children later (six survived). Their smiles represent their dedication to one another. "Dad was a big man- over six feet tall. He had a great sense of humor, and usually a joke or a funny story to tell. Sometimes his jokes were a little on the 'bold' side, which would cause Mom to exclaim, 'Oh, Dear!' daughter Agnes remarked. This photo was taken while Wallace was stationed on a Chesapeake Light in 1950.
Photo courtesy Agnes (Wallace) Haddaway

(Above) Celebrating their first anniversary are Thomas Levi Wallace and Lucy (Whidbee) Wallace. Married in May 1919, they had eight children between 1921 and 1939, two of which died in infancy. Photo courtesy Donna Schlag

"Although I have never been able to return for frequent visits as my siblings do, I still think of the lighthouse as 'My Lighthouse.' And, I think of all that I missed by not being able to grow up on the island in the midst of a large extended family of aunts, uncles, cousins, and maternal grandparents."

My Memories of Cape Hatteras
By Marie (Wallace) Mulvaney

"I was five or six years old when we moved to the Cape Hatteras Lighthouse. My mother and the children lived in Buxton while Dad had been at lights in Virginia and Maryland. They were offshore lights staffed by two or three men. Mr. Unaka Jennette was keeper at Cape Hatteras when we were there. He and his family lived in the keeper's house. We lived in one half of the assistant's house, and Mr. Bill Quidley and wife lived in the other half. Mr. Unaka and 'Miss Sudie' had children about the same age as the children in our family. Rany and Maurice paired up, Olive and I, and Dorcus and Melvina played together. Baby sister, Agnes, was born while we lived there in October 1932. I don't remember what the boys did for entertainment, but I know the girls spent many hours playing with 'paper dolls.' In those days, paper dolls came from catalogs. We cut out the pictures of people- men, women, and children, then we cut out furniture- tables, chairs, and beds, etc. We laid out rooms, folded furniture and people so as to have them in sitting positions. Since catalogs served as toilet paper in those days, girls naturally spent a good amount of time where the catalogs were stored- out behind the house. (Not very sanitary, I'm afraid.)

"Our family had a horse and cart and I remember my mother preparing a picnic, loading the children and food in the cart, and riding out towards the point [Cape Point] to picnic.

"My dad had chickens out beyond the pond behind the house. One chicken became a 'pet' to us, and before we left to go into Buxton, we carried corn out to the chickens and ran while they ate. Otherwise, that particular chicken tried to follow us to Buxton. I'm sure that chicken was our main source of meat at some point! My grandfather always had a garden and he kept us supplied with fresh veggies and my grandmother had two milk cows that supplied us with milk and butter. I remember helping my grandmother churn butter. I believe we only had fresh pork and beef when someone in the villages butchered.

*Keeper Thomas Levi Wallace earned experience as a seaman and surfman early in his maritime career in the U.S. Coast Guard, Later he served aboard light vessels and at various light stations including Cape Hatteras, Hog Island, and Sharp's Island. He retired in 1960 after more than thirty-eight years with the Lighthouse Service. Wallace was awarded the Gallatin Award for his outstanding work, the highest government award given a civilian employee. His big hands and sturdy frame were welcomed additions to any light station where the work was not only mentally demanding, but physically challenging as well.
Photo courtesy Agnes (Wallace) Haddaway*

*At left is Thomas Levi Wallace, and at right is a fellow unidentified sailor. Thomas was age nineteen in 1919. Records indicate that he joined the U.S. Coast Guard in 1919 as a seaman and surfman and later entered the U.S. Lighthouse Service in 1928
Photo courtesy Donna Schlag*

"This was before paved roads and very few people owned automobiles. Those that did had to deal with deep, soft sand in many areas. The road from Buxton to the lighthouse was nearer the ocean than the existing road and was tracks in soft sand. My dad bought his first car while we lived at the lighthouse and that was very exciting!

"My fondest memories are those of playing on the granite blocks at the base of the lighthouse. It seems we spent many hours playing out there. I didn't visit there from 1938 to 1965, but when I got at the base of the light, I knew I had 'come home,' and I have been there at every opportunity since then."

Marie also wrote a special piece on "Thomas Levi Wallace."

"His father, Thomas Wallace, came to the Outer Banks on a sailing vessel in the 1890s. He went to sea with his father at the age of twelve from a village in Massachusetts. He transferred from one sailing ship to another without ever going back home. He settled in Frisco, and became postmaster. He was a self-taught man apparently. He was reportedly very knowledgeable. His mother, Melvina Johnson Tolson, was a young widow with a daughter, Darcas, to care for. They married during the 1890s. My father, Thomas Levi Wallace, was born in March 1900, and was two years old when his father died. His mother married a third time to Jesse L. Foster, and he was the only father [Wallace knew] in the truest sense.

"Years later, they learned of a man, Albert Wallace, from Massachusetts who thought that he was Thomas's brother. Communication was much more difficult in those days, and he supposedly returned to Massachusetts before they could arrange a meeting. So, they never established contact with Dad's biological father's family.

Keeper Wallace's mother, Melvina, and his step-father, Jesse L. Foster, posed for this picture in Buxton. Marie wrote of the time that Keeper Wallace lost his father as a young lad. "My father, Thomas Levi Wallace, was born March 18, 1900, in Frisco, and was two years old when his [biological] father died. His mother, Melvina, married Jesse L. Foster and he was the only father [young Thomas knew] in the truest sense."
Photo courtesy Agnes (Wallace) Haddaway

Agnes (Wallace) Haddaway met Rany Brooks Jennette in 1992 at the double keepers quarters at Cape Hatteras, but it was not their first meeting. They had spent a year living beside one another while both of their fathers were keepers at Cape Hatteras in the early 1930s. Rany, in his National Park Service uniform, told Agnes that he remembered when she had been born sixty years earlier. Agnes's sister, Marie, remarked of that time. "Mr. Unaka and Miss Sudie[Jennette] had children about the same age as the children in our family. Rany and Maurice paired up, Olive and I, and Dorcus and Melvina played together. Baby sister Agnes was born while we lived there in October 1932."
Photo courtesy Agnes (Wallace) Haddaway

"He (Wallace) married Lucy Whidbee in May 1919. From June 1921 to December 1939, they had eight children, two died in infancy.

"When we left Cape Hatteras Lighthouse, mother and the children moved back to our house in Buxton and Dad went to the lighthouse on Hog Island, Virginia. He moved the family there in 1934. He transferred to Sharps Island Lighthouse in late 1937. Since that was a 'water light' in the Chesapeake Bay, the family lived in the little village of Sherwood. He remained as keeper on Sharps Island Lighthouse until its closing in 1951 when he was put in charge of the Tilghman Island Light in Maryland. In 1959, he became keeper of the Bloody Point Lighthouse, retiring in 1960, after more than 38 years with the Lighthouse Service and Coast Guard.

"Lucy died in March 1959 at age fifty-six. Her daughter, Melvina, died in July 1973 at the age forty-five, and son, Maurice, died in February 1981 at age fifty-nine. Thomas Levi died in April 1987 at age eighty-seven.

Keeper Wallace's daughter, Agnes, wrote, "I was fifteen years old in 1947 in Fairbanks, Maryland, and attending high school in my sophomore year in this picture. Today, when I think of family, I think of 'togetherness.' Unlike many families now, we had no outside commitments aside from school and church. Mom was always at home, and when Dad was on leave, they were always together. I constantly had family around for company and entertainment. My favorite memories are of picnics, boat rides, family get-togethers, games, especially dominoes, and snuggling up for bedtime bible stories. Rather than Mom helping Dad, it was Dad helping Mom when he was home on leave. When he was on the lighthouse, all the responsibility for the house and children were hers, of course, but when he was home, whatever they did, they did together. Whether it was cooking, laundry, scrubbing floors, or washing windows, they worked together. Their love for each other was very evident. Dad was a "gentle giant." He was a fair and honest man, respected by all who knew him. He taught us that the most important thing a person owns is his reputation. Totally committed to family, he provided a comfortable life for his aged parents, as well as Mom and us children, requiring little for himself. When I count the blessings of my life, Mom and Dad are at the top of the list. I realize how very fortunate I was."
Photo courtesy Agnes (Wallace) Haddaway

Big sister Marie embraced her little sister, Jessie Mae. The picture was taken in Sherwood, Maryland, in 1945. Nearly a half-century later, Marie's daughter, Beverly (Mulvaney) Davidson, wrote of her grandparents, Keeper and Mrs. Wallace. "They make me smile just to think about them. I am one of the oldest of the nineteen grandchildren, so I got to know my grandfather while he was still fairly young. Although he and my grandmother lived very modestly, there were times when he'd sneak some things for me, like a Papermate pen when I was in the first grade. Although my parents disagreed, my grandfather made up an excuse to take me with him to town, and when we returned I was wearing new Penny Loafers, shiny pennies and all! The dearest thing he did for me was to eat my green vegetables, which I hated, off my plate when no one was looking. Those years for were simple times with simple pleasures. Going to the store with my grandfather where he would buy me the nickel Coke in the small green bottle and a cookie out of the jar or some penny candy out of the candy case - these were special times to me. He was generous, exuded warmth, and he made me feel special."
Photo courtesy Agnes (Wallace) Haddaway

Beverly Davidson, oldest child of Lucy "Marie" Mulvaney (1925), offered information on Keeper Wallace's children. She shared the only known photograph of the entire family. In the picture left to right back row: Albert Maurice Wallace (1921-1981), Thomas Leroy Wallace (1934), Lucy Whidbee Wallace (1902-1959), Thomas Levi Wallace (1900-1987)
Left to right front row: Lucy Marie (Wallace) Mulvaney (1925), Hannah Melvina "Mel" (Wallace) Harrison (1927-1973), Jessie Mae (Wallace) Andrews (1939), and Agnes Mildred (Wallace) Haddaway (1932). Beverly, Wallace's granddaughter commented, "You cannot tell from the photo, but they are a very tall family. My grandfather was about 6'2" and Mom, Mel, and Aggie were all 5'9". Uncle Maurice and Tom were both considerably taller than my grandfather was. The picture of the family was taken before Tom and Jessie finished growing. Tom was the tallest and I think he reached 6'5". Jessie ended up being the tallest of the girls and was at least two inches taller than the other three sisters. I know she was a teenager in the picture and Tom wasn't very old either. My grandmother was about 5'7". 1955
Photo courtesy Beverly Davidson

Agnes is in the arms of her adored brother, Maurice. He was home on leave in Sherwood, Maryland, in 1945. The children enjoyed a home here from 1938-1946 while Keeper Wallace was stationed on a Chesapeake Lighthouse. Maurice served part of his career on a lightship off the coast of Massachusetts from 1941-45.
Photo courtesy Agnes (Wallace) Haddaway

All stories from Thomas Wallace family members 2000-01. Agnes Haddaway shared correspondence and photos of her keeper father. Keeper Wallace's granddaughter, Donna Schlag, daughter of Hannah "Melvina" (1927-1973), provided information from her grandfather's obituary, published after he died at the Meridian Nursing Center, The Pines, Easton, Maryland, on Friday, April 24, 1987. Marie (Wallace) Mulvaney wrote her memoirs for this oral and family histories book
Beverly (Mulvaney) Davidson shared her memories of her grandparents.
Keeper Wallace's signature courtesy Jessie Mae (Wallace) Andrews

A Watchful Keeper
Alpheus B. Willis

His mother, Rowena (Simpson), was the sister of other lighthouse keepers, bringing him into the family of Simpson keepers. Though he suffered with heart problems, he climbed the stairs at Cape Hatteras for four years.

By Cheryl Shelton-Roberts

One advantage Alpheus B. Willis had over any other father was that he could keep close watch on his only daughter, Nora Dare Willis, born 1892, while a certain young man with a fancy for the keeper's daughter walked her home to the Cape Hatteras Lighthouse.

Mary (Stowe) Quidley, Nora's daughter, laughed while she told a story about her grandfather. "He didn't want her [Nora] to have boyfriends. There was one, he'd try to walk her all the way to the lighthouse, but my grandfather got upset. So the boy would walk her only so far. My grandfather [Keeper Willis] would stand at the top of the lighthouse and watch them through his spyglasses. Mom said he saw the boy kiss her one time from up there."

Rowena Simpson, Alpheus's mother, was the sister to the Simpson lighthouse keepers. Alpheus had grown up in a community of light keepers, watching his relatives carry out their duties. Alpheus went on to work for the U.S. Lighthouse Service also.

Mary continued, "My mother married young and so when we tried to call him 'Granddaddy,' he said he was too young to be called that. He told me to call him 'Alphie' and to call Grandmother 'Mama Liza'- that was short for Eliza. As good as I could talk, all I could say was 'Affie' and 'MamaLize,' so that what I called them."

Mary was born in 1910 when there were no cars on Hatteras Island, no electricity, and even owning a horse and cart was a luxury. "Affie didn't want a horse and cart to have to feed and store. And when I was as young as three and four years old and after he left the lighthouse [Cape Hatteras] he tended the beacons out in the water that told you when you were to a shoal. We went out in a small boat and I remember this one beacon that was red. We would tie up to the small building, about three to four feet square up on four pilings. Affie would lift the lamp out of it and trim the wick and fill the lamp with kerosene. If any of the beacons he took care of ever went out or didn't burn right, he had to go right away to fix them. But I don't think that happened often."

Alpheus Willis walked everywhere, as Mary recalled, but not always in comfort. "He must have had heart trouble long before he realized it. I can remember when I was small and see him walk off to the store and he'd have to stop on the side of the road and rest. I'll never forget when he died. It was during an August storm and it was terrible. He tied up near the post office at the mail landing to get protection from the storm. He got out of the boat and walked up to the nearest house, sat down to rest a bit, leaned back, and said, 'I'm gone.' And he was. I was so sad. There weren't any funeral homes and no cars so they laid him out on a cart and brought him home."

Mary also told a story passed down to her by her mother, Nora. While Alpheus Willis was stationed on one of the sound lights, her mother and grandmother, Nora and "Affie," would visit him for several days. Mary's mother, Nora, was an only child and liked to take a friend along. "It was awful lonesome for Mom as a child, you know, out there in the water." On the many trips to the sound light to see her father, Nora had learned the technique of stepping off a boat while it dipped and rose with the current. But the childhood friend hadn't gotten the hang of it and stepped right off into water over her head. "They grabbed her by the hair of her head and pulled her up!" Mary still tells with amusement.

Perhaps this granddaughter's favorite memory of Keeper Willis is that he always made sure that she had a Christmas tree. "There were no lights, of course, but it had decorations and it was always so beautiful to me."

Daisy O'neal, Mary's sister, still resides near the old childhood homes of her parents and grandparents in Hatteras village. Daisy wrote of the time they visited at the sound light, "My mother, Nora, the keeper's daughter, told us the time while they were at the lighthouse [on the water] that she hid from them. And when they found her, they were so happy to find her that they didn't punish her. They were worried she had fallen overboard."

Mary added this memory. "We lived near one another. I'd go between our house and my grandparent's house. Grandparents then were just like parents, we were so close. I remember sitting on Affie's tobacco box at the dresser and my MamaLize was there with me. Most mornings, I walked to their house and she would make my breakfast. She had an iron cook stove and she'd fry potatoes and I'd sit there and just watch her and eat them warm right off the stove. I love these memories."

All stories are from phone and personal interviews with Alpheus B. Willis's granddaughters, Mary (Stowe) Quidley and Daisy (Stowe) O'neal, January 17, 2001.

Timeline

Alpheus B. Willis (1868-1924)
Assistant Keeper 1905-1907 and 1911-1912:

After serving at Cape Hatteras, Willis was sent to New Bern to tend the twenty-one harbor lights that led mariners in and out of the busy port. Though all his service was in the twentieth century, Keeper Willis never once turned on an electric light in a tower. In 1910, the U.S. Lighthouse Service had gone through a third major reorganization. First, the service was known as the U.S. Lighthouse Establishment (1789-1852); then it became the Light-House Board (1852-1910); finally, under the direction of Commissioner George Putnam, the service was known as the Bureau of Lighthouses (1910-1939). Collectively, it was known as the U.S. Lighthouse Service.

Keeper Alpheus B. Willis appeared with his wife, Eliza Ellen (Stowe) (1869-1948), in this undated portrait. Willis served two different times between 1905 and 1912, so we can assume the picture is taken during those years since he is wearing a U.S. Lighthouse Service uniform. Photo courtesy Daisy O'neal

(Below) This is a classic view of the Cape Hatteras Lighthouse and keepers quarters. Taken during the early days of the twentieth century, the photographer has captured the wide expanse of this light station, which approximately eighty-three keepers and their families called "home." This important aid to navigation depended upon a human hand to keep the light in working order from 1870-1936. Photo courtesy Outer Banks History Center, Manteo

Quiet Voices

*From records to date, the following details are what we have on some of the men who served for the U.S. Lighthouse Service at the Cape Hatteras Light Station. For several keepers, we have only their signatures. But after all, the light **was** their signature.*

Nelson P. Angell

From family and Civil War pension records, much more has been learned of this keeper and his family. Nelson Paul Angell was born in Rhode Island round 1831, served in the 2nd MA Inf in the Civil War, and married Czarina "Inez" A. (Locke) (c. 1831 -1911) in Vermont, before they moved to North Carolina after the war. They had one son, Louis Cushman Angell (1858-1892). Nelson served as assistant keeper at Cape Hatteras from 1871 until 1873; the next available record places him at Hatteras Inlet from 1874 until his death in 1887, while still on active duty. Family records state that Louis was a keeper at other sound lights including one of the Royal Shoal screwpile lighthouses in 1874 and then was promoted to keeper in 1885 at the NW Point Royal Shoal Light near Portsmouth Island. Family information states that the Angells took Thomas, a young black boy, with them to Oliver's Reef in 1874. Thomas later was known as "Tom Angell" to Hatteras Islanders and sold ice cream to the public. Keepers' children who loved to go to Hatteras village and visit his ice cream parlor still speak of Tom with great respect.

Margaret Angell Shields Volney-Huff submitted information on the Angell family.

George Albert Bliven

Here is a little mystery. The microfilmed original written registers list George as primary keeper at Cape Hatteras Lighthouse from 21 August 1880 to January 1881 when he was listed as "transferred" and replaced by Augustus Thompson. Some secondary records suggest a birth year of 1849, and others of 1859. If 1859 is correct, it makes it unlikely that he would have been primary keeper at age twenty-one and then serve several years as an assistant at Bodie Island Light Station. The microfilmed registers show him appointed as second assistant at Bodie Island on 2 July 1884, promoted to first assistant on 18 March 1886, and he was still serving when these registers in 1912.

Records and census give confusing birth dates; it would be unusual for him to have served as primary keeper at such a young age and there are no other Bliven families with a son George A. in the census records. However, it is not a precedent because Benjamin C. Jennett served as primary keeper at age twenty-two.

George and his wife Sarah Frances Ward (1866-1926) had at least five children. Sarah reported that two had died before the 1900 census, when three daughters were reported as living. George died in 1920.

George's parents were George Benjamin Bliven (1834-1891) and Mahala Baum (Howard) (c.1837-?). This further makes the son, George A.'s birth date very unlikely in 1849. His father, George Benjamin would have only been fifteen years old. George A.'s parents married in 1880 and had three surviving daughters: Oliva E. (1885-?) Lillian L. (1887-?), and Corolla B. (1895-?).

Jabez Burfoot

Jabez lived past ninety years of age, born c.1878 in Camden Co., North Carolina and died in June, 1969. He married in 1919 to Mary E. Midgett, daughter of John and Levicia [-?-] Midgett, and there is no record of any children. Jabez served in 1907 at Cape Hatteras as an assistant keeper, but most of his working life took place in Norfolk, Virginia.

Ethelburt Dozier Burrus

E.D. was an assistant keeper at Cape Hatteras 1876-1878. He was born 9 December 1856 and was the son of Edmund Dailey Burrus (1820-1862) and Sarah R. (Gaskins) (1825-1877). He married Achsah D. (Williams) in 1877. She was the daughter of Keeper Bateman Attlet and Achsah Maria (Scarborough) Williams. They had eight known children: Ethelburt Dozier Burrus Jr. (1878-1878), Elida Dixon (1879-1913), Lula Dean (1883-1970), Luther Dudley (1884-1962), Mattie Dozier (1885-1947), Calvin Dallas (1889-1955), Almy Dole (1894-1954), Maurice Lennon (1898-1972). E.D. died 6 December 1936.

Harvey L. Farrow

We are unable to positively identify this man who served as an assistant keeper at Cape Hatteras 1873-1875. The only Farrow family in Hatteras in the 1870 census with a young man named Harvey was a black family living very near to other keeper families (Jennett, Gray, Barnett). If this is the same man, he later married in 1874 to Mary E. Banton, had one daughter Florence born in 1877, and had died by 1880 when Mary was called a widow in the 1880 census.

Isaac L. Farrow

The Isaac L. Farrow who served as keeper from 1830-1842 is likely the man b. c.1785 who died c. 1843. Studies continue to match this man with estate records of 1843 to learn more about his family.

Joseph Farrow

Joseph Farrow was appointed keeper in 1808 by President Thomas Jefferson, but no records remain to indicate how long he served. He is likely the man b. c. 1760, son of Hezekiah and Christiana [-?-] Farrow. Joseph's wife was named Rhoda [-?-] and they had at least the following children: William, Wilson, Louisa, Euphemia, Claryssa, and Dorcas. He died in 1822 and is reported buried in the Rhoda Farrow Cemetery in Swan Quarter.

Lorenzo Burrus Farrow

Lorenzo B. Farrow was born in 1811, son of Hezekiah David and Elizabeth [-?-] Farrow. He served as assistant keeper 1864-1867 and died in 1869. The 1850 census lists no children, and in his will of 1868, he named only his wife Christiana and a namesake.

Pharoah M. Farrow

Many myths and folk tales remain concerning this man with the unusual name, but there is no evidence that he was a shipwrecked Arab! Succeeding generations of this surname have named children in his honor, some changing the spelling to Farrow Farrow. He was born about 1775 in the Outer Banks, and died in May 1847 in Kinnekeet, now Avon. A deed remains at the National Archives signed by Pharoah M. Farrow in 1828, selling 40 acres of land, which was added to the four acres formerly purchased of the Jennett family for the lighthouse. Pharoah was keeper at Cape Hatteras for about ten years, from 1821 to 1831. Since he died before the federal census listed family members by name, there is little primary documentation to confirm the number and names of his wives and children.

*This is a postcard printed on the Outer Banks. The identification reads: "Since the English colonists visited Croatan, and until the mid-twentieth century, Hatteras Island was supplied by boat. The Hamlet was a 'Bugeye' captained by Ethelbert Dozier Burrus of Hatteras Village." E.D. can be seen in his captain's hat; the young man is his son, Almy; the other man is from the Smithsonian.
Postcard courtesy Dixie B. Browning*

Abner H. Gray

Abner Gray, born around 1835 served in the 1st NC Inf in the Civil War, and was named assistant keeper at Cape Hatteras lighthouse in 1865 - as his loyalty to the federal government would have been assured. He married Elizabeth H. (Farrow), daughter of Silas and Mary [-?-] Farrow, who was born about 1835, as both Abner and Elizabeth gave their ages as 35 in the 1870 census. Their children in that census were: Elizabeth (1855-?); Louvinia (1859-?) who later married Christopher Farrow, son of Keeper Abraham C. Farrow; and Oliah (1868-?).

Wallace R. Jennett

Wallace Richard Jennett was born in 1829, son of Jabez Benjamin and Salida (Farrow) Jennett. He married Rhoda Jennett, daughter of his cousin, Keeper Joseph Claude Jennett and they had six children born 1853-1868. Wallace was appointed an assistant keeper in 1867 and was promoted to primary keeper in 1873, serving in that position for four years.

Isaac Chauncey Meekins

Isaac (1868-1948) was a brother to Keeper Ephraim Meekins, both sons of Daniel W. and Sarah "Sally" (Etheridge) Meekins. Isaac served in the US Life Saving Service, and also served briefly as an assistant keeper at Cape Hatteras lighthouse in 1905, when his brother Ephraim was primary keeper.

William B. O'Neal

William signed his name with no apostrophe or capital "N". He was the son of the keeper William O'Neal who served 1853-1860. William B. was born c. 1833, and is likely the "W.B." who served as an assistant keeper in 1854, and again as "William B." in 1867. He married Dorcas Jennett, daughter of Keeper Joseph Claude Jennett.

Ephraim H. Riggs

Born in January, 1853, Ephraim married Terah L. Jennett, the daughter of another Cape Hatteras keeper, Wallace R. Jennett, and they had five known children. Riggs was obviously an educated person, as he was listed as a teacher in the 1880 census, when he was also serving as a census enumerator at Hatteras. A political activist, of the Republican party as was his father-in-law, Ephraim was involved in a heated contest with fellow Keeper Alpheus W. Simpson, an equally avid Democrat, in an election for the State Legislature. Riggs also served as a Notary and his signature remains on many archival documents of the time. He was an assistant keeper at Cape Hatteras 1889-1892.

W.G. Rollinson

William Gibbons Rollinson was born in Frisco in 1873, son of Erasmus H. and Emma C. (Devine) Rollinson. He married Mariah D. Whidbee in 1900, and they had three children. He had a long career in lighthouse service, and was an assistant keeper at Cape Hatteras 1905-1906. Other stations included Hatteras Inlet, Bluff Shoal, and Cape Lookout.

A.G.B. Salter

Albert G. Browning Salter went by the name of "Browning" in many records. He was born in Hatteras in 1852, the son of William and Salina [-?-] Salter. He married twice, first in 1877 to Fannie E. Rollinson, with whom he had three children. After Fannie's death, he married Magnolia [-?-], with whom he had at least three more children. Browning served eleven years as an assistant keeper at Cape Hatteras, from, 1877 to 1888.

Sanders Burdon Smith

Sanders was born 6 May 1867 in North Carolina. He served as assistant keeper at Cape Hatteras for seven years 1892-1899. From 1909 until after 1912, he listed as "Acting Laborer" at the Cape Channel Beacons. He was married on Christmas Day 1895 to Charlotte (Austin) who was born in 1867. They had one known child, Louise Catherine, born 17 December 1910. Sanders died 19 June 1929.

Malachi Daniel Swain

Malachi was an assistant keeper at Cape Hatteras for four years 1913-1917. He was born 26 March 1868 and died 20 June 1927. He married the lovely Letitia English (Fulcher) (1869-1921), granddaughter of Keeper Benjamin T. Fulcher. Her parents were the Rev. George Leffers Fulcher (1838-1898) and Cynthia Harriet (Stowe) (1848-?). Malachi and Letitia had five known children: Martha Alivia (1892-1980), Frances (1894-1980), Arthur Jennings (1898-1963), Malachi "Mack" (1910-1985), and Myrtle (1912).

Malachi Daniel Swain was photograhed with his wife Letitia English (Fulcher), the granddaughter of Benjamin T. Fulcher. Malachi and Letitia married in 1889. Photo courtesy Saundra Swain

William G/ Willie Gardner Tolson

W.G. Tolson was an assistant keeper at Cape Hatteras in 1905. In the 1920 census, he gives age fifty, making his birth year about 1870, with wife Charlotte, six daughters: Martha, Fannie, Katie, Cora, Annie, Anges, and son Washington D. In the 1910 census, Willaim G. Tolson gives age thirty-nine, making the birth year about 1871. The 1900 census has a W. Tolson, single, age twenty-four and born around 1876, with sister Annie age seventeen, born January 1883. In the 1880 census, George W. Tolson has a son Willie G., age seven, born around 1873 and daughters Fannie age five, and Annie, age one, born around 1879.

If these all refer to the same person, the census taker(s) didn't help much determining birth dates!

There were nine known children: Bertha (c. 1902), Missouri F. (c. 1905), Martha W. (c. 1907), Fannie V. (c. 1909), Katie (c. 1911), Cora (c. 1913), Annie M. (c. 1915), ?Anges L. (c. 1917), Washington D./? Leston (1919).

John T. Twiford

A "J.T. Twiford" is listed on the Lighthouse Registers with two days' service as an assistant keeper at Cape Hatteras in 1912. In 1918, living in Stumpy Point, John Thomas Twiford listed his work as US Lighthouse Service, serving as a keeper in Baltimore, Maryland. No family information has been discovered.

Victor Lawson Watson

Born in 1874, Victor is listed in the 1900 census as single and living with his parents, Israel Burrus Watson (1835-1911) and Margaret Ann (Mann) (1851-1932), along with his siblings in Lake Landing township in Hyde County. He is on the official records for Cape Hatteras keepers from 1907-1909. In 1910, he was serving as an assistant keeper at a station not named while living in Straits township in Carteret County. In 1920 he was back in Lake Landing, living next door to his father and is called "keeper, lighthouse," but the station again is not named. Around 1909, Victor married Lena (Reid) (1891) and they had six known children: Floyd Winslow, (1910), Durward Lawson (1911), Dorsey Eugene (1913), Melceina Reid (1915), Walter Israel (1920), and Joseph Dancy (1922-1999). Victor died in 1925.

Miles F. Whedbee

Miles was born in 1852, son of James Whidbee, and served a very brief term as an assistant keeper at Cape Hatteras, recorded as less than a month in 1907. But he was well acquainted with the keeper staff, as his half-sister Mariah had married William G. Rollinson, who had been a keeper at Cape Hatteras in 1905, and later at the Hatteras Inlet station.

John E. Whitehurst

John was an assistant keeper at Cape Hatteras Lighthouse 1879-1880. He is listed as such at age twenty-four and single in the 1880 census. He married Liddie Jane (Rollinson) (1858-1945), the daughter of George Smith Rollinson (1820-?) and Eliza (Austin) (1823-1880) in 1882. There is no information on children; they do not appear in Hatteras in the 1900 census.

Andrew Williams

Based on a stated age of 50 in the 1860 census, Andrew Williams was born about 1810. While he was serving as a keeper that year, he told the census taker that his occupation was "a nautical life." Andrew married Christian Flowers and they had six children. Two sons served in the Civil War in the 1st NC Infantry - Evan Garland (1837-1877) and Ervin Hooper (1845-1919). Other children included Margaret (1842-1917), Sarah S. (1847-1917), Franklin (c.1852-?), and Zion (c.1856-1881).

Bateman Attlet Williams

B.A. Williams was assistant keeper at Cape Hatteras 1860-1865, during which time the light was temporarily extinguished during the Civil War. Born in c.1822, B.A. married Achsah Maria (Scarborough) (1832-1910). They had seven known children: Mary (c.1850); Louisa (c.1851); James Dickson (1853-1897), the father of James Oliver Casey who became an assistant keeper from 1920-1928; William (c.1855); Hosanna Credle (1856), Achsah D. (1860-1903) who married E.D. Burrus, a Cape Hatteras keeper 1876-1878; and Urias Blount (1865-1933).

Nasa S. Williams

Nasa was born about 1818, and he served in the Civil War as a pilot for the *Delaware* in 1862, for which he later received a military pension. From 1864 to 1871, he served as an assistant keeper at Cape Hatteras, and his wife, Chrissa Naomi, was of the Jennett keeper family.

Sandra Clunies compiled this information to date from a variety of primary and secondary sources and information submitted by family members.
All signatures appearing in this book are authentic.

A Keeper's Descendant Is a Keeper of History

My Keeper Heritage

With Beatrice (Barnette) McArthur

Beatrice "Beatie" (Barnett) McArthur is a fellow founder of the Hatteras Island Genealogical and Historical Society (HIGHS). She described the goals of this organization: "History is People. To determine the history of this Island and surrounding areas and its people; to protect, preserve, and promote our history. To preserve the history of these men and their families, the HIGHS members give of their own time and money for research, organization, and preservation of the genealogy of Hatteras Island families."

When asked about the founding of HIGHS, Beatie shared "Thinking that history is nothing more than people and what they do and why and how, and the results of what they do for good or bad, I found eight other amateur genealogists, and we became a committee to trace eighty-one family names. Therefore, the HIGHS is a group of committees with individual ones focusing on its own area of expertise, but each of us do contribute to the other if we find anything we think is pertinent. My area is genealogy and lighthouse-related topics. Earl O'Neal of Ocracoke has contributed much to the information on the keepers' descendants. This project has brought us information on many branches of families we are researching that we would have never found otherwise. Some of the families go back to the colonists, and we are taking the eldest that we know and are following him to the latest descendant born this year. Earl takes what we find and keeps it in order for the preservation of the family information for future generations."

Nearly an octogenarian, Beatie is a walking genealogy chart and Hatteras history book. She is a direct descendant of at least six Cape Hatteras Lighthouse keepers and is the daughter of Avilla (Credle) and Joseph Dailey Barnett. Both of her grandfathers were named Walter L. Barnett, therefore keeping middle names is important to distinguish men of the same name.

Walter Loran Barnett, her maternal grandfather, was born in the double keepers quarters in 1876, the son of Keeper **Oliver Neal Barnett**, who was appointed to Cape Hatteras Lighthouse in 1873. Walter Loran Barnett's wife was Lona Leigh Jennett, a granddaughter of keepers **Bateman A. Williams** and **William B. Jennett**, and a great-granddaughter of keepers **Benjamin T. Fulcher** and **Joseph Claude Jennett**.

Walter Lambeth Barnett, Beatie's paternal grandfather, was First Mate on the LV 105 when it was destroyed by German U-boat gunfire in 1918. Barnett served at area sound lights also, and was son of keeper **James Jennett Barnett**, who served at the Cape Hatteras Lighthouse in 1907.

The following chart, prepared by project genealogist Sandra MacLean Clunies, illustrates the relationships in a visual format:

> *"'That history is nothing more than people and what they do and why and how, and the results of what they do for good or bad is the concept upon which the HIGHS is founded.' I deserve no more credit than my coworkers."*

A partial ancestry chart of Beatie McArthur's links to six Cape Hatteras lighthouse keepers through her two grandfathers named Walter L. Barnett, whose stories follow. The keepers' names are in bold italics.

- *Joseph Claude Jennett* — keeper 1843, 1849
- *Benjamin T. Fulcher* — keeper 1860
- *William B. Jennett*
- Sabra Fulcher
- *Bateman A. Williams*
- *James J. Barnett*
- *Oliver Neal Barnett*
- Isaac L. Jennett
- Hosanna C. Williams
- Walter Lambeth Barnett
- Walter Loran Barnett
- Lona Leigh Jennett
- Joseph Dailey Barnett
- Arvilla Credle Barnett
- Beatrice Barnett McArthur

Beatie is a lightning rod for Hatteras memories. She grew up listening to stories from her great-grandmother, Hosannah "Hosie" (Credle) Williams, her grandmother, Lona (Jennett) Barnett, and her mother, Arvila (Credle) Barnett. She heard eye-witness accounts about how the wives of lifesaving service men helped their husbands. When the men went out on a rescue, the women packed up the children. There is little wonder why Beatie describes her great-grandmother, Hosie, as "a spicy old girl, but delightful. She had fourteen children and reared nine, so I guess she had to be spicy. Her husband, Isaac Littleton Jennett, was gentle as the proverbial lamb. Most of these families were like that. The men had to develop patience because of their jobs in the Life Saving Service and the Lighthouse Service."

It was no easy task in the late 1800s and early 1900s to put children into wagons and go to the beach and wait for the surfboat to return. The tradition was a duty and held as seriously as a contract. Rescues were frequently done in the worst weather conditions and children had to be bundled up, food packed, a horse and cart obtained, and the families traveled together to the beach area closest to the lifesaving station that was involved in the rescue. Often the families went to the lighthouse and allowed the children to play in the yard if weather permitted it. One mother looked after the children while another went to the top of the lighthouse and watched for the surfboat. If it were spotted, the news rang out to the other surfmen's families. When the men returned with survivors to be taken care of, the women helped provide dry clothing, food, and comfort to the suffering.

In the following, Beatie shared her personal recollections about her lighthouse families. In these delightful accounts, we first meet her great-grandfather, James Jennett Barnett and next, his son, Walter Lambeth Barnett, who was Beatie's grandfather. Finally, Beatie wrote of her great-grandfather, Oliver Neal Barnett and his son, who was also Beatie's grandfather, Walter Loran Barnett.

James Jennett Barnett III
(1844-1937)

Walter Lambeth's father was James J. Barnett, Beatie's great-grandfather and a Cape Hatteras assistant keeper in 1907. Barbara Williams submitted a photo of J.J. Barnettt during the 1930s. He was quoted to have said shortly before his death at age ninety-three, "Don't need glasses anymore. Getting new fuzz on top of my head- when I finish that, I will start growing new teeth." At ninety years of age, this old salt built a skiff in his back yard.

Born in Tyrrell County, he resided in Currituck County where he was by occupation a sailor. He enlisted in Company B of the 8th Regiment of the Confederate States Army the first of August 1861. He transferred to the Confederate States Navy on or about 10 January 1863.

His first wife, Salome Dailey (1845-1886), was the sister of famed Benjamin B. Dailey of the U.S. Lifesaving Service. She and James J. married in May 1869.

Beatie commented on this part of her ancestry. "I was descended from his first wife, Salome Dailey. Salome was descended from Joshua Halstead Dailey, whose father was Edmond Dailey. Edmond was the first teacher in Ocracoke

James J. Barnett was father to Walter Lambeth Barnett of the LV 71 fame, destroyed by Germans in warfare off the East Coast in 1918. At seventeen, James was in the Confederate Army and at nineteen, he joined the Confederate Navy. James was an assistant keeper at Cape Hatteras in 1907 at sixty years of age. Though blurred, this image depicts this "old salt." Photo courtesy Barbara (Barnett) Williams

and afterwards he taught in Hatteras village. His son, Joshua, was one of several teachers on Hatteras Island; therefore, Salome must have been more educated than most women of her time. Salome died in 1886 when her eldest child was sixteen and her youngest was only four years old. My great-grandfather then remarried Olive Frances (Farrow) Gray. James was a loving and patient man and he had a great part in carrying on for Salome and helping Olive. Both 'Grandpa Jim' and 'Grandma Ollie' were delightful people. He loved his son, Walter- all the children were lovely."

Walter Lambeth Barnett
(1871-1957)

All the following is by Beatie McArthur

Walter was not a native of Dare County, although his father, James Jennett Barnett, while visiting in Hatteras, met and married Salome Dailey of Hatteras. His uncle, Stephen D. Barnett, was Master of the schooner, *Mary Louise*. Hatteras was a port-of-call for many trips through Hatteras Inlet. On one of these trips, Stephen met and married Rebecca Gaskins. In those days, it was customary for the wives and children to travel on the ships with their husbands. She served as teacher to her children and the crew, as well as nurse and friend to all. It has been said that while the ship was taking on cargo the Chief, from one of the islands came on board with his son who was very ill. Rebecca cured him with medicine from her medicine chest. The Chief tried to buy her from her husband. He offered a peck of gold, but captain Stephen wasn't selling. It was after one of these trips that the *Mary Louise* was wrecked. Stephen and Rebecca and their infant were drowned. The infant was never found.

Walter came from a family of shipbuilders and river lighthouse men [screwpile lighthouses on the sounds and rivers rather than on the coast]. True to form, while visiting the Island, he met and courted Chloe Midgett, granddaughter of Little Bannister Midgett of U.S. Lifesaving fame. She agreed to marry him only if he would build her a house. She wanted her own family, and did not remain in a house full of half-brothers and half-sisters while Walter was away on lighthouses for months at a time. And so, on his time off, he built a two-room house and a "necessary." They were married 11 July 1897.

Probably the most severe storm on record ever to strike Hatteras Island was the hurricane of 1899. This strong storm dragged along the Outer Banks on August 16-18 of 1899. Extreme wind velocities on the 17th were recorded at 140 miles per hour. Tides were estimated at eighteen feet. Hurricanes were unnamed at that time, but this one was called San Ciriaco. Diamond Shoals Lightship No. 69, of which Walter was a crew member, broke from its permanent anchor at the shoals and washed ashore at Creeds Hill west of Cape Hatteras. No crewman was injured, and when the tides went down, Walter walked home to Buxton. There he found that all was well, and his first born, Joseph Dailey Barnett, was twelve days old. His uncle and neighbor, Benjamin Baxter Dailey, had looked after Chloe and had named the child.

In September 1929, the *Carol A. Deering*, later called "The Ghost Ship of Diamond Shoals," became a mystery yet to be solved. She was a five-masted schooner on the shoals with all sails set. Walter, then Master Barnett, boarded her with part of his crew, and found not a living soul- only a cat. He took the cat back to the lightship and later took it home where Chloe fed it with any other cats that came around the yard. The cat had six toes on each foot and, to this day, many six-toed cats roam the woods.

During World War I, in 1918, few people in the United States knew of the devastation caused by German U-boats just a few miles off our coast. Freighters and tankers were riding the Gulf Stream to take supplies and fuel to Europe. The U-boats (submarines) were sinking them here with a great loss of lives. It seemed that the whole ocean was afire. One ship was torpedoed near the lightship. Walter radioed headquarters and the sub issued a warning and started firing on the lightship. Walter and his crew took to the lifeboats and were allowed to row ashore while they watched their ship sink to the bottom. They came ashore near the lighthouse here and walked home.

From all accounts that I have heard, Captain Barnett must have been a patient and caring master. His theory seemed to be that training his crew in the knowledge and efficiency of their positions could save their lives, the lives of their crewmembers, as well as their ship. He carefully selected educational books for the ship's library, as well as books suited to their talents. In short, he encouraged his men to learn how to use their isolated time to their own advantage.

Captain Barnett retired in 1933 after nearly thirty-five years of service. He was back to stay with his beloved Chloe, his seven children, many grandchildren, and great-grandchildren, still loving and patient as always. And about that two-room house- as the children came along and grew, so did the house. He added five more bedrooms, a "sitting" room, three porches, and three kitchens. One of those had to be a dining room, and another separated by a "dog-trot" for Chloe's "fish-cooking" kitchen. Also, he added a bathroom when the Island got "city water." No more "necessary".

Oliver Neal Barnett
(1829-1892)

Oliver, like most of Hatteras Island men, joined the N.C. Union Volunteers during the War of the Rebellion (Civil War). Oliver was stationed at Fort Hatteras, where records report he enlisted 20 June 1863, discharged 27 June 1865. Complexion: dark. Hair: black. Eyes: dark grey. Height: 5 ft. 8 1/2 inches. He was a Private in the Co. I, 1st Regiment under Captain Graves. He was severely injured while mounting a gun on a carriage. Also, he received hearing damage and never fully recovered from these injuries.

After the war, he was unable to work at his trade as master carpenter, and he was employed as assistant keeper at the present Cape Hatteras Lighthouse, then newly-built in 1870. His family then lived in the assistant keepers quarters, and his son, Loran, was born there.

Nolie Midgett, twenty-four, and Laurette Bragg, daughters, were present at the death of their father in 1892. They thought he had typhoid fever with symptoms of high fever and delirium. When widow Mary Louise applied for Oliver's pension, she couldn't prove marriage to him. The Courthouse had burned and all records were destroyed. The minister and all witnesses had died. Several leading men on the island wrote glowing letters as character witnesses for both of them. Also, from war records as proof of birth of Walter Loran: Nancy Williams, age 33, Buxton, and Zorada Bonner, age 36, Hatteras, were present and witnessed the birth of Loran on 21 August 1876. Nancy was a member of Oliver's family and Zorada was a nurse.

Oliver Neal Barnett was a deeply religious man and was the interim minister in the Northern Methodist Church. His house was on the ridge behind the cemetery where he now lies with his wife, Mary Louise Fulcher, and some of his children. Beside the house he had a clearing with an altar where he worshipped every day. He was a Justice of the Peace, and his beautifully written signature is on many marriage licenses as well as witness to wills and deeds. Reports from many sources, handed down through the generations, were that he was a well-beloved community leader.

Walter Loran Barnett
(1876-1944)

Walter Loran Barnett was born 21 August 1876 in the double dwelling house on the grounds of the Cape Hatteras Lighthouse where his father, Oliver Neal Barnett, was an assistant keeper who died in 1892. Loran, then sixteen years old, lived with his mother, Mary Louise (Fulcher) and, to

Walter Loran Barnett was born in the double keepers quarters on the grounds of the Cape Hatteras Lighthouse in 1876. Like many other Hatterasmen, when he became of age, he joined the U.S. Lifesaving Service. He received a Lifesaving Medal for the rescue of the crew of the German steamer Brewster *in 1909.*

help provide for her, he took odd jobs wherever he could. One of the things he did was to chop wood to keep the fire going to boil the tar for the men to put on their nets for preservation for fishing. While doing this, he cut off one of his big toes. The men found the toe, dipped it in the hot tar, and replaced it, using a rag for bandage. Although he never recovered feeling in the toe, it healed very well but left a black ring around it. His grandchildren, over and over, begged him to show it and tell how it happened. We thought him a hero in many ways, and he was!

He had a marvelous sense of humor. Also he was very musical. He sang bass, and his tone was true and clear. He owned a small concertina, which he played while singing hymns and folk songs. His favorite was "Lorena." He was kind, patient, gentle, brave, and courageous, known to fear only two things: any size mouse and his beloved wife Lonie (Lona Lee Jennett (1880-1956), herself the descendant of four Cape Hatteras keepers).

Like many other Hatterasmen, when he came of age, Loran joined the U.S. Life Saving Service, a forerunner of the U.S. Coast Guard. He was stationed at Little Kinnakeet Lifesaving Service Station from 1899 until 1904. His family lived in the small village there during the duty months. The village and the trees are now long-gone due to storms.

In 1905, he was transferred to the Cape Hatteras Lifesaving Service Station where he stayed until the early 1930s when he retired. While stationed there, he was one of eleven men who were awarded the Medal of Honor for the rescue of the crewmen from the German steamship *Brewster*, which was bound from Port Antonio, Jamaica to New York. The account of the rescue, as recorded in the U.S. Coast Guard Record Book follows: "On November 29, 1909, the German steamer *Brewster* stranded on the SE point of Inner Diamond Shoals seven miles from the Cape Hatteras Life Saving Station. The wreck was discovered at daybreak of the 29th. Without delay, three lifesaving crews started to her assistance. The weather was very rough and the seas were breaking over the vessel fore and aft, making it out of the question to board her. A lifeboat was anchored as near as possible to leeward and the crew drifted a line to her by a buoy. With this line the seamen were hauled into the lifeboat one at a time. The entire crew of 33 were saved although the vessel was a total loss." On this Medal it says "In testimony of heroic deeds in saving life from the perils of the sea." It says, "To W.L. Barnett for gallant conduct, wreck *Brewster*, November 29, 1909." When the station crews went out in the terrible storms to a wreck, their wives brought out the entire family to wait it out on the beach. Arvilla, the eldest daughter, just past six years old at the time, well remembered the *Brewster* trip. "For several weeks afterward, Pop could not sit or feed himself due to blisters and raw places on his hands and behind."

– Beatrice McArthur

In the files of the HIGHS is the following "Old Naming Pattern" for children.

The piece reads, "Though not an invariant tradition, it may give a clue about the name of grandparents whose names are often so elusive in genealogical research.

The first son was named after the father's father.

The second son was named after the mother's father.

The third son was named after the father.

The fourth son was named after the father's eldest brother.

The first daughter was named after the mother's mother.

The second daughter was named after the father's mother.

The third daughter was named after the mother.

The fourth daughter was named after the mother's eldest sister.

It was also a common practice, especially among Quaker families, to give their children Biblical names.

Beatie McArthur is a living treasure of Cape Hatteras as she commits her time and talents to preserve its past for the future generations.

Sandra MacLean Clunies gave editorial assistance on this chapter.

Taming the Troublemaker
Lightships of Diamond Shoals

A brief history and navigational explanation

By Charles and Shirley Votaw and quotes from Allene (Quidley) Gaskins,
C.C. Austin, Belinda Farrow, Ben Price, and Mike Shepherd

Mariners are keenly aware of the expert seamanship and, to some extent, good fortune needed to avoid disaster at the hands of the invisible, undulating, underwater sand trap known as "Diamond Shoals." Three distinct ridges of sand lie in wait for any vessel that ventures too close to the Cape Hatteras shoreline.

Several Cape Hatteras Lighthouse keepers began their U.S. Lighthouse Service career aboard the Diamond Shoals Lightship. With a light at each of its two masts, the lightship was considered an extension of the land-based beacon to mark a safe passage around the hazardous shoals eight and more miles off Cape Hatteras. The men stationed on the lightship endured hardships; there was mutual respect between the crew at sea and the keepers on land.

The confluence of the Gulf Stream flowing from the south and the remnants of a cold current from the north have made for great challenges concerning weather. Further complicating the situation are shoaling ridges of sand that stretch outward from Cape Hatteras, eight miles to the inner shoals and about fourteen miles to the outer shoals.

For years, the only warning and point of reference for the shoals was the Cape Hatteras Lighthouse, but the 1803 lighthouse, only ninety-five feet tall until it was heightened to 150 feet in 1854, was not very helpful since its was not always clearly visible. The shortcoming was immediately recognized. Within three years of finishing the original tower, Congress ordered a survey to explore the feasibility of building a light "on the tip of Hatteras Shoals (Diamond Shoals), which have been long a terror to navigators." in 1806. No attempt was successful. The interim solution was to place warning buoys, but they often were torn from their position, confusing mariners. A lightship was the only viable solution.

The history of lightships on Diamond Shoals reaches back to the first one placed there in 1824. With only a tentative mooring in the sand at the edge of the inner shoals, the "Cape Hatteras" Lightship had to re-anchored several times. It stood brave vigil and beamed a warning to passing ships until June of 1827 when a storm broke the 320-ton vessel from her moorings

> "Between 1824 and 1827, the Diamond Shoals Lightship was hit by storms and dragged off station twenty-two times."

Several lightships have served off Diamond Shoals. Over time, the number of crew and amount of time on-and-off-duty have varied in the U.S. Lighthouse Service. During the 1800s, when crew members were expected to stay on board as long as three, even four months, there was a high rate of turnover. The duty evolved to one month on and two weeks off. Each lightship served at various places along the East Coast, exchanging places with another lightship when repairs were needed. As an extension of the land-based Cape Hatteras Lighthouse, great efforts were made beginning in 1827 to place a lightship permanently on Diamond Shoals since no attempt to build a traditional lighthouse there ever succeeded. The U.S. Coast Guard finally tamed the troublemaker by erecting a Texas oil rig-style light tower in 1967 and the last Diamond Lightship went home.
Photo courtesy U.S. Coast Guard

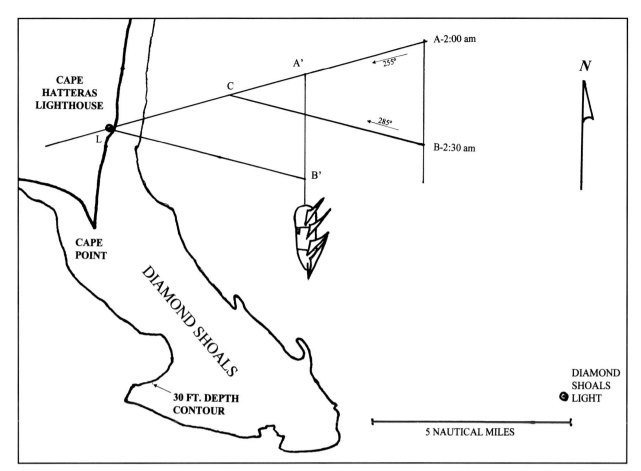

For example, as night falls and we lose sight of familiar daymarks, the ship may need to move a little further from the land and keep a steady course parallel to the shore. If we become unsure of our distance offshore, it may be necessary to slow the ship and take depth soundings to avoid running aground on one of the shoals that protrude from the shore. It is much better if we can spot the lighthouse because this will provide a safe passage at the higher speed.

While going due south, if we sight the lighthouse at an angle 75 degrees off our starboard bow at 2 am, then we can know that we are on a line that runs through the lighthouse at an angle of 75 degrees from north. But we will not know how far away from the lighthouse we are. Some time later can take another reading as we move along the line to the south. The new reading is 285 degrees clockwise from north or 15 degrees abaft of our starboard beam and the time between readings has been 30 minutes. Our log measurements indicate that our speed is 5 knots so we have traveled 2.5 miles in that half-hour.

If we extend a line 2.5 miles south of point A and then draw a line that bears 285 degrees from point B, it will intersect the line L-A at point C. This is far short of intersecting at the lighthouse and it indicates that we are not at point B but are traveling south on a line that is much closer to the shore than we thought. We must slide the triangle ACB down the line A-L until point C is on top of L. Our true track is A'-B'. The bad news is that if we do not quickly alter course to the east we'll run aground on Diamond Shoals.

We were lucky tonight; the visibility was good enough to let us see the light at about five miles. Some nights the fog is so thick we cannot see the light at two miles and the only safe procedure is to anchor and wait it out. A lightship on Diamond Shoals would give us a clear marker at sea and increase our chance for a safe passage around the shoals. Chart by Charles Votaw

and pushed her back to shore. Over the next seventy years lighthouse officials made many attempts to place other lightships on the shoals; but no attempt was permanent.

The fear and frustration associated with trying to make a lightship "stick" can best be appreciated if one understands the ship navigator's job. Lighthouses were not just "mile markers" to show how far down the coast one was. They also provided a means for knowing how far seaward one's vessel lay from the lighthouse.

A ship's navigator depended on the lighthouse so he could know the ship's position at all times, including knowing how much room the ship had to compensate as a margin of error. The advantage of passing a lighthouse that is clearly visible for twenty or thirty minutes is that it reduces navigational errors to near zero. This allows the navigator enough time to read the bearing between the ship and the lighthouse several times. These bearing angles, the ship's course, and speed permit the navigator to pinpoint the ship's position each time bearings were taken.

From the above illustration it is easy to see that the better place for the lighthouse is at the end of the shoal or beyond it. When visibility is less than ten miles, the safe course around Diamond Shoals would never bring you within sight of the Cape Hatteras Lighthouse. How could a light be placed closer to the outer edge of these dangerous shoals? The first lightship was on station there in June 1824. It was thirteen miles east-southeast of the Cape Hatteras Lighthouse. Attempts to improve the anchoring system over the next two years were not satisfactory, and in August 1827 the lightship again broke its mooring. This time it washed ashore six miles south of Ocracoke Inlet and the vessel had to be scrapped. There was no light on the shoal for many years, but in the 1870s buoys were tried, but again without success.

Seventy years passed until a serious attempt was made to place a lightship on Diamond Shoals. Within two years, in 1899, the inevitable happened when a monstrous hurricane slammed into the Outer Banks. After the storm subsided, lookout F.J. Rollinson of the Creeds Hill Lifesaving Station spotted a ship beached about a mile to the southwest, about 3.5 miles south of Cape Hatteras Lighthouse. Surfmen launched their boats and when they reached the stranded vessel they saw "Diamond Shoal" emblazoned on her side. The hurricane winds had broken her mooring and dragged her to shore, but all nine crewmen had survived and were rescued in the breeches buoy. The surfmen had to re-rescue the lightship's crew several more times during the salvage operations; but, undaunted, the crew floated the lightship back out to her station on Outer Diamond Shoals.

The efforts of these two groups of men showed great cooperation between the two sister services, the U.S. Lighthouse Service and the U.S. Life Saving Service (USLSS). As stated in the following letter of November 21, 1899, from the 5th District Lighthouse Inspector to the Lighthouse Board in Washington, the USLSS was reimbursed for expenses:

Respectfully referring to the Board's letter of October 26, 1899, transmitting an account for meals furnished to the officers and crew of Diamond Shoals light-vessel No. 69, N.C., by the keeper of Creeds Hill Life Saving Station, I have the honor to state that a check in settlement thereof has this day been mailed to H.W. Styron keeper of the life saving station above mentioned...." [Homer Styron was the nephew of Cape Hatteras keeper Benjamin T. Fulcher]

The first lightship on the shoals faithfully continued her lonely vigil until 1901. Light Vessels (LV) 71 and 72 replaced her and stood watch on Outer Diamond Shoal from 1901 until 1918. That year, LV 71 made the ultimate sacrifice and earned a special place in the annals of maritime history.

On the afternoon of August 8, 1918, having recently transferred, First Mate Walter Lambeth Barnette skippered LV 71. When a German raider submarine, U-boat 104, began firing at a merchant ship about a mile and a half away, Barnett radioed a warning to area ships. The Germans reportedly fired six warning shots across the bow of the lightship to cease the warning, and then turned to chase the merchant ship.

Barnette ordered "abandon ship" and he and the crew launched the lifeboats. The Germans returned, and as the crew of the LV 71 rowed safely towards shore, the lightship was destroyed. (For additional information on Walter Lambeth Barnette, see the story on him written by his granddaughter, Beatrice McArthur)

In concluding this brief history of the lightships on Diamond Shoals, it can be said that the greatest effort was made to supply a lightship there. A lightship remained a welcomed warning until a Texas oil rig-type lighthouse was built by the U.S. Coast Guard. For the first time, man had successfully tamed the troublemaker. It was hard duty in spite of the more modern conveniences. Personnel had a front-row seat to the moods of the stormy Atlantic and all the fury of the winds and waves. Salute to all who pulled duty on Diamond Shoals!

Now we turn to first person memories from family and crew members who served at various times from 1918 to the 1960s.

Guy Chestwood Quidley
By Allene (Quidley) Gaskins

Guy Chestwood Quidley was Quartermaster on the Diamond Shoals Lightship before and during World War II. His daughter, Allene, recalled growing up on Hatteras Island and the sinking of the lightship.

My Daddy, Guy Chestwood Quidley (1896-1977), was Quartermaster on the Diamond Shoals Lightship when the Germans sank it in August 1918. He said he was down below shaving when the Submarine surfaced within one hundred yards from the lightship and began firing its deck gun. The Submarine gave chase to a passing freighter.

At that time, First Mate Walter Barnett ordered the crew to abandon the ship. They took to the lifeboat and started rowing toward the beach. While they were rowing toward the beach the submarine returned and fired at the lifeboat. He said they could hear the bullets hitting all around them, but due to the waves on the shoals, they were missing the lifeboat. So the sub's crew returned to the deck gun and finished sinking the light ship.

My mother-in-law, Rosa Gaskins told me they could hear the gun shots at her home in Hatteras, which was a short distance from the beach in Hatteras. All of the crew on the Diamond Shoals Lightship were saved. My father was the last one alive until he died in August 1977

When Dad was off-duty at home, he planted collards, turnips, tomatoes, string beans, peas sweet potatoes, Irish potatoes, squash, bell peppers, beets, lettuce, corn, mustard greens, cucumbers, watermelons and cantaloupe. My mother canned enough to last until the next summer. We had pears, peaches, figs and grapes for desserts. My father raised our chickens, so we had eggs; also he hunted, fished, oystered, and clammed. He raised cattle and pigs for our meat, which had to be salted to keep. My Mother made nearly all our clothes.

We had oil lamps for light, wood stoves for heat and to cook on which my father had to cut trees down and then cut it in pieces to fit in the two stoves.

We had outside toilets, also hand pumps for water. We were poor as far as money, but we were rich, too, with plenty of love and food and clothes.

C.C. Austin
Hurricane of 1933

Although duty on a lightship during stormy weather on Diamond Shoals was less dangerous than during wartime, it still demanded a high level of courage and endurance. "Never abandon the ship" took on poignant meaning for a lightship's crew. No matter the roughness of the storm or threat by mountain-high waves, a crewmember must stick with his vessel - it was his only hope of survival. Hurricanes posed the toughest of conditions for lightships; one might compare a lightship to a toy boat in a huge pond when hurricane-force winds and swells rushed upon them. George Putnam quotes Master Claudius Cecil

Austin's personal account of riding out a 1933 hurricane on his light vessel stationed at Diamond Shoals in his Sentinel of the Coasts: The Log of a Lighthouse Engineer (Norton, 1937)."

"On the morning of [September] 15th the weather showed indication of a hurricane. At 8 a.m. wind forty and forty-five miles per hour, increasing, barometer falling. I got engine under way and began to work ahead slow. From noon to 4 p.m. wind east-northeast between fifty and sixty miles per hour, increasing, barometer falling. Seas getting rough and washing ship badly.

At about 2 p.m. station buoy sighted for the last time as the weather was thick with rain and spray. I judge the ship began to drag anchor at about 4 p.m., wind increasing to about seventy miles per hour. I began to increase the speed of the engine from forty to sixty revolutions per minute. From 8 p.m. to midnight, wind east-northeast, between seventy and eighty-five miles per hour, barometer falling. Seas were getting mountainous high and washing the ship terribly. Engine speed increased to ninety revolutions per minute.

September 16th, between midnight and 1 a.m. ship went into breakers on southwest point of Outer Diamond Shoal (having dragged the fifty-five-hundred-pound anchor and twenty-four thousand pounds of chain the five miles from her station). Wind about one hundred and twenty miles per hour. The first breaker which came aboard broke an air port in the pilot house which struck me (master) in the face and around the neck and on arm, cutting face and neck badly. This same breaker carried away one ventilator close to the pilot house. Mate S. F. Dowdy tried to get a stopper in the hole in the deck and was washed against a davit and broke some ribs. He was almost washed overboard. From 4 to 5 a.m. wind decreasing to about fifty miles per hour, barometer falling to 28.19 (lowest point).

We laid in the breakers from 12 midnight until 6:30 a.m., breakers coming aboard, breaking up everything on upper deck, washing boats, ventilators, awning stretchers away, bending awning stanchions inboard. Taking water in around umbrella of smokestack and through ventilators to such an extent that the water was rising at times above the fire-room floor with all pumps working, and every means we had to keep the water out of the ship. At 5:30 a.m. day began to break, so I could see the conditions outside. I could see an opening about south-southwest from the ship that looked like a chance to get away. Breakers coming over at intervals and I decided that it was the only chance out. I told the mate to get ready to slip the mooring, as we had to get out of that place, for when the wind comes from the west it would carry her into the breakers and finish her up. I slipped the mooring at 6:30 a.m. and got the ship outside the breakers, at about 7:15 a.m. being in the center of the hurricane. I had just got the breakers behind me when the wind struck from the west at about ninety miles per hour. I ran the ship southeast until I was sure I was all clear and then ran northeast thinking the hurricane would pass. I ran this course for a while and it did not get any better. I considered it was moving very slow (the barometer was rising fast) so I changed my course to south and ran this course until I ran out of the hurricane.

Claudius Cecil Austin (1887-1965) began his career as a U.S. Lighthouse Service employee until it merged with the U.S. Coast Guard in 1939. In this image, he wore his Coast Guard uniform as Chief Boatswain (Warrant Officer rating) around 1942. He is with his wife, Bessie Etheridge Austin. Known as "C.C.," he received a well-deserved commendation from then President Franklin D. Roosevelt in 1933 for "...exceptional character of the services performed in saving this vessel, and in the protection of the shipping along the coast..." when C.C. mastered the Diamond Shoal Lightship through the hurricane of 1933.
Photo courtesy granddaughter Winifred (Austin) Minson and his daughter, Edith (Austin) Cosme

September 17th, 5 a.m. wind northwest, strong gale, but decreasing. At 6 a.m. I called the mate and told him to get the crew out and see if he could get the wireless antenna fixed up so that we could establish communication. (There had been no radio communication since Friday evening.) About 9 a.m. I got radio compass bearings which put the ship approximately sixty miles east-northeast from Cape Hatteras Lighthouse; at 4 p.m. radio bearings placed the ship about one hundred and ten miles east-southeast from

Cape Henry. All the crew were at hand at all times and ready to do everything they could to help save the ship, both deck and engine force. During the storm one of the fusible plugs in the boiler blew. They let all steam from the boiler and opened up the furnace, went inside and took out the fusible plug that had blown and put in a new one, and closed the furnace and got steam on the boiler in the strength of the hurricane. I consider this a brave deed, and M. W. Lewis and J. J. Krass, firemen, and A. D. Ameyette, seaman, are due all credit for accomplishing this job. I consider each and every man of the crew did all in his power, and through their bravery, energy, and willpower we brought the ship through the hurricane and safely into port. The vessel I consider a most excellent seaworthy ship to come through such a severe hurricane with such comparatively slight damage as was sustained; so much water came aboard that at times there was three feet of water in the engine-room bilges."

C.C. Austin received the following letter of commendation from President Franklin Delano Roosevelt. The letter was framed and placed aboard the lightship.

"I have read with keen satisfaction the report of the heroic work done by the officers and crew of Diamond Shoal Lightship during the hurricane of September 15th and 16th. I am fully appreciative of the exceptional character of the services performed in saving this vessel, and in the protection of the shipping along the coast; and I wish you would convey to them my personal commendation for the manner in which they performed their dangerous duties during this storm."

(signed) President Franklin D. Roosevelt

Clyde Farrow, former keeper at Ocracoke Lighthouse, was a crewmember onboard LV 105 with C.C. Austin. He often related stories of those horrendous days to his wife, Belinda.

"My husband, Clyde Farrow was on the lightship with C.C. Austin the day of the hurricane (she pronounced it as islanders do: 'hur-uh-kin'). He told me that when they were being dragged across Diamond Shoals after the winds shifted that the sand was rolling around in the water like it was boiling. The winds were awful and the waves were the strongest he'd ever seen. The wind bent the lightship's railings all the way down to the deck. The ship was keeled over so far that he walked on the walls. Clyde came home all beat up. The President [Roosevelt] gave him a pin of accommodation and a nice letter telling him how proud he [the President] was of him. My Clyde died Father's Day 1981."

Interview October 20, 2000

This is a picture of LV 71, a few months before it was sunk in 1918 after giving warning to ships in the area of enemy activity. Walter Lambeth Barnett was skipper of Light Vessel 71 the day a German raider submarine destroyed it and a passing merchant ship. Few Americans knew of the war activity off the East Coast, especially the Cape Hatteras area, a scene that would be repeated in WWII.
Photo courtesy U.S. Coast Guard

Aboard in the 1950s
By Ben Price

Ben Price was on the Diamond Shoals Lightship from 1954 to 1956. At that time, there were twelve to fifteen men stationed on the ship. The work schedule was thirty days on the ship, followed by fourteen days off. There was a crew of eight aboard at all times. Most crewmen were young, but the officers were older and more experienced. The thing Ben remembered most clearly was the boredom. After the ship was cleaned in the morning there wasn't much for him to do until mealtime. Ben was one of the reluctant cooks. The captain, on at least one occasion, was heard to say," [Darn], Ben burned the stew again!"

Fishing helped to relieve the boredom and augment the food supply. Ben remembers pulling in a sixteen-foot hammerhead shark. Some days he only had to toss in a hook and catch plenty of fish. Other days, no matter what he offered, he couldn't catch a thing. The lightship was anchored near a station buoy. In the winter the Gulf Stream heat would cause foggy conditions for days at a time and the foghorn would sound night and day. Ben's bunk was right next to the foghorn, making sleep difficult.

Sometimes, during winter northeasters, they would drag anchor and move off station. Once, the wind was blowing the ship into the station buoy and the captain, afraid the buoy would pierce the side of his ship, considered sinking the station buoy. Just when they were poised to fire on the buoy, the wind shifted and all was well. During another storm, Ben remembered looking out of the porthole and seeing a wall of water fifty feet high. They kept heading into the wind to keep from capsizing. The anchor line broke in the strong wind and the gusts pushed them fifty miles out to sea. The U. S. Coast Guard found them and towed them back into position.

The worst storm Ben remembered, or the most regretted by the crew, was the storm that caused their utility boat to capsize while transferring supplies. All of their supplies plus all the new movies went down. The crew was saved, but they had to watch old movies for two weeks until another supply ship came with more movies. Ben left the lightship in 1956 to attend a business school in Groton, Connecticut.

The Diamond WAL 390 in the 1960s
By Mike Shepherd

Mike Shepherd was stationed on the Diamond Shoals Lightship WAL 390. "W" is a designation for Coast Guard and "WAL" stood for "lightship." He wrote of his experience.

There were many different classes of lightships ranging from 96 feet to 148 feet. Their task was to mark the location of a reef, shoal, or an important navigational point. To be readily visible, they were painted bright red with a white superstructure and had their names painted in large letters on their sides. They anchored at a charted position and became a 'fixed' mark.

Lightships were designed to ride out any storm. As with buoys, position was everything in life to a lightship. Her position on station must be cut in sextant angles and the ship was secured to a heavy mushroom anchor. The duties of the crew parallel those of the personnel at a light station. A "watch" was always maintained to see that the light, fog signal, and radio beacon operated exactly on schedule. In addition to these duties, there were the normal tasks, which must be accomplished on any ship at anchor: auxiliary watches in the engine-room and the ceaseless battle against corrosion on deck.

Compensatory leave was granted to all personnel on the same basis as that for isolated light stations. When one liberty party departed another returned. On the Diamond we would get two weeks off and spend four weeks at sea. Of course, this was not always the situation. If bad weather set in, or the tender that was to pick us up got involved in continuous search and rescue assignments, it could take several days, even weeks, before we were picked-up. For example, if the tender was four days late we only get ten days leave. I remember one time spending seven and one half weeks at sea because of bad weather, and only getting twelve days leave.

I was a "Fireman/Engineman (FN/EN)" when I served on the Diamond. My duties were to stand engine watches, making sure that the generators were running properly. We had four diesel generators and would have one on line all the time. During the day we did maintenance work in the engine room and worked four-hour watches at night. In fact there was always someone on watch. I always remember the foghorn!
Fifteen-second blasts every sixty seconds, sometimes for days. We learned to talk in forty-five second intervals.

In November 1963, the day we returned from leave was the day President Kennedy was killed. Since we had been up most of the night aboard the tender when we got settled in back aboard the Diamond the Chief let everyone turn in. I was one of the only two people who were not sleeping when the news broke about JFK. I was on the mess deck reading and listening to the radio when I heard the announcement; I ran up to the bridge and asked the seaman standing the deck watch if he had heard, he hadn't. We then woke up the Chief, he heard the radio, and he ordered the deck watch to lower the flag to half-mast. For five days all of us were glued to the TV. The day after JFK was buried, we lost TV reception. It seems that the weather held so we could see what the rest of the world was also watching."

From 1918 to 1966, a number of lightships stood defiant watch on Diamond Shoals, and a buoy marked the area during World War II. In 1966, Light Vessel 189 slipped her mooring and sailed away in farewell. Her services were no longer needed. Diamond Shoal Tower, a "Texas tower design" or described by others as a Gulf oil-rig structure, had taken over the lightship's duty of warning mariners away from the shoals.

Built for the U.S. Coast Guard, Diamond Shoal Tower is the first offshore lighthouse to be completed there. Four steel pilings driven deep into the sand 12 1/2 miles south-southeast of Cape Point raise the square tower 125 feet above the water. Automated in 1977, its 1,000-watt bulb flashes a warning every 12 1/2 seconds from a digitally controlled beacon that is now solar powered. As long as its footing remains firm in the shifting sands off Cape Hatteras, this unmanned, ghostly structure will improve mariners' chances of making it safely past the long-feared and highly-respected Diamond Shoals.

Information from personal interviews and Lighthouse News *Vol. III no. 4 of the Outer Banks Lighthouse Society.*

A Navy Pharmacist Mate, a Midwife, and a Medical Doctor
Delivered Babies and Provided Medical Care 1890s-1930s

M.B. Folb
(1892-1983)

In the 1920s, M.B. Folb, Chief Pharmacist Mate, U.S. Navy, was known to Hatteras Islanders as "Dr. Folb" or just "Doc." He delivered 300 babies and made good old-fashioned house calls to those in need.

Folb came off a WWI destroyer to his new assignment in 1920. He was to minister medically to the small number of Navy personnel at both the radio and the radio compass stations in Buxton. Upon arrival there, he discovered that he was the only certified medical person on the island.

M.B. Folb helped Hatteras Island families during the late 1920s and early 1930s. Keeper Unaka Jennette's son, Rany, stated, "Doc Folb, a young Pharmacist's Mate at the Naval radio station, along with 'Miss Rovena,' a midwife, took care of most of our severe illnesses and performed many miraculous wonders with their limited skills and 'modern' medicines. 'Doc' will always be remembered by folks along the Outer Banks- we always considered him as one of us as long as he lived. He died at age ninety-four."
Photo courtesy Reese Folb

Folb wrote in *The Navy Hospital Corps Quarterly October 1927*, "There were respiratory diseases to combat; several epidemics of influenza to take care of; villages to be immunized against typhoid; immunizations against diphtheria to be given; all sorts of foreign objects to be removed from children's ears, noses, and other orifices; and help lectures to be given at the schools. A Red Cross Chapter was formed called the 'The Cape Hatteras Island Chapter'; a nurse was procured from Atlanta, Georgia, to give modified home courses in home nursing and hygiene; and a Red Cross loan locker, containing sheets, hot water bottles, ice caps, air rings, etc. was provided for each of the four villages.

"There were many cases beyond the ken and ability of the writer [Folb], and circumstances- weather and the urgency of the case permitting, they were sent off to some hospital by boat or by Naval plane," Folb added. He wrote of one difficult situation in which he made a breech delivery while the mother suffered a seizure.

Lighthouse keepers' children of the 1920s and 30s, whose families depended upon him as their access to what medicine had to offer, referred often to "Doctor Folb." Diphtheria was a leading killer of adults and children alike. One such epidemic, in 1929, was averted by his plea to the Navy for help. Within six hours, serum and a doctor were flown by seaplane from Chesapeake, Virginia, a reaction time difficult to match today. Doc's and the Navy's generosity saved many lives by getting help to the island quickly.

Though he delivered hundreds of babies along the Outer Banks, he is perhaps also remembered as somewhat of a transportation expert. Folb wrote, "There were no true roads in those days- just two ruts in the sand. Before the Fords came, the men drove two-wheeled sulkies, or rode horseback. The sulkies had broad, iron tires so as not to sink into the soft sands. The Coast Guard stations used Clydesdale horses to pull their boats in times of rescues. Their boats had no motors and were launched by hand and rowed into the breakers, the men at the stern using a sea oar instead of a rudder." Folb concluded, "In March 1923, I introduced balloon tires on the island. Captain Unaka Jennette, who was then keeper at the lighthouse, was the second man to put 'balloons' on his car, and Fate Midgette was the third- then the deluge of cars and balloon tires…I used oversized tires at 14 pounds pressure instead of the 60 pounds in the clincher tires of that time."

Dr. Folb credits the automobile and balloon tires with bringing the modern world to Hatteras Island. Doc deserves his own credit for bringing "modern" medicine to its residents.

Rovena Rollinson Quidley
(1864-1955)

"Generations of Hatteras Islanders knew her and venerated her as 'Miss Rovene'," said Ben Dixon MacNeill, author of The Hatterasman.

Rovena, who played as many roles in the Hatteras Island community as there are ways to spell her name (Rovena, Rovenia, Rovine, Rovene), was born just four months after Lincoln's assassination in 1865. Descendants of the 300 and more babies she helped bring into this world from the 1890s through the 1930s have described her in generally the same terms. Known to many island children as "Grandma Rovene," she was old, dressed in many layers of clothes, wore small, black, lace-up shoes, a dark hat, and told scary stories to her brood. Whenever anyone was ill, she went to the home and stayed with the patient overnight if needed. She carried with her various self-made homeopathic remedies to help ease pain or fever. In her house "in the woods," she is also remembered today for her well-fed animals and fig trees.

Her obituary was written by MacNeill, a friend, and it appeared on the front page of *The Coastland Times* on Friday, September 9, 1955. "She was a neighbor, friend, and sound counselor, gentle and kindly and keenly intelligent."

Rovena married David Gardner Quidley, a widower, when she was only sixteen. She and David raised five lighthouse keepers: William Edward Quidley, David's son by his first marriage to Miranda Farrow; three of their sons Thomas, Dave (their first Dave died young and they gave the subsequent boy his name), and Guy; and another young man who had been taken into their home and raised as their son, Amasa J. Quidley. Other children, orphaned by tragic illnesses including tuberculosis, pneumonia, and influenza, were taken into Rovena's home as part of one big family.

One of Rovena's sons, Thomas Daniels Quidley (1882-1980) spent his summers helping on board the Diamond Shoals Lightship with his father, Dallas Sr., a temporary, part-time crewmember on board. Thomas also served as substitute keeper for James Wilson Gillikin when he was sixteen years old. An oral history was recorded by his grandson, Dallas Quidley, Jr., "T.D." carried kerosene to the top of Cape Hatteras Light, learned to light the lamp and extinguish it daily, cleaned the prisms and polished the brass. Not only did he retire as a respected keeper from the Lighthouse Service in 1941, but he also influenced many other men to join the U.S.L.H.S. Rovena's boys were part of her legacy given to the island and our maritime heritage. Thomas's son, Dallas Sr., was the last as keeper at Roanoke Marshes Lighthouse when his U.S.L.H.S. career ended in 1944. [Source: details taken from recorded interview with TD Quidley by Dallas Quidley Dec 2, 1970; letters from Dallas Quidley 6/99-2/00; interview with Dallas Quidley at the editor's home January 10, 2000.]

At her funeral, the Group Commander of the U.S. Coast

A picture of Rovena and a child, Carol Quidley Paul, circa 1955 shows her love for children. "Rovena's elongated nose and chin is a family characteristic," Dallas Quidley Jr. commented on this photo from his private collection.

This is a portrait of Rovena's son, T.D. Quidley (1882-1980) who served as a substitute on the Diamond Shoals Lightship with his father, Dallas Quidley, Sr., and filled in for Keeper Gillikin at Cape Hatteras starting when he was sixteen years old. T.D. enjoyed a successful and long career in the U.S. Lighthouse Service and influenced others to join the service. Circa 1909 Photo courtesy Dallas Quidley, Jr.

Guard Station on Hatteras Island and other coastguardsmen served as pallbearers. They had one thing in common: Rovena had brought them all into the world. She was buried next to her husband in the Quidley cemetery in Buxton.

When Rovena was eighty-five-years-old (about 1950), her sons were concerned that her house was too far away, about a mile from the nearest neighbor on the sound. They moved it next to one of her sons along the highway, and the story is told that the fearless Rovena rode atop the moving house with a forked limb, pushing up power and phone lines so that her house could slip under them. She walked the mile back to her old home site to care for her garden until her death.

Rovena's step-great granddaughter, Sabra (Gray) Jennette, spoke of this remarkable woman who loved children and animals. "Grandma Rovena had just about everything she needed right there on her place. She had a big pasture she kept the cows in down there. And she had her own milk cows with a screened-in small house and she kept her milk out there. Did her cows just graze like the free-range animals of the island? HERS didn't, no my!" Sabra said, "She'd buy five or six bags of stuff for them, cottonseed meal and all that. And I bet she spent more on those cattle than she did to feed herself. She was old as long as I remember. I know she'd tell stories and when she'd spend the night with us and those stories would make your hair stand on end! I believe she made those things up, but they'd scare you to death! She had big fig trees down there on that shore. There were a lot of them. She'd preserve lots of vegetables."

Jackie Jennette, Sabra's daughter, added, "She'd get the kids to go down and pick them for her."

"She was really good to everyone," Sabra concluded.

Dr. Joshua Judson "Josh" Davis
(1868-1949)

In 1894, "Dr. Josh," drawn by his love of the sea and the Outer Banks, moved his family to Buxton near the Cape Hatteras Lighthouse, and became the first resident physician on Hatteras Island, serving the islanders until 1910.

Dr. Josh was born on a farm near Elizabeth City in 1868. He graduated from Elizabeth City Academy and was admitted to the University of Virginia Medical School in 1889. He transferred to the University of Maryland Medical School, from which he received his M.D. degree in 1891. In 1892, he married Margaret E. (White), or "Miss Maggie," as all knew her (1872-1968), and they began a long journey together as parents and co-workers.

Their home in Buxton was a stopping place for important visitors to the island including Dr. H.H. Brimley, curator of the N.C. Museum of History; Thomas A. Edison, the inventor; and A.H. Fessenden, who conducted wireless experiments at the cape. Miss Maggie wrote that she remembered seeing a picture of Thomas Edison's beautiful wife that he had placed on the bureau in her guest room.

Maggie wrote that the hurricane of 1899 wreaked havoc on the island. It beached the Diamond Shoals Lightship, drowned many cows, cattle, and sheep, and was followed by an epidemic of typhoid. Dr. Josh worked feverishly to help all who needed it, including their own children. Persevering like native islanders after severe flooding, the Davis family moved their home, along with its drenched contents, to Buxton Woods to gain higher ground.

Dr. Josh treated patients from Oregon Inlet to Hatteras village, travelling by sailboat "or a few beach carts," Maggie remembered. "He learned to steer the boat and became a good sailor. He made trips from Chicamacomico to Hatteras and sometimes as far as Ocracoke. We got mail once a week if the weather was favorable... He treated for sore fingers to typhoid fever and anything between." This included toothaches and pulling teeth.

For sixteen years, Dr. Josh gave Hatteras islanders his best medical expertise and, in 1910, he relocated his eleven children (a twelfth was born after the move) to Beaufort. All twelve Davis children, often home-schooled by their teacher/mother, attended college. The success of their children, including a director of the N.C. Museum of Natural History and two Rear Admirals, is a great tribute to Dr. Josh and Maggie.

In her lifetime, Maggie had witnessed the advent of new medical cures, the onset of radio and aviation, and she lived to see John Glenn launched into space on her own color television.

Information from The Heritage of Carteret County *by Maurice Davis and Iva Davis Holland 1982. Comments on Dr. and Mrs. Davis by their granddaughter, Sally Davis, in correspondence with the editor in 1997-2001. Dr. Davis's granddaughter, Jean Lewis, shared family information and pictures.*

Dr. Joshua Davis was a welcomed sight for many Hatteras Island families. He made house calls, travelling by sailboat or horse and cart. "He learned to steer the boat and became a good sailor," Miss Maggie wrote of her husband. The Davis family lived in Buxton from 1894 until 1910, the year the family moved to Beaufort, North Carolina.

Dr. Joshua Davis and his wife, "Miss Maggie," are at their home in Buxton. Dr. Davis was the first resident, certified doctor on the Outer Banks. He trained at the Virginia Medical School and the University of Maryland for his degree in 1891. Drawn by the lure of the sea, he moved to Buxton and over a sixteen years, he delivered babies, comforted and treated the ill, and even took care of surfmen and those rescued from shipwrecks. Date unknown.

Children of Dr. Josh Davis and Miss Maggie are left to right: Graham, Roy, Lloyd, Mary, and Harry. After the 1899 hurricane, Dr. Davis moved from the beach to higher ground in Buxton Woods. The ancient, giant dogwoods provided excellent climbing; notice that the boys' knees are well worn from serious play. Mary appears quite contrary in having been stopped from play for this picture. About 1909, Harry was the victim of a shotgun accident while he was trying to shoot some crows and eventually lost his leg despite his father's medical efforts. The incident led Miss Maggie to insist that her family, then eleven children, move to Beaufort in 1910. Circa 1903
Photos courtesy Jean Lewis, granddaughter of Dr. Josh and Miss Maggie

Life and Living
1830-1930
By Margaret N. Harker, M.D.

These times were difficult, especially in isolated regions like the Hatteras Light Station.

In the mid-nineteenth century, in English cities, the average age of death was 36 years for gentry, 22 years for trades people, and 16 years for laborers. More than half of the children of working class parents and one-fifth of the children of gentry died before their fifth birthday. This situation did not change for a long time. In the United States in 1900, the average life expectancy was approximately forty-seven years. There are birth and death records for forty-five of the eighty-five keepers and assistant keepers at Cape Hatteras. Of this group, the average age at death was 67.5 years, with a range from 28 to 92 years!

There were no antibiotics. Quinine was known to help prevent and cure malaria. When supplies were not obtainable (as during the Civil War) useless tinctures of dogwood, poplar, and willow tree bark mixed with whiskey were substituted. Aspirin, known since 1853, was widely used. The use of opiates of all kinds for all reasons was prevalent. These could be obtained by mail from numerous sources, including Sears. Coca-Cola contained cocaine! Strychnine tablets were in the Light Stations' medicine chest. Deaths from cholera, diphtheria, typhoid, malaria, yellow fever, tuberculosis, and dysentery/ diarrhea were common. Poor sanitation practices, flies, and mosquitoes all combined to make people sick. In the Civil War, two soldiers died of disease for every one killed in battle. The first North Carolina State Board of Health was established in 1877, with an appropriation of one-hundred dollars and appointment of the N.C. Medical Society as its board.

Anyone claiming to be a physician could practice as such until the 1888 U.S. Supreme Court ruled that States could require licensing of physicians. Standards for Medical Schools improved. Most medical care was provided in the home. Hospitals were rare and not always desirable places to be. Midwives of varying capabilities and knowledge routinely attended home deliveries. Surgical procedures in isolated areas were also preformed in the home. Ether, used since 1846, and chloroform, used since 1851, were the only available general anesthetics. Lessons from the Civil War and World War I greatly helped the modernization of public health, sanitation, and medical practices. Many of the causes and proper treatment of sickness and injury were known by the mid 20th century and rapid advancements occurred.

The government-issued *Instructions for Light-Keepers and Masters of Light-House Vessels and Prevention of Disease and Care of the Sick and Injured, Medical Handbook for the Use of Lighthouse Vessels and Stations*

In 1881, a medical handbook, The Ship's Medicine Chest, *was prepared for use aboard ships that had no physician present. Since that time, numbers of revisions have been made. In 1904, George W. Stoner, Surgeon, United States Public Health Service, prepared the* Handbook for the Ship's Medicine Chest. *In 1912, W.J. Pettus, Assistant Surgeon General, revised this book again. The 1915* Medical Handbook for The Use of Lighthouse Vessels and Stations *was revised (from the 1912 Ship's handbook), by W.G. Stimpson, M.D., Assistant Surgeon General, United States Public Health Service. A Supplement on* FIRST AID TO THE INJURED, *by R. M. Woodward, M.D., Surgeon, United States Public Health Service was included. The document could be procured for 50 cents! Commissioner of Lighthouses, G. R. Putnam wrote the introduction.*

(published at various times) are reflective of these events. They are impressive compendiums. They contain up-to-date practical advice regarding medical care and sanitation. There are lessons therein for today. They provide yet another view of the resourceful and responsible light keepers and their families.

The organization of medical care for the Lighthouse Service is not clear, as many documents have been lost from the U.S. Archives. The 1915 handbook did state that:

Pictured above is the medicine chest from the Ponce de Leon Inlet Light Station, similar to the one issued to Cape Hatteras. Each light station was given a U.S. Lighthouse Service medicine chest. The primary keeper, or a person whom he designated, held the responsibility for its safekeeping, stocking, and was the one who dispensed medications. Photo by Bruce Roberts

"Sick or disabled persons employed on vessels of the Lighthouse Service will be admitted without charge to relief stations of the United States Public Health Service upon application of their respective commanding officers."

There is no mention in available records and handbooks of Lighthouse Stations' personnel having, or not having, access to such admission; nor is there mention of just how the keepers "called the physician." It seems there must have been some sort of "Rule or Regulation."

In a letter written October 3, 1916, by David Williams, keeper, Ocracoke, NC to the Superintendent 7th Coast Guard District, Elizabeth City, N.C., the keeper refers to a circular letter of August 4th, 1916. According to records, he was actually the first Chief of the Coast Guard station there, but signed off as "Keeper." The Lighthouse Service was then under the Bureau of Lighthouses; in 1939, it was under the Coast Guard.

"As I red in the list that the station crew be treated by Dr. Jesse B. Bulluck, at Atlantic, N.C., and as transportation of physicians to stations must be furnished by the facilities afford. The distance between station No. 187 and the doctor office at Atlantic is thirty miles which wood take me in the boat nine hour in the best weather to get the Dr. and lots of times should not go and come at all. Now as thear is a Doctor one half mile of this station which is Doctor J.B. Angle that has treated this station before. I wood ask you to take the matter up with the department and se if station No 187 and No. 188 could be treated by Dr. J.B. Angle as it is 60 mile to and from this station to Atlantic to Doctor."

There is no further information regarding this matter.

As with most research, historical, genealogical, scientific, etc., there are at times more questions and puzzles found than there are answers. There are always lessons to be learned from the past. Following are partial contents and some comments about the Lighthouse Medical Handbook from 1915. Hopefully, the reader will find the same admiration of and interest in the keepers and their families that the author has found while studying the medical challenges of those days.

Of the many and at times quite detailed instructions found in these handbooks, the following are of particular interest and fascination. Often the instructions for treating

LIGHT STATIONS' MEDICAL SUPPLIES 1915

ITEM	AMOUNT	POISON	NOTES	CONTENTS/ USE
Absorbent cotton	1 pound			
Alcohol	1/2 pint		*Listed only*	
Aromatic spirit of ammonia	4 ounces			
Aspirin, 5 grain tablets	100			
Belladonna plaster	1 yard		1 year	
Bicarbonate of Soda	4 ounces			Baking soda
Bichloride of mercury, 7.3 grain tablets	100`	X	One tablet to a pint of water	Antiseptic
Bismuth subnitrate, 5 grain tablet	100			
Borax	4 ounces		*Listed only*	
Boric acid, powdered	1/2 pound			Boracic acid
Bromide of potash, 5 grain tablet	100			
Brown Mixture lozenges	100			*colds,cough / licorice,opium, gum &sugar*
Calomel, 1/10 grain tablets	100		1 year, amber colored bottle	
Camphor and opium pills	100	X		
Camphorated oil	4 ounces			
Carbolic acid, liquid, pure	1/2 pint	X		
Castor oil	1/2 pint			
Charcoal	4 ounces		*Listed only*	
Chlorate of potash, 5 grain tablet	100			
Compound cathartic pills, vegetable	100		*Listed only*	
Copaiba, 5 minim tablets	100			
Cresote, Beechwood	1/2 ounce	X		
Dobell;s Solution	1/2 pint			
Ear drops	1 ounce		*Listed only*	Carbolic acid, glycerin, well mixed
Epsom salts	1 pound			
Essence Jamaica ginger	4 ounces		*Listed only*	
Essence of peppermint	2 ounces		*Listed only*	
Essence of pepsin	4 ounces		*Listed only*	
Flaxseed meal	1/4 pound		*Listed only*	Linseed meal
Formalin	1 pint		1 year	
Iodide of potash, 5 grain tablets	100			
Laudanum	2 ounces	X	1 year	
Lead and opium wash	1/2 pint	X	Shake well before using	
Magnesia, calcined, heavy	4 ounces		*Listed only*	
Mustard	4 ounces			
Oil cloves	1/2 ounce		*Listed only*	
Olive oil	1 pint			Sweet oil
Paregoric	4 ounces	X		
Permanganate of potash, 5 grain tablets	100		*Listed only*	
Peroxide of hydrogen solution	1 pint		1 year	
Picric acid, 1/2% solution	1/2 pint	X		
Quinine sulphate, 5 grain tablet	100			*Prevention and treatment of malaria*
Salicylate of soda 5 grain tablets	100			
Salol , 5 grain tablet	100		*Listed only*	
Sirup of ipecac	4 ounces		*Listed only*	
Soap liniment	1 pint			
Strychnine sulphate, 1/60[h] grain tablet	100	X		
Sun Cholera Mixture, 15 minim tablet	100	X		
Sweet sprit of niter	4 ounces		1 year, dark colored bottle, listed only	
Tannic acid	4 ounces		*Listed only*	
Tincture of green soap	4 ounces		*Listed only*	
Tincture of iodine	4 ounces	X	1 year	
Tincture of iron	4 ounces		*Listed only*	
Tincture of myrrh	4 ounces			
Turpentine	1.2 pint		*Listed only*	
Unguentine	1/ pound		*Listed only*	For burns, scalds, etc.
Vaseline	1.2 pound			
Zinc sulphate, 15 grain powder	6 powders	X	One powder in water	White vitriol/ to produce vomiting

Instructions regarding the contents of the medicine chest were found in the medical handbook. These instructions varied with differing editions of the handbook. The 1915 edition included storage recommendations and renewed caution for those marked "1 year." Bulky items were not recommended to be kept in the actual chest. Rough-surfaced bottles were to be used for poisonous medications and they were to be clearly marked. Of interest, this handbook had directions for calculating reduced medication doses for children. This formula was based only on the age of the child.

LIGHT STATIONS' SURGICAL SUPPLIES, ETC.

ITEM	AMOUNT	NOTES/ INSTRUCTIONS
Adhesive plaster, 10 yard reel, 1 inch wide	1	
Applicators, small, wooden	1 dozen	*Listed only*
Atomizer. Devilbiss	1	*Listed only*
Bandages 2 inch by 3 yards gauze and muslin 3 inch by 5 yards 4 inch by 5 yards	1/ dozen each	*Listed only* *Listed only*
Bandages, Plaster of Paris, 3 inch	2	Each contained in an air and moisture proof container *Listed only*
Bandages, triangular (Esmarch's bandage)	6	With figures printed on them showing the various ways they can be used. *Listed only*
Camel's-hair brushes	3	*Listed only*
Catheter, rubber, No. 20 F.	1	1 year
Corkscrew	1	*Listed only*
Forceps, artery (hemostatic forceps)	1	This can be used to grasp a bleeding vessel until it can be tied, or until the doctor arrives. A catch holds the grip of the forceps. Sterilize by boiling. *Listed only*
Forceps, dressing, or dissecting	1	Will be found convenient in cleaning up a wound and applying dressings; also in removing splinters, etc. Sterilize by boiling. *Listed only*
Fountain syringe, 2 quart	1	1 year *Listed only*
Gauze, picric acid	5 yards	Good dressing for wounds and scalds. *Listed only*
Gauze, plain, sterile	5 yards	
Hot -water bottle, rubber, 2 quart	1	1 year Metal bottle preferred *Listed only*
Medicine droppers	6	*Listed only*
Medicine glass	1	*Listed only*
Nail brushes	2	*Listed only*
Safety pins, large	2 dozen	*Listed only*
Scissors, dressing, surgeon's	1	For cutting gauze and bandages. Sterilize by boiling *Listed only*
Shears	1	For cutting cotton and muslin, etc. *Listed only*
Splints, wooden	3	Straight and angular splints made of thin board, as described in chapter on "Fractures" *Listed only*
Spool of silk ligature, medium size	1	
Surgical needles	2	In glass -stoppered bottles
Thermometer, clinical	1	Fahrenheit
Tooth forceps, incisor	1	*Listed only*
Tooth forceps, molar	1	*Listed only*
Wire gauze	2 pieces	Made of heavy mesh malleable wire. When well padded can be wrapped around a fracture for temporary dressing. *Listed only*
Yucca palm	2 sheets	A thin fiber board. Can be wrapped around fracture for temporary dressing *Listed only*

Instructions in the handbook regarding these supplies pertain to storage of supplies and replacement of "1 year" items. Gauze and bandages were kept in paraffin-paper packages, sealed after sterilization (instructions were not noted here). Catheters and rubber goods were to be kept in sealed paraffin packages or envelopes, slightly dusted with sterile talcum on the inside of the package. Scissors and instruments not in cases were recommended to be coated with paraffin.

illness required one to have the diagnosis first! A feat for the keepers, their families, and the physicians!

A clinical thermometer was included and instructions on its use provided. In 1886, the modern clinical thermometer replaced the previous foot-long one that required 20 minutes to register a patient's temperature! Great store was (and still is) placed upon fever patterns for the diagnosis and prognosis of many conditions. Oddly enough, actual note of the fever pattern of malaria was not presented. Quinine was known and recommended for the cure and prevention of malaria.

"In going to a malarial region, treatment should be commenced several days before arriving at port. To each man on board should be given at least 10 grains (0.6 gm.) of quinine daily for a period of one week. The allowance may then be reduced to 5 grains (0.3 gm.) a day. The bowels should be kept freely open."

By 1915, Diphtheria was known to be caused by a germ, and an antitoxin was available. Diphtheria examination packages apparently were supplied free by most drug stores.

"These packages hold two glass tubes, one of which contains blood serum and the other a sterile swab. The tubes are closed by cotton plugs. These should be removed, the swab wiped over the throat, and then gently rubbed over the blood serum. The swab should then be replaced into its own tube, the cotton plugs of both tubes replaced, and the tubes mailed to the health officer of the city or district. A postal card will be mailed by him the next day to the sender stating whether or not the person from whom the specimen was taken has diphtheria."

Antitoxin for diphtheria was first produced in sheep in 1894, and then in horses. It was available in ship's medicine chests, along with tetanus antitoxin and smallpox vaccine, according to *The Ship's Medicine Chest and First Aid at Sea*, 1929 edition. It is not known if these were available to the keepers, and if so when.

How did the keepers manage all this at isolated light stations such as Hatteras?

Coughs and colds were treated by rubbing with soap liniment and taking Brown Mixture tablets, and Epsom salts (to keep the bowls open). Perhaps the last was needed because the Brown Mixture contained opium (all opiates cause constipation). Fresh air but not a draft was recommended. Good ventilation is recommended throughout the handbooks. Also used were hot mustard footbaths, hot lemonade and tea, aspirin, and induction of "a good perspiration."

Tuberculosis is also discussed in the 1915 Handbook. A poignant description follows:

"The patient has a slight cough, feels weak, and indisposed to do anything, loses weight, and has very little appetite. If the temperature is taken in the evening, it will be found that he has a slight fever. In a few weeks or months the emaciation becomes more marked, the fever is higher, there are sweats at night, severe cough, shortness of breath, and a large amount of mucopurulent matter is expectorated. There may be severe diarrhea from extension of the disease to the bowel, or the larynx may be involved, causing the voice to be husky and swallowing extremely painful. The patient's sleep is disturbed by the coughing spells, which are violent and protracted. As the disease progresses the symptoms increase in severity and the patient is confined to his bed until death brings him relief from his suffering."

By 1915, the causative organism for tuberculosis was known. (Koch discovered the tubercle bacillus, (Mycobacterium tuberculosis) in 1882). X-rays (discovered by Wilhelm Konrad von Roentgen in 1895) helped to follow the progress and severity of a patient's illness. Treatment included moving the infected person to a sanatorium (often mandated by law). Numbers of the "gentry" went to healthier climates, mountains, etc. The regular folk went to sanatoriums, such as the one in Wilson, N. C. Good nutrition and isolation of active infectious cases, which were determined by examining sputum with special stains under a microscope, were the mainstays of treatment. Some surgical procedures, such as collapsing the lung and multiple rib removals, were also employed. No specifically effective "magic bullet" was available until the discovery of Streptomycin by Selman Waksman at the University of California in 1943. Other medications soon followed and it no longer took months and years of confinement in sanatoriums to become non-contagious.

A resident of Harker's Island remembers her stay for eight months at the Wilson facility in the 1950's. She was *"taken"* after her Dr. made the diagnosis of TB. She had her own room of about ten by twelve feet *"at the end of the hall after you came in the front door, for the contagious."* She was not allowed out of that room for three months.

At some time she was on the third floor and could go to a window and look down upon her family. Her husband came every Friday from Harker's Island. She had a "thing" on the table to spit in, took bitter-tasting pills, and regular X-Rays. She reports:

"It was very strict then, but a good thing. The whole family and neighbors had to take tests. They said you had to eat your way out of here. There were tears dropping on my plate. I knew I had to eat."

She weighed 133 pounds at the start and 167 pounds when she went home. While there, she made an apron and a quilt (a Chinese girl had a cart from which she sold articles for making various crafts). She got home, took her medicine, took X-Rays, and sent in sputum samples. She is a fine example of grit and grace. Her special sorrow was having to send her faithful husband to a nursing home. He died there. Most of the sanatoriums closed. The Wilson sanatorium is at present a special hospital for the physically disabled mentally ill.

Much of the handbook is devoted to bandaging and the treatment of wounds, dislocations, and fractures. Detailed instructions are provided. Many of these treatment principles hold true to this day.

Several questions and lessons arise from even this brief review. How many poisons reside in our own medicine chests, or under our sinks? Overuse of antibiotics are rendering us vulnerable to resistant strains of germs, creating the same conditions as when keepers' families had little or no medical defense again tuberculosis and pneumonia. Common sense serves us well: pay attention to fresh air, good nutrition, exercise, and our environment. Recently, North Carolina experienced the severe hurricanes of Floyd and Dennis. Many people became as isolated as the keepers were, and realized how fragile is our present day way of life and living. We would fare well is we were as self-reliant and responsible as the keepers and their families.

– Margaret Harker, M.D.

KEEPERS OF THE LIGHT
By Bett Padgett

Adam climbed the steps each night around the twilight hour
He'd go into the lantern room on top of the light tower.
And when the flames were all aglow in the quiet of the night
His mind would wander far away to his children and his wife.
For this was not a place for families on the rustic shore.
Adam worked alone and listened to the ocean's roar.

Unaka climbed up different steps inside a different tower.
The lenses sparkled brightly, shone through a stronger power.
His sons and daughters by his side to help him with the chores.
But when angry storms came from the sea they'd be sent far
    from the shore.
For this was not a place for families when the seas were mad.
Unaka would guard the tower with all the courage that he had.

They were the keepers of the light, they kept the Hatteras
    flame a-burning
So that sailors in the night would know of treacherous shores.
Through storms and angry oceans they kept the light in motion
So it could shine forever more
Upon the sailors at the sea and all of those on shore.

Many Keepers in between the first one and the last.
Each one with a story that tells us of the past.
Of pirate ships and mysteries and many happy hours
Of wartimes and of hurricanes, how waves crashed into the
    tower.
We know these men worked from their hearts and how they
    were so brave.
We've heard of tales so long ago of many lives they've saved.

The keepers' hands are many hands now not just one or two.
Our spiraled friend will keep us all safe the night through.
The light shines out upon us, like a blanket in the night
Where all of us can gather and friends can reunite.
This is a place for families and through the shifting sands
She brings us all together no matter where she stands.

> We are the keepers of the light;
> We'll keep the Hatteras flame a-burning
> So that sailors in the night will know of treacherous
>   shores.
> Through storms and angry oceans, we'll keep the light
>   in motion
> And it will shine forever more
> In the hearts of those at sea and all of us on shore.

From the CD Bett For Ever

Index

Keepers:

Angell, Nelson P. .... xx, 106
Austin, Homer T. .... xx, 2-3
Austin, Julian H. .... xx, xxiii, 8-19
Austin, M. Wesley .... xx, 4-7
Barnett, Hezekiah .... xx, 112-114
Barnett, James J. .... xx, 4, 112-114
Barnette, Oliver N. .... xx, 70, 79, 112-114
Baum, Thomas H. .... xx, 20-23, 76
Bliven, George A. .... xx, 106
Brady, John D. xx
Burfoot, Jabez W. .... xx, 106
Burrus, Ethelburt D. .... xx, 106
Casey, James O. .... xv, xx 24-38, 59
Daniels, Joseph B. xx
Daniels, Louis G. xx
Farrow, Abraham C. xx
Farrow, C.P. xx
Farrow, Harvey L. .... xx, 107
Farrow, Isaac .... xx, 107
Farrow, Joseph .... xx, 107
Farrow, L.B. .... xx, 107
Farrow, Pharoah .... xvii, xx, 107
Fulcher, Amasa G. .... xx, 34-35
Fulcher, Benjamin T. .... xii, xx, 36-37, 52, 56, 57, 112
Fulcher, C. xx
Fulcher, Charles H. .... xv, xx 38047
Fulcher, Christopher xx
Fulcher, Martin L. .... xvii, xx
Fulcher, Randolph P. .... xii, xx
Gaskins, Adam .... xvi-xvii, xx
Gillikin, James W. .... xx, 48-50, 94, 95
Gray, Abner H. .... xx, 108
Hause, Selwyn xx
Jennett, Benjamin C. .... xx, 52, 57, 92, 93
Jennett, John B. .... xx, 52, 54-56, 92
Jennett, Joseph C. .... xx, 52, 112, 57, 93
Jennett, Joseph E. .... xx, 52
Jennett, Wallace R. .... xx, 52, 108, 94
Jennett, William .... xii, xx, 52, 112
Jennett, Zion B. .... xx, 52, 53, 92, 93
Jennette, Unaka B. .... xii, xviii, xx, xxii, 52, 94, 57-65
Meekins, Ephraim .... xx, 66-67
Meekins, Isaac C. .... xx, 66, 108
Midget, John E. .... xx, 57, 59, 70-75
Miller, Christopher C. .... xii, xvii, xx, 22, 36, 37, 55, 56, 76-79, 94
O'Neal, E.D. xx
O'Neal, E.F. xx
O'Neal, W.B. xx
O'Neal, William xx
O'Neal, William B. .... xx, 52, 108
Quidley, Amasa J. .... xx, 80-81
Quidley, John B. .... xx, 82-83
Quidley, William E. .... xv, xx, 57, 59, 70, 84-91
Riggs, Ephraim H. .... xx, 94, 108
Roach, Louis C. xx
Rodgers, George W. xx
Rollinson, Sylvester xx
Rollinson, William G. .... xx, 94, 95, 108
Rue, Oscar xx
Salter, A.G.B. .... xx, 109
Scarborough, Henderson xx
Scarborough, R. xx
Shepperd, John S. xx
Simpson, Alpheus W. .... xx, 52, 92, 93
Simpson, Amasa J. .... xx, 52, 92
Simpson, Fabius E. .... xx, 92
Smith, Sanders B. .... xx, 68, 94, 109
Smith, Tilman F. .... xx, 92, 93, 96-97
Stowe, John M. xx
Swain, Malachi D. .... xvii, xx, 109
Thompson, Augustus C. xx
Tolson, W.G. .... xx, 110
Twiford, J.T. .... xx, 110
Wallace, Thomas L. .... xx, 98-103
Watson, Victor L. .... xx, 110
Whedbee, Miles F. .... xx, 94, 110
Whitehurst, John E. .... xx, 110
Whitehurst, Joseph B. xx
Williams, Andrew .... xx, 110
Williams, B.A. .... xx, 111, 112
Williams, Nasa S. .... xx, 111
Willis, Alpheus B. .... xx, 94, 95
Willis, David xx

Other Topics:

Austin, Cecil Claudius 118-120
Barnett, Walter Loran (Walter L.) 79, 112
Barnett, Walter Lambeth (Walter L.) 112-114, 120
Baum, Wayland 20-23
Benjamin T. Fulcher Family Tree 37
Bloody Point Bar Lighthouse (screwpile, Maryland) 98, 102
Bodie Island Lighthouse 11, 12, 15, 18, 68, 70, 82, 93, 108

Brewster	70, 76, 78, 79, 115
Cape Charles Light Station (Virginia)	8, 82
Cape Lookout Lighthouse	49, 50, 82, 95, 108
Carol A. Deering	114
Christmas	6, 8, 10, 26, 27, 44, 59, 86, 87, 103, 104
Contents of light station medical chest	128-129
Creeds Hill Lifesaving Station	70, 114, 118
Croatan Lighthouse (screwpile)	20, 22, 23, 66, 68, 80
Currituck Beach Lighthouse	2-7, 77 80
Davis, Dr. Joshua	125-126
Defender	76
DELCO	43
Diamond Shoals	xiii, 8, 12, 26, 29, 34, 66, 77, 84, 90, 96, 116-121
Diphtheria	
1803 Cape Hatteras tower	25, 35, 37
Ephraim Williams	61
Farrow, Clyde	120
Folb, M.B.	59, 122
Fresnel lens	viii, xxii, 6, 13, 16, 23, 25, 35, 36, 37, 64, 72, 84, 96
Gallatin Award	19
Gaskill, Vernon	11, 12
German U-boat	6, 39, 45, 114, 118, 120
Giant, Poem by Sybil Austin Skakle	xix
Gull Shoal Lighthouse (screwpile)	38, 42, 80
Gulf Stream	114, 116, 121
Harbor Island Lighthouse (screwpile)	34, 48, 49, 82
Hatteras Beacon (Cape Hatteras Beacon Light)	xii, 4, 6, 96
Hatteras Inlet Lighthouse (screwpile)	xii, 93, 95, 106, 108, 110
Hatteras Island Genealogical and Historical Society (HIGHS)	iv, 112, 115
Hattie Creef	22
Holly (USLHS tender)	6, 20-22, 54
Hog Island Lighthouse, Virginia	98, 100, 102
Hoopers Strait Lighthouse (screwpile moved to St. Michaels)	38
Hurricane 1933	118-120
Incandescent oil vapor lamp (IOV)	v, 12, 26, 33, 39, 64
Influenza	122, 123
Jasmine (USLHS tender)	57
Jennett, Jabez Benjamin	52
Jennette Family Tree	53
Jennette, Rany B.	xv, 8, 31, 51, 87, 89, 98, 100, 101, 122
Keepers duties	xxii
Keepers list	xx-xxi
Keepers of the Light, Lyrics by Bett Padgett	131
Lighthouse Keeper, Poem by Renae Brabham	xxiii
Lightship (light vessels)	116-121
Long Shoal Lighthouse (screwpile)	23
Louisiana	7
Maple (USLHS tender)	57, 58, 88, 90, 91
Mary Louise	113, 114
McArthur, Beatrice (Barnette)	37, 112
Measles	9, 29
Medical chest	127
Medical handbook	126
Middle Ground Lighthouse (Chesapeake Bay)	2
Miller, Baxter Benjamin	76, 79
Miller, Seymore Horatio	76, 78, 79
New Bern Harbor Lights (post beacons)	54, 55, 56, 105
North River Lighthouse (screwpile)	95
Ocracoke Lighthouse	6, 96, 120
Outer Banks Lighthouse Society	iii, iv, vii
Pamlico Point Lighthouse (screwpile)	25, 27, 30, 32, 74
Quidley, Rovena	40, 41, 54, 80, 86, 123-124
Quidley, T.D.	123
Relief LV 80	59, 90
Roanoke Marshes Lighthouse (screwpile)	30, 42, 64, 123
Roanoke River Lighthouse (screwpile)	9, 11, 48, 80
Royal Shoal Lighthouse (screwpile)	106
Sharp's Island Lighthouse, Maryland	15, 98, 102
Simpson, Amasa W. Sr.	92
Simpson Family Tree	94
Summer of 1946, Poem by Sybil Austin Skakle	xviii
Tilghmans Island Lighthouse (Chesapeake Bay)	98, 102
Tuberculosis	11, 14, 16, 21, 70, 73, 75, 86, 87, 123, 126, 130-131
Typhoid	114, 122, 124, 126
U.S. Coast Guard	5, 11, 18, 29, 41, 60, 63, 70, 71, 98, 100, 115, 116-120
U.S. Lifesaving Service	5, 68, 76, 79, 113, 115
U.S. Lighthouse Service, terms used for	xv
U.S. Lighthouse Service (USLHS) or Lighthouse Service	xii, xiv, xv, xxii, 11, 63, 68, 134
U.S.L.H.S. library of books (circulating case of reading material to light stations)	40
U.S. Navy	122
Violet (USLHS tender)	58
Wade's Point Lighthouse (screwpile)	68
Whooping cough	28, 48

Biographies

Cheryl Shelton-Roberts is cofounder and former five-year President of the Outer Banks Lighthouse Society, a non-profit group dedicated to preserving the lighthouses and artifacts of the old U.S. Lighthouse Service. She is editor of the society's newsletter, the *Lighthouse News*. She is author of LIGHTHOUSE FAMILIES, a highly acclaimed book about keepers' families who served and lived at lighthouses all over the United States. Cheryl is a native North Carolinian, a teacher for two decades, and continues to record oral histories of lighthouse families. She and husband Bruce published MOVING HATTERAS: RELOCATING THE CAPE HATTERAS LIGHT STATION TO SAFETY for the National Park Service. They also have been contributing editors and consultants for newspaper and magazine articles on lighthouses, as well as for documentaries including the PBS LEGENDARY LIGHTHOUSES and the History Channel's MODERN MARVELS.

Bruce Roberts was former Director of Photographer and Senior Photographer at *Southern Living* Magazine in Birmingham, Alabama. Before joining *Southern Living* he was a member of the legendary early 1960's photo staff of the *Charlotte Observer*, which pioneered the use of the 35-mm camera and natural light for newspaper photography. During this time he received numerous awards for his photography in state and national competitions. Bruce freelanced for TIME LIFE BOOKS, *Sports Illustrated*, and as well as both *Time* and *Life Magazines*. His photography has appeared in a number of best-selling lighthouse books including AMERICA'S LIGHTHOUSES, a full-color guide to all of America's lighthouses. He and his wife, Cheryl Shelton-Roberts, live in Morehead City, North Carolina, where they continue to work together on publications about lighthouses and the South and remain active in projects for the Outer Banks Lighthouse Society.

Sandy Clunies holds the Certified Genealogist credential from the Board for Certification of Genealogists. She has published research in many journals, written articles for many publications, and lectures regularly on a variety of topics at regional and national conferences. She is an adjunct faculty member of the National Institute on Genealogical Research at the National Archives. Recently, Sandy retired from federal service to establish a research company with a special focus on the records of the U.S. Lighthouse Service, and has served as a consultant to the Harbour Lights Company.